1995

Living in the margins

LIVING IN THE MARGINS

Racism, sexism and feminism in Australia

Jan Pettman

ALLEN & UNWIN

First published in 1992
Allen & Unwin Pty Ltd
8 Napier Street, North Sydney NSW 2059 Australia

National Library of Australia
Cataloguing-in-Publication entry:

Pettman, Jan Jindy, 1944–
    Living in the margins: racism, sexism and feminism in
    Australia.

    Bibliography.
    Includes index
    ISBN 1 86373 005 2.

    1. Minority women—Australia—Social conditions.
    [2]. Aborigines, Australian—Women—Social conditions. 3. Sexism
    —Australia. I. Title.

305.4880994

Typeset in 10.5/11.5pt Sabon by Adtype Graphics, Australia
Printed by Kin Keong Printing, Singapore

Contents

Introduction

Living in the margins is a series of interconnected essays which focus on the intersections of race, ethnicity, class and gender, and look especially at representations and experiences of Aboriginal women and women from non-English-speaking backgrounds in Australia.

Political and academic representations of race, ethnicity and gender frequently suggest these as alternative or exclusive identities, as Aborigines and members of ethnic communities *and* women, as if women aren't more than half of the first two categories, and as if women don't come from very different racialised or ethnic backgrounds. These categories are also often represented as natural and fixed, disguising the politics of their construction and their shifting and relational qualities.

Minority women are frequently subject to 'normalised absence/ pathological presence' treatment (Phoenix, 1985:51). They are rendered largely invisible within academic studies for example; or where they are represented it is often as problems or victims, in ways that deny them agency and purport to explain their experiences within culturalist frames. These representations can also contain them within racialised or ethnic categories in such a way as to disguise their other identities and interests, as workers, welfare consumers, mothers and so on, and so disguise connections that women and others may have across the boundaries.

This book begins by examining the politics of boundary making, and the rather different processes of colonisation and migration which have shaped Australian society, and asks where the women are in constructions of nation, race and ethnicity. Chapter 2 analyses the experiences of Aboriginal women within the context of colonisation and ongoing racism, and asks how these differed from Aboriginal men's experiences. It also investigates Aboriginal women's relations with white men and with white women, and the complexities of race in sexual politics. Chapter 3 analyses the experiences of ethnic-minority women in the rather different context of labour migration, and focuses on the post-war period, when increasing numbers of migrants came from non-English-speaking backgrounds.

Having set the scene, the next chapters seek to draw more connections, to analyse both differences and commonalities in the lives of women who are identified as Aboriginal, ethnic or migrant, and other Australian women. Chapter 4 focuses on racism and sexism, and on the ways in which Aboriginal women and ethnic-minority women experience simultaneous oppression. It asks how their experiences of racism and cultural difference differ from those of 'their' men; and how their experiences of gender and sexism differ from those of majority-group women. Chapter 5 examines different women's experiences of the state, and state policies for managing difference and 'special needs'. Chapter 6 looks at concepts of culture, community and identity, and examines constructs of Aboriginality and multiculturalism, asking again where women are in these constructs. Chapter 7 analyses the construction of academic knowledge about Others, and investigates the absence or marginal presence of Aboriginal women and ethnic-minority women in academia. Chapter 8 examines issues of sisterhood in view of the differences among and between women, while also identifying shared interests and seeking a more inclusive feminism.

The big categories of nation, race, ethnicity and gender disguise differences within the categories and commonalities across their boundaries. This book seeks to deconstruct the categories and analyse the politics of their making. The focus moves over a wide terrain, highlighting women's differential positioning within those categories. It also examines differences among women, and interests and affiliations they may share. Given the usual academic segmentation between Aboriginal Studies, Migration or Multicultural Studies and Women's Studies this is a hugely ambitious task, especially when I draw on theoretical and comparative material to inform it. Thus this project is in no way definitive. It provides further reflections on representations of difference, and on ways of talking about multiple oppression and the mutually constitutive relations of race, ethnicity, class and gender.

Part of the project of thinking about differences is to develop a language beyond the simplistic and often obscuring labels usually available to us. It proved difficult to find appropriate words in many circumstances. Here I use the term Aboriginal women to include

Torres Strait Islander women, while acknowledging that they are in some ways different again; and also recognising that some Aboriginal women prefer to name themselves differently, for example as Koori women in the case of some from south-eastern Australia, or by their particular group. Others prefer to stay with Aboriginal, as it signals indigenous status and claim, while some others, or the same women in different situations, call themselves black, used as a political colour in terms of race power in Australia.

To refer to those women who are variously designated migrant, and/or ethnic or of non-English-speaking backgrounds, I often use the term ethnic-minority women, to signal their positioning away from public power in Australia, although some women from this category are well placed in class terms. An appropriate term for English-speaking background, majority-group or dominant-group women still eludes me, although especially in relation to Aboriginal women and in the context of colonisation where 'white' is a political colour, it is possible to refer to 'white women'. At times when referring to both Aboriginal women and women from non-English-speaking backgrounds I shorthand to minority women, and I attempt to use 'women' as an inclusive category which embraces women of very different backgrounds and experiences.

The 'battle for the name' (Banton, 1987c) is indicative of the theoretical and conceptual problems in a project around difference. It is also crucial in the politics of boundary making and the naming of oneself and others, which are central themes of this book.

In addition to the widely scattered materials that are referred to within it, the book draws on many years of conference, work and coffee conversations with colleagues, allies and friends. My involvement in in-service programs, departmental training programs and associations of practitioners in equal employment opportunity and cross-cultural work and in political and community organisations has frequently tested my hunches and given me insights into the experiences of other women who either are Aboriginal, migrant or ethnic-minority women, or who work extensively with women from a variety of backgrounds. I also draw on long years of tertiary teaching in Aboriginal Studies, Multicultural Studies and Women's Studies areas, where I learnt much from my students and colleagues. Most recently I have been pushed along in interesting ways by the Women, Race, Ethnicity and the State workshop organised at the Peace Research Centre at the Australian National University in April 1989, and by Jackie Huggins and others who worked with me at the Deakin Women's Studies Summer School course on Marginalised Women in 1990. Helen Meekosha and Nira Yuval-Davis have shared writing projects and more with me. My brother David Hollinsworth and I have been in continuous conversation about the politics of race over many years, and while other colleagues have read parts of the manuscript, he read the whole thing. So too did Jan Larbalestier. My thanks to both of them and to those at Allen & Unwin who have helped me through.

There are many friends who have urged me on and encouraged me. Karen Bowland and Carol Staples helped with the word processing and supported me at work. My extended family kept the meals and good times going at home. Special thanks to my mother Frances, who helped compensate for my house neglect, to Judith for coffee and friendship, and with my love to Tasha, Dominic and Mike.

1 Making Australia

The history of Australia is in part a history of displacements—of disruption, journeys, and resettlement in strange places.

Australia was founded through invasion, conquest and the dispossession of Aboriginal people,[1] many of whom were then forcibly removed from the places where old identities and knowledge made sense. Australians not of Aboriginal descent, and some relatives of many who are, are migrants or the descendants of relatively recent migrants. Many migrants also had experience of invasion, civil war or oppression in their home countries, or migrated to escape the dangers of minority status (Storer, 1985:5; Langer, 1990:6). Even those who came voluntarily, to better themselves or to secure a better future for their children, often faced problems in the process of migration.

Representations of Australia as extraordinarily peaceable are only possible by denying the violence of colonisation and the turbulent histories that lie behind many migrations here (Castles et al., 1988:1). The conflicts, traumas and grief in many Australians' past may partly explain the profound insecurity about national identity, and a widespread defensiveness about being Australian (Shortus, 1988).

Yet the journeys were also escape for some, and adventure or new opportunities for others. Colonisation disrupted old identities and social relations, but also provided the space to develop new ones, and enabled new connections and categories to be made. Thus 'Australian' as much as 'Aboriginal' or 'ethnic' came into being as part of the process of movement and change.

1. Aborigines is used in this book to include both Aboriginal people and Torres Strait Islanders.

National, racial and ethnic categories are often ungendered, so that women are rendered invisible within them, or else presumed to occupy the same places and have the same experiences and social interests as 'their' men. Thus they are often invisible or marginal within Aboriginal Studies, Multicultural Studies or Race Relations; or they are made visible only in an add-on lecture or extra chapter or essay topic. In Women's Studies, race and ethnic differences may not be considered, so the women often turn out to be white (cf Hull et al., 1982). Where minority women are made visible it is often as problems or victims (cf Gilroy, 1987:11), in ways that deny them agency, and imply that it is because they are Aboriginal or Asian, for example, that they have problems or are discriminated against. Thus Aboriginal and ethnic-minority women are often contained within the 'normalised absence/pathologised presence' couplet that sums up the representation of minority women in other countries (Phoenix, 1985:51).

Nationality, race, ethnicity and gender are all crucial dimensions of social identity and of social inequality. Minority women experience cultural difference, racism and sexism simultaneously (King, 1988). Racism and cultural difference are experienced in gendered forms; and sexism affects Aboriginal women, ethnic-minority women and dominant-group women in different ways.

Gendering issues to do with nation, race and ethnicity means asking questions about differences between women, and also what women may share across these differences (*Signs* editorial, 1988:3). As a basis, this chapter will begin by examining the politics of boundary making, and then look at the construction of nation, race and ethnic community, before asking where the women are in these constructions.

THE POLITICS OF BOUNDARY MAKING

We begin by problematising the categories of nation, race and ethnic group, drawing attention to the politics of their making within the context of relations of domination, subordination and resistance (Green and Carter, 1988; Anthias and Yuval-Davis, 1983).

There is often an ill fit between the categories, social identities and individual lives (Mason, 1990). It is also necessary to avoid privileging any one aspect of people's multiple identities, although in particular contexts one identity may be uppermost.

Nationality, race and ethnicity are not natural categories or prede-termined identities, but rather political constructs whose member-ship and meaning are contested and shifting (Miles in de

2

Lepervanche and Bottomley, 1988). Nationality, race and ethnicity are ways of naming people and of representing social identities and interests. They also have real material consequences for those who are so named and represented (Pettman, 1988c; Hall, 1988a).

Nation, race and ethnicity are ways of drawing boundaries that simultaneously include and exclude people (Miles, 1987a:24). They are imagined communities (Anderson, 1983) in the sense that they exist largely in people's heads, naming groups that are far too large to know each other personally; yet they presuppose connectedness and belonging among in-group members.

Nation, race and ethnicity are ideological collectivities that are made and change in struggle between different, shifting groups of people. They are discursive formations, which signal languages through which to name and explain differences (Goldberg, 1987). They are mobilised identities (Ballard in Jennett and Stewart, 1987; Rowse and Moran, 1984:230) for they are activated and used as political resources to preserve privilege or to back claims.

But nation, race and ethnicity are not only imagined, or part of political discourse. There are real and sometimes deadly conse-quences for those who are named as belonging to, or outside, par-ticular boundaries. Nation, race and ethnicity are constructed through, and as, relations of dominance and subordination (Hall, 1980). They are social constructions, and they both constitute and represent unequal power relations. The ideologies of nationalism, racism and ethnic difference appear to naturalise the boundaries, as if they are birth identities (Green and Carter, 1988). In so doing they naturalise the role and power of dominant groups by representing their race and culture as the norm, and others as deviant, where they are represented at all. Racism and its representations of others become common sense (Lawrence, 1982; Cohen, 1988), but a 'common sense racism which holds the norms and forms thrown up by a few hundred years of pillage, extermination, slavery, colonialism and neo-colonialism' (Trinh, 1987:11).

National, racial and ethnic boundaries and identities are not simply imposed from above by the powerful. These impositions are also resisted, subverted and exploited by the weak (Carroll, 1972), by those in minority positions, who then use difference to mobilise in support of their own claims. Nationality, race and ethnicity structure relations in ways that contain people and help determine their oppor-tunities, rights, or the lack of these things (Bhabha in Rutherford,

3

1990:208). But within the structures and the sets of relations different individuals and groups act, even in circumstances not of their choosing (Rutherford, 1990:20).

The consequences for people named as within or outside the boundaries vary (Pettman, 1988b:19). Boundaries drawn by dominant-group members around themselves 'in the course of, or for the purpose of, domination' (Bannerji, 1987:12) imply that inclusion is good and exclusion bad. Boundaries drawn by dominant-group members around and imposed on others often makes inclusion bad, for it locks the dominated into a form of identity enclosure (Trinh, 1987:16). The dominated may in turn mobilise in defence of their own interests, either disputing the imposed boundaries or categories, or seizing the category and infusing it with new and oppositional value and meaning (Gilroy, 1987:66).

The categories that are imposed in dominance or mobilised in resistance are not homogenous. Category boundaries create false differences and mask real ones (Quintanales in Moraga, 1983:153). Nation, race and ethnic categories disguise interests that may be shared across their boundaries, by women, by workers, by employers, for example. They also disguise differences within the categories, including those of age, class and gender, and also of sexuality, ideology and affiliation or association on other grounds. Individuals within the boundaries have multiple identities, and are themselves fractured by representations of categories like Aborigines, migrants and women, as if these are alternative or exclusive identities (Bannerji, 1987:12; Spivac in Gunew and Spivac, 1986:137).

Nation making

'Inventing Australia' (White, 1981) is a popular cultural activity, which was highlighted in 1988 by the Bicentenary of white settlement in Australia, with its official slogan as 'the celebration of a nation' (Alomes, 1988:329).

The Bicentenary itself became a site of struggle over different definitions of national identity and preferred future directions for Australia (Mercer, 1987; Lattas, 1990). It generated images and counter-images about being Australian. Officially celebrating Australian History, it also generated counter-histories, making visible particular fragments or constituencies usually excluded from the language and image of the nation. (Note Murphy's 1986 observation of historians as prophets who are primarily responsible for articulating national and cultural images; see also Lattas, 1990.)

The most conspicuous counter-history was that of ongoing Aboriginal history and the forging of Aboriginal nationhood (Mansell, 1989). This history spoke the language of invasion, conquest and dispossession by British colonisers. It spoke too of ongoing, unceded Aboriginal sovereignty, of struggle and of survival against the odds (e.g., Treaty '88 Committee publications; see also Jennett, 1987:67). It called into question the legal and moral bases of 'Australia', and dominant representations of Australians as one people.

Nation making claims a community, but 'Australia' has long excluded many within the boundaries of the state from that community. Nation making refers to the national political project, and its making of 'the people' as a social category (Rowse and Moran, 1984:231). It involves determinations of who 'we' are, and where we belong; and simultaneously defines 'them' and the difference that threatens us (Pettman, 1988b). 'Like all imaginings, [nationalism] consists, in equal parts, of fabrication and intervention, memory and amnesia, solidarity and murder' (Anderson in Guidieri et al., 1988:406).

The Australian national political project historically has been an exclusive one—masculinist, racist and Anglo-supremacist (de Lepervanche in Yuval-Davis and Anthias, 1989). Aborigines were excluded from the beginning of settlement by the formulation of the colony of New South Wales as *terra nullius*—unoccupied country (Reynolds, 1987). Violence, restricted citizenship and institutionalisation were the strategies to build the nation and the state as white (Evans, 1975; Beckett, 1988b). Immigration and citizenship restrictions also operated to keep foreign 'others' out (Sherington, 1990).

Nation making and state making are related but not equivalent processes. Making the nation, calling up the people, determining who 'we' are, requires considerable ideological work (Lattas, 1990; Gilroy, 1987; Hall, 1988a). The state in Australia has been centrally engaged in the process of defending its own territorial boundaries, and seeking to administer all who are within those boundaries. Succeeding federal governments have determined who is entitled to Australian nationality, to citizenship and to a range of other social and political rights, by virtue of birth, or through immigration and 'naturalisation' after a period of residence. The state polices its nation through immigration and citizenship policies, as well as through its management of different groups and of inter-group relations within its boundaries (Jupp in Najman and Western, 1988).

The state claims responsibility over the whole of the territory within its jurisdiction, but the intensity of the state's gaze varies in terms of both space and people. Whilst Australia did not experience long periods when the frontier was beyond government reach, in places local settlers and state agents, notably the police, exercised considerable local power historically; and frontier conditions continued in parts of Australia into the twentieth century, in fact until quite recently in parts of the north (Larbalestier, 1988).

In 1901, with the federation of the rather fractious colonies after a period of energetic nationalist mobilisation, 'Australia' was founded. The motto of the popular nationalist *Bulletin* in the 1890s—'Australia for the white man'—summed up a political project that lasted until after the Second World War. Notions of race were intertwined with loyalty to Britain, kith and kin, which took many young men to the killing fields of the empire. Racist and imperialist ideology mixed with versions of a new man in the Antipodes, but the man was still white and English speaking.

McQueen (1970) identified racism as intrinsic to Australian nationalism, expressed especially against Aboriginal people, through fear of Asia, and in sub-imperialistic designs on the Pacific. The social significance of whiteness and of being part of or close enough to the dominant language and culture were made brutally clear. Becoming Australian was a highly exclusive enterprise.

The national political project was also both militaristic and masculinist. The birth of the nation was through the ritual of the blooding at Gallipoli and its destruction of young men; it was not a celebration of the life-giving powers of women (de Lepervanche, 1989). Men were the brave warriors who would defend the virtuous (white) women (cf Elshtain, 1987), reinforcing a division between the public and the private which confined women to the less political, less important, domesticated aspects of life. It also militarised notions of citizenship and made women's relationship with the state problematic, even where they enjoyed the vote (Pateman, 1988). Women were rarely visible within nationalist representations (Summers, 1975; Curthoys, 1970; Saunders, 1990), although they became visible in panics about immigration and population as 'breeders of the white race' (de Lepervanche, 1989:165). Representing white women as reproducers of the nation and defenders of its morals entailed among other things the policing of white women's relations, especially their sexual relations, with 'inferior races'.

Colonisation and the settler state

Making Australia required Aboriginal dispossession. Aboriginal people were the subject of large-scale violence, and in their defeat were frequently displaced from their home-places (Broome, 1982).

They were also systematically excluded from the emerging nation: physically, through their confinement to reserves and settlements; legally, through their subjection to a separate and inferior legal status; and culturally and psychologically, through an extraordinary forgetfulness, a voluntary amnesia which rendered them invisible within the nation (Stanner, 1969; Smith, 1981). On the occasions they did appear they were contained within representations of the exotic and/or the primitive. Australian History could begin with Captain Cook discovering Australia, and with valiant white men struggling to tame an empty and forbidding continent.

Colonisation created Australians, and it also created Aborigines (Reece, 1987; Attwood, 1989). Before colonisation, Aboriginal people identified themselves with a particular country or place, and with a range of kinship and religious affiliations and relations. Through colonisation, Aborigines came to be named and managed as a racial category, or else as two categories where their administrators distinguished between 'mixed race' and 'full bloods' (Rowley, 1974). These categories were ascribed characteristics based on notions of blood, and informed by ideologies of scientific racism which were used to rationalise Aboriginal dispossession, exclusion and exploitation.

A nation of immigrants?
Australia was forged through colonisation. A focus on this process generates a model of Aborigines and the rest, variously represented as whites, Europeans, or even Australians. 'The rest' are all immigrants or the descendants of relatively recent immigrants.

'The rest' are not homogenous. Many potential migrants were long excluded from coming by racially and culturally restrictive entry regulations, and some who did manage to migrate were and in some cases still are marginal in Australia. From the 1950s entry gradually became less discriminatory, and then from the early 1970s non-discriminatory in terms of race and country of origin (Sherington, 1990).

The immigrants provided labour to build a nation which was also a part of an international capitalist system (Collins, 1988; Miles, 1987b). The new nation had a class structure and race, cultural and gender relations that reflected the dominant groups and their interests, and the society was stratified in terms of race, ethnicity, gender and class.

Aboriginal people only came to be officially counted in census data in their own country in 1967. Shifts towards a more inclusive citizenship policy had been evident from the 1950s, but the expectation was that Aboriginal people and migrants from non-English-speaking backgrounds would assimilate. Thus difference was to be denied or diluted and rendered safe by 'them' becoming like 'us', adopting 'Australian' values, lifestyle and culture, without Australia having to change. It was not always clear what Aboriginal people and migrants were being asked to assimilate into.

Assimilation was undermined by dominant groups' hostility to the provisionally admitted others. The latter understandably sought their own forms of association and identity, which offered some welcome and security. From the late 1960s especially, both Aboriginal groups and ethnic minority groups organised on the basis of their difference, and the exclusion and exploitation they experienced. From the 1970s some degree of cultural difference has been officially accepted as a basis for identity and claim and for government provision through policies directed separately to Aboriginal people, or to 'ethnic communities', whilst Australia has been declared a multicultural society (Foster and Stockley, 1988).

Thus race and cultural difference are accorded recognition in Australian politics today, this time seen either as markers of disadvantage or as positive cultural attributes. But the nature and bases of the communities which are called up are rarely subject to analytic scrutiny, nor is it clear where and how they relate to notions of nation.

In the process we are left with rather different models of Australian society. The dominant model continues to be an Australia which is white, English-speaking and probably male, although nowadays some recognition may be given to others—Aborigines, migrants, and women, often seen as alternative categories, each with an ambiguous relationship to being Australian. A colonial model anchors Australia in a division between Aboriginal people and the colonisers/migrants, but may read this division in terms of cultural difference, or alternatively as relations of domination and subordination in which the organising concepts are indigenous status, colonisation and racism. The multicultural model may obscure the power of dominant groups and see Australia as a mix of cultures and plurality of interests. A more radical model of the political economy of migration posits unequal power and the exploitation of migrant labour. It is not clear how these different models fit in relation to each other; nor where the women are within them. Feminist models tend still to represent a binary opposition between men and women, or juggle both class and gender. They too frequently have difficulties theorising about more than one or two oppressions at once (Broome in Jennett and Stewart, 1987).

Race making

Race and ethnicity are often represented as if they are alternative bases for labelling people, and for self-identification. Thus race is associated with physical characteristics like skin colour, and ethnicity is associated with cultural characteristics like language. In Australia there is a common alternative distinction where 'race' refers to Aboriginal people and the context of colonisation, while 'ethnicity' refers to people of non-English-speaking backgrounds, located within the process of migration. These academic and popular representations reflect the political and administrative divide between Aboriginal Affairs and Multicultural or Ethnic Affairs.

Since race is frequently associated with characteristics like colour, hair type or facial features, it is often presumed to be 'real' and immutable, and spoken of as if it is a birth identity (Green and Carter, 1988:5). Indeed the political significance of race lies precisely in its capacity to make differences and inequalities seem natural, to locate them within biology or primordial time, and so to mask the social and political processes—and interests—that create and reshape 'races'.

Even the most cursory review of the language of race reveals widespread slippage between biological characteristics and learned, cultural ones (Cowlishaw, 1987). The boundaries drawn around different groups labelled as races change over time, as too does the ideology used to inform the meaning given to racial differences (Mason, 1982; Banton, 1987b). In the nineteenth century 'scientific racism' authorised common-sense notions of physical and cultural differences. The result was an elaborate model of a hierarchy of races, used to justify colonisation and early capitalist notions of progress. These ideas were widely utilised in Australia, especially in the process of rationalising Aboriginal dispossession (de Lepervanche in Bottomley and de Lepervanche, 1984; Marcus in de Lepervanche and Bottomley, 1989).

Different groups were racialised at different times. Thus in Australia in the late nineteenth century not only the Chinese but also the Irish were represented as belonging to a race apart, presumed to have essential qualities by virtue of their birth identities. In the 1930s Italians were not white enough; and post-Second World War migrants from southern Europe were also singled out, though more often using language or country of origin to predict otherness. 'Asians' became the most visible non-Aboriginal targets of racism in the 1980s, while Muslim and Arab Australians are the most recent groups to be racialised and victimised (HEROC, 1991).

Thus racism draws shifting boundaries around different 'races'. The markers used to signify membership of or exclusion from particular races vary. Possible markers include skin colour, religion, country of origin, and language. But it is the process of signification—the labelling of others as members of the out-group—which is politically strategic, and not the particular marker or supposed difference in itself (Miles, 1987a:26). Racism is often associated with colour, but this is only one, although perhaps the most obvious one, of the possible markers of racialised difference. Colour has been significant in classifying people in Australia as Aboriginal or not, and also in a presumed linking of colour with culture (Tonkinson in Howard, 1989:141; Cowlishaw, 1986:3). Colour can also be used as a marker by Aboriginal people among themselves (Trigger, 1989).

Political mobilisation around imposed race categories can make black a political colour, signifying shared experiences of discrimination, exploitation and resistance among those who are labelled as not-white. White is also a political colour, signifying inclusion in public power, although both definitions of whiteness and white people's access to power and privilege may vary considerably. The political significance of whiteness remains under-theorised (Kovel, 1988). Some whites also become targets of racism, either because of their presumed country of origin or religion, or because of their political, social or family association with racialised others.

The language of race and racism also changes over time (Prager, 1987:62). The 'new racism' uses the language of nation and utilises cultural rather than biological criteria for identifying difference (Barker, 1981; Gordon and Klug, 1986). It asserts that defence and closure against others and preference for one's own is natural.

The new racism is not simply a clever exercise in political manipulation or a disguise for racist sentiment. It represents the redefinition and defence of 'the people', of national boundaries, belongingness and identity under seige. It uses the language of war and invasion (cf Gilroy, 1987). It rose to prominence in Australia and in other western countries in the wake of large-scale labour migrations and of the crisis in international capitalism that generated massive economic restructuring and rising unemployment.

The new racism in Australia was signalled by the so-called Blainey debate in 1984 (Markus and Rickfels, 1985), and incorporated attacks on both 'Asian' immigration and Aboriginal land rights. These attacks were coded in terms of 'our' way of life, citing 'community attitudes' in a way that constructed a narrow and exclusive community, and asserting that special provision for Aboriginal people or migrants amounted to reverse racism. In the process the ambiguous citizenship of non-dominant groups was again demonstrated. While the arguments purported to be about cultural difference, the deterministic association of culture with race or country of origin reflected a tapping into the old racism (de Lepervanche, 1980; Cowlishaw, 1986).

The language mobilised in resistance to racism also changes over time. Those subjected to racialisation and marginalisation often change their names to signal their desire for a change in status (Banton, 1987c:170). For example, some Aboriginal activists described themselves as black in the late 1960s, identifying with the struggles for civil rights in the United States, but by 1972 they increasingly used the language of indigenous status and identification as a fourth world people, signalling the claim to special status and their still-unresolved part in the colonial adventure. Since then Aboriginal people have spoken of themselves variously as a nation, race and culture (see chapter 6). Some Aboriginal people use the different names that Aboriginal people give themselves in different parts of Australia; for example Koori in south-eastern Australia (Fesl, 1990).

Noting these shifts in the meaning and language of race reminds us that race and particular races are social and political constructions (Pettman, 1988c). It is necessary to analyse the processes behind their construction and naming, and the reproduction of the ideology behind those processes. Such analysis must be placed in a historical and material context, for it is the interplay of ideology and material relations that determines the meaning of race, and the status of those who are categorised as belonging to particular races.

A focus on the political construction of race highlights the power relations that underpin race relations. Green and Carter for example talk of 'race-making', through which increasing numbers of immigrants are seen to constitute a 'race problem', and numbers themselves become a threat (1988:15; see Pettman 1988c).

Gilroy, writing about blacks in Britain, identifies an 'alternate current of racism between problem and victim status', and examines the ways that representing blacks as problems and victims, as objects, pushes them out of history, rendering their race and inferior status as natural, as something pertaining to them (1987:11). He analyses race as a political category whose meanings are determined in political struggles. He develops Omi and Winant's notion of 'racial formation', through which races become organised politically.

This concept supports the idea that racial meanings can change, can be struggled over. Rather than talking about racism in the singular, analysts

11

should therefore be talking about racisms in the plural. These are not just different over time but may vary within the same social formation or historical conjuncture. (1987:38)

The notion of racisms (see also Hall, 1978:26; 1980:336) underlies both the changing historical and material circumstances in which the politics of race are conducted, and the changing meanings and language of that process. Racism may refer to the ideology used to distinguish and to devalue 'others', and also to the actual consequences of their being so labelled and treated. Thus racism is both an ideology and a social practice. In its practice it structures social relations of dominance, subordination and exploitation (Hall, 1988a).

Racism as ideology and as practice takes its form from its particular historical and social context. We will explore the nature of racisms in Australia in subsequent chapters.

Making ethnicity

The federal 1975 Race Discrimination Act refers to race, colour, ethnicity and country of origin. In various government and other pronouncements, confusion between race and culture abounds.

Political recognition of difference in terms of Aboriginality, ethnicity and multiculturalism raises conceptual as well as political problems. Race is no longer an officially endorsed basis for discrimination or exclusion: indeed anti-discrimination legislation now protects those who were until recently victims of legislative racism. But as race became unfashionable, ethnicity became fashionable (de Lepervanche, 1980). Although race as a biological concept was then officially discredited, those groups that had previously been racialised were now reconstituted as cultural groups. As the old boundaries remained the same, this often meant that cultural referents continued to signify race, and to validate the boundaries that had been drawn in dominance and for the purposes of control (Cowlishaw, 1986).

'Ethnicity' became part of the political language of difference in Australia in the 1970s, recognising that neither Aborigines nor many migrant groups were going to assimilate and fade away. Migrants or New Australians became ethnics. 'Ethnic community' usually refers to migrants from non-English-speaking backgrounds (de Lepervanche, 1984:171; Jupp, 1988). Ethnicity thus involves 'migrantness' as ideology (Morrissey in Bottomley and de Lepervanche, 1984:186), a process by which some rather than other migrants become 'ethnic'.

In terms of power relations, ethnicity signals minority status, and mobilisation against the penalties of that status (Pellizzi in Guidieri and Pellizzi, 1988:156). Ethnic groups are not pre-migration identifiers but new social forms, shaped by members' experiences of exclusion and/or exploitation, and of treatment by the state as different. Thus ethnicity does not express culture in and of itself, but rather the political signification of culture within social relations of dominance (Pellizzi in Goldberg and Greer, 1990:45). Yet in debates about migration and multiculturalism, culture and ethnicity are frequently represented as birth identities, as something pertaining to people simply by virtue of their or their parents coming from a particular country of origin. In this representation culture becomes something static and shared equally by all those labelled as members of the category. Yet the boundaries that are represented as immutable are fluid, and informed by shifting and contradictory associations.

The politics of boundary making are disguised by the assertion of discrete and different cultures and racial and ethnic groups. Differences within the groups and interests that some members of subordinate groups share across the boundaries are also disguised. So too is majority-group hegemonic race and ethnicity. Thus race and ethnicity become something only minority groups have. The race and ethnicity of the dominant groups is normalised and naturalised, as if they are somehow outside culture and politics, and simply represent 'society' (cf Julien and Mercer, 1988:6).

In 1973, Minister for Immigration Grassby in the Whitlam Labor government first declared Australia to be a multicultural society, and also asserted that 'we are all ethnics'. While intended to remind dominant groups of their own cultural histories, this representation disguises the power relations involved and depoliticises cultural difference (see chapter 6). It may be more useful to recognise that

we all speak from a particular place, out of a particular history, out of a particular experience, a particular culture, without being contained by that position ... We are all in that sense *ethnically* located and our ethnic identities are crucial to our subjective sense of who we are. (Hall 1989b:4)

Race and ethnic identities represent distinct social interests, with a close relationship between identity and power (Rowse and Moran, 1984:230). Identities are mobilised as political resources and as backing to claims in dominance and resistance, but in language that disguises the positional, relational and contingent nature of identity.

Ethnic identities, which for Hall include 'race', are also crucial in positioning individuals in complex power relations within society. We all speak from a particular place, but some places are more powerful than others. The state and ideology-making institutions like education and the media can constitute racialised subjects and represent difference as deviance. Access to positions with power to validate and enforce meanings are unequally distributed, and correlate with race and ethnicity—and gender.

WHERE ARE THE WOMEN?

The crucial dimension of gender is often missing from representations of nation, race, ethnicity and cultural difference. So it is necessary to ask where women are in national, racial and ethnic processes and collectivities, and how race and cultural differences are represented in women's and feminist writings.

Nation, race and ethnicity entail the drawing of boundaries and the determining of characteristics through which to allocate or withhold membership of the different collectivities. These collectivities must be reproduced ideologically, materially and biologically. The gendered roles of women are a key, even when not intentionally or explicitly articulated.

Yuval-Davis and Anthias (1989:7) identify five ways in which women are represented in national processes:

1 as biological reproducers of ethnic collectivities—evident historically in Australia through the representation of white women as the breeders of the nation, and through the restrictions on non-white women's immigration into Australia;
2 as reproducers of the boundaries of ethnic/national groups—evident in policing of boundaries through anti-miscegenation legislation; and the defence of dominant groups' purity through the designation of most children with one Aboriginal parent as Aboriginal;
3 as transmitters of culture and ideological reproducers, through their roles in the upbringing of children and as community managers whose labour and skills maintain 'cultural' organisations and associations;
4 as signifiers of ethnic/national difference, both to their own group, and to outsider groups. Thus a 'good' Italian girl or Muslim woman may be expected to behave in certain ways to be considered as part of the community. Dominant groups also signal the outsider status of other groups through the symbolic representation of non-white women as different from their own-group women; and
5 as participants in national economic, political and military

struggles—relevant in Australia in the central role played by Aboriginal women in holding their families and communities together in the face of dispossession, racism and poverty; and in some migrant women's roles in resistance and feminist struggles before and after migration.

Here women's roles in biological, social and cultural reproduction of collectivities of which they are members are made visible. So too are ways in which collectivities reproduce and define themselves through, among other things, sex roles and sexual division of labour, and through representations of women. 'The family' is rightly seen (although often in distorted or patriarchal ways) as a marker of national, racial and ethnic difference, and minority families may operate as places of escape from and resistance to dominant social relations. Alternatively minority families may be stigmatised and subjected to surveillance that places them under stress and makes intervention against them a constant danger (see chapter 4).

Women are not just ideological constructs of their own or others' collectivities, nor boundless or selfless labourers for their community's good. Particular women may or may not see themselves as belonging to a 'community' identified on grounds of race, ethnicity or cultural difference. They may resist both insider and outsider constructions of them or attempts to confine them within particular boundaries. Representations of race and ethnicity as fixed and bounded rather than changing and contested in both their membership and their meaning also disguise women's continuing negotiations and active engagements in boundary and identity making. In Australia today 7 million Australians come from three or more different ethnic backgrounds, and many women through intermarriage and other relationships have living connections with more than one ethnic group (Price, 1989), including Irish, Scottish and Welsh as separate categories.

Women are socially constructed in terms of race, ethnicity and cultural difference. While they may frequently be invisible within these representations of difference, asking 'where are the women?' reveals distinctly racialised or culturalised gender stereotypes. Gender is constituted in and through racial and cultural difference, and race and cultural difference are experienced in gendered forms. We will be pursuing these complex constitutions throughout this book.

Asking where women are in the collectivities of nation, race and ethnic group includes interrogating their relations with men of their group/s, and with women both within and across the boundaries. The task involves analysing multiple oppression, and identifying women's experiences of difference, while also retaining sight of the structures and power relations in which the politics of difference are played.

2 The colonial encounter

Some Aboriginal women assert that racism rather than sexism is their primary problem, and that their being Aboriginal rather than their being female is what places them socially (O'Shane, 1976:64; but see O'Shane in Mitchell, 1984; Huggins, 1987). Others argue that racism and sexism equally determine their lives (Watson in Scutt, 1987; Kelly in National Women's Conference, 1990:104). Certainly Aboriginal women have been centrally affected along with Aboriginal men by invasion, colonisation, dispossession, displacement, institutionalisation, exploitation and ongoing racism. But it is necessary to look at those processes and ask whether Aboriginal women have experienced and continue to experience colonisation and racism in ways similar to or in some ways different from Aboriginal men.

This chapter will not attempt to retell the whole 200 years of Aboriginal/white history; but rather sketch an overview of colonial relations and institutional racism in which Aboriginal women have been entrapped, before looking specifically at the experiences and representations of Aboriginal women, and their relations, historically and currently, with 'white' women.

THE CONSTRUCTION OF COLONIAL RELATIONS

Aboriginal women's status today can only be understood in terms of colonisation, the fatal impact of two very different peoples, cultural systems and systems of production. White invasion signalled a conflict over political control, superseding the sovereignty of a large number of land-owning groups by colonial and then state and federal governments, and the development of a colonial structure in which the relations between the colonisers and the colonised were typified by domination and subordination (Pettman, 1988a). The colonisation of Australia also meant the imposition of a capitalist system of ownership and production on the then-existing hunting and gathering economy (Drakakis-Smith, 1981; Jennett in Jennett and Stewart, 1987). Colonisation was and centrally still is a bitter conflict over land ownership and land use (Maddock, 1983). The very process of white settlement and the development of modern Australia necessitated dispossessing Aboriginal people, for the two modes could not co-exist (Larbalestier, 1990:84), although in places a gradual, partial or contradictory displacement occurred.

The frontier spread in fits and starts over the continent (Reynolds, 1972; Broome, 1982), bringing with it in varying degrees the violence and resistance of the killing times, before Aboriginal defeat and dispossession was secured (Reynolds, 1981; Read, 1988). Until recently Australian History has been largely silent about both the violence and the resistance. From the 1970s different histories, usually written by white academics, began to tell different stories. For example, Rowley (1974a) broke the silence with descriptions of the horrific destruction of Aboriginal people along the frontier and after settlement, telling of them as victims of colonisation (Attwood, 1989). Then revisionist historians wrote another history, signalled by Reynolds' *The Other Side of the Frontier*, documenting Aboriginal resistance (see also Robinson and York, 1977). These histories contested images of Aboriginal people as pathetic or as caught up in cultural disintegration in the face of an overwhelming power, technology and ideological assault. Sometimes the cost of Aboriginal inclusion in Australian history appeared to be romanticising Aboriginal men as fighters, presaging an Anzac tradition (Rowse, 1986). More recently a number of historians have stressed accommodation along with resistance (Reece, 1987; McGrath, 1987; Reynolds, 1990).

In many of the earlier representations of Aborigines as victims or as resisters Aboriginal women were invisible, and both Aborigines and whites were often treated as homogenous categories (Reece, 1987). There was at times insufficient recognition of both the variety of experiences in different localities and times, and of the ambiguous and often contradictory nature of the colonial exchange on the ground (Reece, 1987; Attwood, 1989; Rowse, 1986).

After the violence came defeat and often dispossession and displacement, although in places where whites did not want the land (yet) Aboriginal communities were less disrupted.

There was a dramatic decline in Aboriginal population, from a contested estimation of 500 000 in 1788 to an officially recorded 277 645 in the 1986 census (Butlin, 1983; ABS, 1989). This latter figure is based on self-identification, and probably significantly under-represents the numbers of people of Aboriginal descent.

Over huge tracts the land was lost to Aboriginal people, who especially in the 'protection'/segregation period from the late nineteenth century were removed to reserves away from their country (Rowley, 1974b; Beckett in Howard, 1989:124; Markus, 1990). In the pastoral north, where more extensive use was made of Aboriginal labour, some Aborigines managed to remain for decades or even generations on their land. The seasonal nature of labour demands and the pastoral industry's exploitation of aspects of Aboriginal culture allowed a degree of cultural maintenance. It also constituted Aboriginal labour in the pastoral industry as a super-exploited segment of the labour force (Jennett, 1987:59), maintaining the Aboriginal camp as a source of cheap casual labour and of sexual partners for white men (Larbalestier, 1988; Beckett, 1988b:7).

Aborigines in the pastoral industry also learnt new and valued skills and had access to some European goods. They might continue to live in or on or near their own country, and had some protection against marauding whites, in some circumstances at least. But power always rested ultimately with the whites in a situation where the distant state and its more immediate police and Aboriginal 'protectors' were firmly on the side of the colonisers (Larbalestier, 1990).

In the more settled south-east, where agriculture or close settlement developed, Aborigines were frequently forcibly removed from their country (Markus, 1990). In some places the combination of violence, disease and malnutrition destroyed all members of the group. Elsewhere Aboriginal people were often contained within government reserves and missions described by Beckett as 'a total structure of domination orchestrated by the state' (1988b:8; see also Rowley, 1974b; Peterson, 1985). They were managed and administered as a 'race' category, even where that administration also recognised distinctions of 'blood', or issued exemption certificates to those who were 'advanced natives' on condition of their breaking with their communities and families (Tatz, 1979; McCorquodale, 1986).

In this situation Aboriginal people's place in 'Australia' was ambiguous and often contradictory (Beckett, 1988b). They were excluded from citizenship, from the labour market in many situations, and from other legal and social entitlements. They were an entrapped minority (Rowley, 1987:7) in their own special status, and institutions were developed to administer them separately. But both Aboriginal men and women were also often exploited and forced to labour for little return, often for rations or keep on reserves or for white employers. Aboriginal women were also exploited sexually by white men, including those who were charged with responsibility for their welfare (Evans, 1975; Rosser, 1985; McGrath, 1987).

The situation varied from state to state (Rowley, 1974b; Broome, 1982), but Aborigines everywhere suffered from both neglect and vulnerability to state intervention. Moves towards assimilation for Aboriginal people began to take effect in the 1950s and 1960s, discriminatory legislation was gradually repealed, and Aborigines were expected to become ultimately indistinguishable from other Australians. Responsibility for preparing Aboriginal people for assimilation became the excuse for heightened surveillance and control by the state (Beckett, 1988b:10; Morris, 1990).

Assimilation was not official policy for long. The Whitlam Labor government adopted a policy of Aboriginal self-determination in the early 1970s, succeeded by self-management under the Liberal–National government (Bennett, 1989). 'Race' remained a category for managing and servicing Aboriginal people.

Aboriginal people have not been passive recipients of state or dominant-group constitution. From the earliest physical resistance (Reynolds, 1981), through passive resistance to incorporation (Alexander, 1984), to more recent organisation and participation in the political processes of the Australian state, is a whole history in itself (Bennett, 1989; Bandler, 1983; Perkins, 1975). In the process and through a kaleidoscope of policies and practices, a highly complex and dynamic relationship developed between Aboriginal people and the state (Beckett, 1988b; Jennett in Jennett and Stewart, 1990).

Aboriginal people have always been seen, and see themselves, as different, but they are constituted differently at different times. The process of constructing 'Aboriginality' is a complex interaction between Aboriginal and state action and reaction. It has been described as ethnogenesis (Jones and Hill-Burnett, 1982), as 'inventing Aborigines' (Reece, 1987) and as 'the making of the Aborigines' (Attwood, 1989). Aborigines made and continue to make themselves, but within structures, relations and discourses not of their making. The imposition of boundaries, the criteria and the consequences of exclusion or inclusion are still largely beyond their control.

Aboriginal people have been both excluded and incorporated in an uneven and ongoing process, and considerable ideological work has been done along the way to explain who 'they' are. Related to this work are debates about the nature of colonial power, Aboriginal–white relations, the mode of incorporation of Aboriginal people into the new regime and economy, and the degree of agency that Aboriginal people have had. These debates will be briefly considered next.

The generation of public knowledge about Aboriginal people includes various writings and rewritings of Aboriginal history, each of which has different implications for understanding gender in Aboriginal and Australian history.

Australian History was until recently winners' history, within which Aborigines were absent or rendered occasionally visible for national authenticity or exotic purposes. Yet in the last twenty years Aboriginal history has been significantly rewritten, and Aboriginal people have become visible in new ways (Rowse and Moran, 1984:264; Attwood, 1989). But while Women's Studies is now largely taught by and written for by women, albeit women from particular backgrounds, Aboriginal history and Aboriginal Studies are still dominated by non-Aboriginal people, especially in terms of research and academic writing. Here there are highly political questions about who should and who can write Aboriginal history; about who is authorised and entitled to speak for whom, and who is knowledgeable about what (Pettman 1988b).

Within Aboriginal society women's business is frequently constructed as in some ways separate from and different from men's business (Gale, 1978, 1983; Bell, 1983; Mundine, 1990). Aboriginal women are still largely invisible within Aboriginal history (Curthoys, 1983:109), or else are contained within academic writings specifically about Aboriginal women, often written by white women anthropologists and historians. Langton (1981; 1988) and Huggins (1987; 1987/8) are among the exceptions here. Many white academics are now self-conscious about the way they authorise what they say about Aboriginal people, for example, through reference to Aboriginal informants or by virtue of their own standing in Aboriginal society (see Bell, 1983; 1989). There are questions here about whether white women are better able to talk with, learn from, and work with Aboriginal women than white men are, and in turn whether some white women are better at working with (some?) Aboriginal women than other white women are. Thus Hamilton's review (1986) of Bell's *Daughters of the Dreaming* comments on her situating herself as the right kind of woman to find out about Aboriginal women. Bell later suggests that radical feminists, with their understandings of separatism, are better placed than are socialist feminists to work with Aboriginal women (1989). Responses to this article highlighted the question of whether some issues should be dealt with or can only be dealt with by Aboriginal women (see chapter 7).

White academics are inevitably located within a set of social relations in which whiteness and Aboriginality are still of determining significance. Exchanges between white people and Aboriginal people, including white women and Aboriginal women, are saturated with interchanges and exclusions of past generations. Some white academics seek collaborative ways of working and voicing (for example Laurie and McGrath in White, 1985; see Pettman, 1988b:9–10). These collaborations are often fraught with difficulties (Huggins and Tarrago, 1990), including those to do with unequal power relations and with the problematic nature of experience and memory (Goodall, 1987), to which we will return later.

Yet even while academic production of Aboriginal history and Aboriginal studies remains largely in white hands, there have been significant challenges to the dominant versions of Australian History and society. Why? What has generated the radical, revisionist and oppositional histories? They are clearly informed in part by developments within various disciplines. The growth of feminist scholarship, social history, and the new ethnography question receive notions and critically examine the construction of categories. Marxist analyses make visible the generative role of economic processes and relations between classes, noting material factors that constitute and in turn are constituted through ideology.

Non-Aboriginal writers of Aboriginal history may well have a politics in support of Aboriginal rights, although the extent and forms of their engagement will vary. Increasingly visible Aboriginal protest and political organisation has challenged dominant representations of Aboriginal history and society. Non-Aboriginal academics working in these areas have had their outsider expert status called into question by those who claim the privilege of experience and of identity with the category that is being written or talked about (Atkinson et al., 1985; Huggins, 1990).

Aboriginal history is still with us in the sense that it tells Australians how they got to where they are now. It is the other side of and constituted through 'white' history in the process of colonisation and the structuring of social relations today. Issues of Aboriginal dispossession and claim and of colonisation are still unresolved in Australia. Hence academic writings and representations about the nature of pre-colonial Aboriginal society, the violence of the frontier, the mode of incorporation of Aboriginal people into colonial and contemporary society, their communities and the nature of

Aboriginality, are not simply 'academic'. Rather they play a part in the politics of language and contest—about Aboriginal status and rights now, about whose country it is, and who should have rights within it—that underlie debates about immigration, multiculturalism, and social justice generally (Pettman, 1988b).

Each writing of history, each representation of Aboriginal people is an ideological and interpretive event. Each is informed by a particular political project (Rowse, 1988:21), even if conventional academic discourses disguise the particular position of writers. Sometimes the project is more explicit, or at least in evidence. Thus Attwood discusses the oppositional white historians who sought 'to produce a politically useful past' (1989:136), and those revisionist white historians who represent Aboriginal people as active historical agents. For example, Reynolds writes of Aboriginal resistance and adaptability and of whites' seizing of the land, aiming to convince a white audience of both the humanity and the just claim of Aboriginal people (see Curthoys, 1983:100).

Rowse (1986) has criticised Nathan and Japanangka (1985) for their telling of the forcible rounding-up and institutionalisation of the Pitjantjatjara people, arguing that they reinforce representations of Aborigines as mere pawns and victims of white agency and coercion; a representation he sees as motivated by the need to demonstrate that the people were forcibly removed from their own country. Evidence of their choosing to leave might be used to undermine their land-rights claims (see also Long, 1989). Rowse (1988) also questions McGrath (1987) in her rather different reading, when she argues that Aboriginal men and women in the pastoral industry between the wars were not truly colonised, for their own resistance and the seasonal demands and the relative autonomy of the camp allowed for the maintenance of a dynamic Aboriginal culture. Rowse argues that Aborigines taking what pastoralists allowed them to take, in an arrangement that provided the latter with a cheap and superexploitable labour reserve, hardly constitutes resistance or autonomy. Rather he sees McGrath's reading in terms of a contemporary political project to assert continuity of Aboriginal culture as a basis for current claim, shaped in part by land rights legislative requirements and by popular perceptions about 'real' Aborigines.

Aboriginal historians are many, but rarely placed within the academy or able to publish their knowledge in academic forums except through collaboration with white academics, for example, through journals like *Aboriginal History*. Those few Aboriginal historians who have credentials in academia have their own projects.

Aboriginal contributions to Aboriginal history have fundamental cultural and political purposes. 'We are reclaiming our right to identify and define ourselves ... We, as Aboriginal people, can begin to rectify the white misconceptions about our history by writing it ourselves' (Atkinson et al., 1985:40).

While Aboriginal historians are beginning to be heard outside their own communities (Huggins, 1987/8:5), Aboriginal contributions to public readings of Aboriginal history come more from family or community histories, or from auto/biographies, including some of people who have played a role in key political struggles and confrontations with the state (e.g., Bandler, 1983; Tucker, 1987; Mum Shirl, 1989; Perkins, 1975).

The rest of this chapter will pursue aspects of Aboriginal women's history, and the implications of contested readings for political projects today, looking at debates about Aboriginal women's role and status in traditional society and the effects of colonisation on Aboriginal women. It will examine historically-informed representations of Aboriginal women's sexuality, their experiences of work, and white women's involvement in the colonial project.

ABORIGINAL WOMEN IN TRADITIONAL SOCIETY

'Tradition' is a difficult concept. It is called up in contemporary politics as a contested social construction (see chapter 6). We cannot know what traditional Aboriginal society was like before white colonisation, although we do know that Aboriginal people across the continent shared many things including their mode of production, land use, and many aspects of social organisation. We also know that the details of organisation and ritual varied considerably from place to place. 'Traditional' society is still seen as existing in the more remote parts of Australia. It was those places that were favoured for anthropological fieldwork (Cowlishaw, 1987), which itself then played a crucial role in the reconstruction and representation of Aboriginal culture. Anthropological writings were usually set well behind the frontier, and their gaze was upon societies already profoundly affected by colonisation.

Anthropologists' accounts were shaped by their own cultural experiences and expectations, including those of gender in their own societies. Within these accounts women's roles were often invisible or misrepresented, reflecting the prominence of male white anthropologists and the sexism of their perceptions, as well as the fact that their informants were usually Aboriginal men (Berndt in Gale, 1978; Bell, 1983).

Here, as in popular representation, is the familiar normalised absence/pathologised presence of minority and colonised women. Where visible, Aboriginal women were frequently represented as degraded and abused chattels, mistreated by Aboriginal men; or as dusky temptresses who were to blame for white men's straying (Evans 1982:11). These representations legitimised white government and mission interference in Aboriginal life and white men's exploitation of Aboriginal women.

There is extensive debate about the role of Aboriginal women traditionally. Merlan (1988) identifies several models of gender relations in recent literature on Aboriginal women, including a popular representation by some white women anthropologists of 'unequal but non-colonising participation', as opposed to models of subordination. She also critically examines Bell's (1983) construction of Aboriginal women as independent, parallel and equivalent in social and ritual power. She notes how the separation of the sexes in certain Aboriginal domains is seen as absolute and immutable.

Bell is a white woman anthropologist who has written to recover Aboriginal women's self-perception of being 'boss for themselves' (1983:11), arguing women's substantial independence in economic and ritual terms, with separate gender-specific power bases (1983:23). Bell maintains that Aboriginal women would not agree with popular anthropological characterisation of their lives as impoverished and male dominated. She notes but downplays the impact of colonisation and tensions between women and men, and puts emphasis upon strong women with an autonomous base.

Hamilton (1986) challenges Bell's reading of Aboriginal gender politics, and her implicit rejection of universal male domination (interesting in view of Bell's comments on radical feminism, see Bell, 1989). Hamilton questions the possibility of autonomy existing within a framework of male domination. She observes that Bell represents women as central, not presenting her analyses as of a contained women's space. Hamilton argues rather that Aboriginal women are still entrapped in a world of men, and that both masculinism and the impact of colonial relations reveal a different picture. She further argues that Bell, in her concern to 'put women back into the account' and accord respect for Aboriginal women's representations of their own role and ritual, fails to observe how certain forms of Aboriginal performance have been rewarded in travel, money, recognition and land rights status. Many external factors encourage Aboriginal women to focus on their own ritual activity, as actors in the contemporary political scene.

This focus is analysed in Lilley's (1989) examination of the instrumental purposes served by representations of Aboriginal women's spirituality by one set of claimants in a land rights dispute between different groups. Gungarakayn women reconstituted themselves in an idealised version of a past constructed in the context of requirements of land rights legislation and hearings. The women making these representations were urban-based and linked with academic institutions and radical Aboriginal community organisations. They were also drawing on non-Aboriginal concepts and visions in their construction of gender, using colonial, anthropological and feminist discourses as 'a way of talking *about* their society and not only *within* it' (Lilley, 1989:88). Their evidence and this analysis further highlights the contemporary and political uses of tradition.

Debates about Aboriginal women's role in traditional society are thus part of an ongoing political contest. Aboriginal women argue for their rights as landowners who have been excluded from political, legal and bureaucratic processes of negotiation between white men and Aboriginal men (Gale, 1984:4, 165; Mundine, 1990:167). The debates also inform arguments about Aboriginal women's status now, and whether that status is worse or better as a result of colonisation; and the extent to which contemporary relations reflect 'traditional' forms.

The debates about women's status traditionally are also significant in terms of feminism and its wider concerns. Some Aboriginal women argue that they, unlike white women, have not been oppressed within their family or community, but that traditionally they had and some still have their own bases and rights (Huggins, 1987; Mundine, 1990; Kelly, 1990). This in turn has implications for feminist representations of patriarchy as universal (Hamilton, 1986). Aboriginal women's readings of their own role in traditional and contemporary society challenge some of the core concepts of some feminist analyses. Hamilton (1988:63–4) notes the vast gap between Aboriginal women's representation of themselves in autobiographical writings, and academic, including white feminist, representations.

SEXUAL POLITICS

The violence and dispossession accompanying colonisation affected Aboriginal women along with Aboriginal men, but held special dangers and perhaps different possibilities for Aboriginal women.

The shock of colonisation was traumatic, although its speed, force and deadliness varied from place to place. Displacement was physical but also social, cultural and emotional. It ruptured the close association with kin and place, including the places where Aboriginal women's ceremonies made sense and the women's camps could be securely maintained. The devastation went beyond the initial violence, to the destruction of whole groups through introduced diseases, and forceable removal.

The violence and maleness of the frontier (with a ratio of 38 men to 1 woman—presumably meaning white women—Broome, 1982:38), and the exploitation and rape of 'the others'' women as part of the spoils of war are stark (Evans, 1982:12). But Aboriginal women's vulnerability to exploitation and sexual abuse continued long after frontier conditions had apparently ceased, as it continues today (Sykes, 1975; Evans, 1982; Burgmann, 1984).

Complex issues to do with rape and notions of complicity and consent are raised here. Sexual relations in colonial and/or racist societies can hardly be free or equal, for the power relations are structured in such a way that the colonised women are usually terribly vulnerable. Racist and sexist representations of Aboriginal women have tended to label them as immoral and highly sexed, as prostitutes (Sykes, 1975:321; Evans, 1982:7, 11; Burgmann, 1984:26). These representations are compounded by the devaluing of women and the tendency to blame the victim, which is part of rape politics in Australia generally (Scutt, 1980). Here again racism and sexism reinforce each other, and are experienced by Aboriginal women in a brutal interaction.

Where 'rape' did appear as a political issue in colonisation it was usually as a supposed threat against white women from Aboriginal men (Evans, 1982:27). While this has not been a strong visible feature of Australian History, Harris's evidence reveals it in colonial Queensland, where Aboriginal men's sexuality was constructed as a threat to white women, again seen as white men's property (1982). Meanwhile the far more frequent rape of Aboriginal women by white men was hardly commented on, although some contemporary white reports of mistreatment of Aboriginal women have been recorded.

Sexual politics in colonial situations generally, including that of Australia, involved the related construction of black masculinity as bestial and a threat to white womanhood, and of black female sexuality as loose and wanton, placing black women beyond protection (Sykes, 1975; Harris, 1982; Hooks, 1981; cf Hall, 1984; Carby, 1986). White women's sexuality was denied, as was the possibility of their seeking out or welcoming Aboriginal men, so that any apparent relationship was defined as rape (McGrath, 1987:73; Harris, 1982). White women were expected to be God's police, a civilising influence on the frontier (Summers, 1975). But some representations blame white women for deteriorating race relations in colonial situations and for enforcing race boundaries. Such blame disguises and romanticises the male power and violence of the frontier. White women were themselves confined and controlled within different gender boundaries drawn in patriarchal racism, even where they also acted as boundary police (Inglis, 1974; Knapman, 1986; Haggis, 1990).

Rape is not a sexual act but a crime of violence and a political-power act. In colonial situations the cry of rape was used to signal moral panics, for the purpose of controlling white women's, black women's and black men's bodies and associations (Pettman, forth-coming, a). White men protected 'their' women while simultaneously controlling them and monopolising sexual access to them. They stigmatised and intimidated black men, while maintaining their access to and abuse of black women. Thus boundaries were drawn around black men and around white women, while white men were free to cross these boundaries without assuming responsibility for either black women or for their own children born to those women. Those white men who did support their Aboriginal families were often persecuted and stigmatised (McGrath, 1987). These complex relations are often more represented in fiction and family histories than in academic writings (Langford, 1988; Morgan, 1986).

These boundaries are still potent in Australia today. Popular rep-resentations of Aboriginal women as 'available' and of Aboriginal men as aggressive and threatening reproduce a strong mix of racism and sexism. Aboriginal victims of racist violence and Aboriginal women who experience sexist violence often go unrecognised and unsupported. Failure to deal with this mix also means that some feminist calls for more policing to make the streets safer for women may appear to Aboriginal men and women, especially those in the inner cities or country towns, as supporting further police interven-tion and harassment of their already-besieged communities. It means, too, that Aboriginal women may be reluctant to name dangers of violence, rape and child abuse within Aboriginal families, lest such naming confirm the construction of Aboriginal men as brutal and savage, or provide excuses for further state intervention against them (Langton, 1989; Thomas, 1988:760; see also chapter 4).

ABORIGINAL WOMEN AND AGENCY

Representations of sexual relations on the frontier and after raise questions to do with Aboriginal women's agency and choice (Ryan 1986; Jennings and Hollinsworth, 1987/8). While many Aboriginal women were dreadfully abused and others were casually used and abandoned, there are also examples of closer relations between

Aboriginal women and white men (Langford, 1988; McGrath, 1987). Some white men who did acknowledge paternity and got on with their Aboriginal families were ostracised by the white society and at times harassed by the state and its agents.

The politics of contesting representations become clear. Once Aboriginal women's absence or invisibility is noted, they may be made visible only as victims of Aboriginal men and/or white men. Ryan contests this reading, suggesting that some Aboriginal women chose and manipulated relations with white men in the Tasmanian exchanges. She argues further that Aboriginal women's relations with sealers in particular were ultimately positive. The sealers, through their sexual and economic relations with Aboriginal women, enabled Aboriginal Tasmanian society to survive (1986:39), contrasting with the total destruction wrought by pastoralists. She further suggests that representations of Truginini as a traitor to her race are based on a sexist reading of relations which condemned her because she acted without the permission of Aboriginal men (1986:39).

Colonial conquest always involves complex sexual as well as racial politics. In places Aboriginal men encouraged sexual relations between 'their' women and the intruders, in an attempt to incorporate the latter into Aboriginal kinship relations and obligations, which most refused to acknowledge, reading the 'offers' simply as prostitution or trade in women. But some settlers did enter into reciprocal obligations and relations in return for both Aboriginal women's sexual services and other Aboriginal labour and support. In various situations, Aboriginal women appeared as buffers or brokers, and had to negotiate relations in which social, police and political power backed the settlers.

McGrath, drawing on reminiscences of older Aboriginal ex-pastoral workers, notes the difference between Aboriginal women's and Aboriginal men's stories about sexual politics (1987:89). Some of the women recall particular white men or a series of adventures with some affection and pleasure. Aboriginal women may have had opportunities to benefit from moving across the racial boundaries, opportunities not generally available to Aboriginal men. They secured access to some goods and to a relatively protected base through their buffer or intermediary role between the Aboriginal camp and homestead. Yet the women who might have gained through access to some white goods and protection were never secure in that access, and were especially vulnerable to increasing interference by the state in its self-appointed role of guardian of 'mixed race' children (McGrath, 1987:90; Thomas, 1988:769).

THE STOLEN GENERATIONS

The state has interfered constantly in Aboriginal families through its forced movement, control and surveillance of Aboriginal people, and most brutally through the seizing of Aboriginal children (Jacobs, 1986; Read, 1984). One out of every six or seven Aboriginal children in New South Wales were 'taken into care' compared to one in every 200 non-Aboriginal children. Aboriginal children are still 'taken into care' in overwhelmingly disproportionate numbers (Tomlinson, 1986; Carrington, 1990; Cunneen, 1990:45).

Almost every Aboriginal family knows someone who was taken away. The stories told by Edwards and Read (1989), who are part of Linkup, an organisation dedicated to assisting Aboriginal people find their lost families, are often heart rending. These stories also demonstrate the permeability of Aboriginal communities (Merlan, 1986:116) and their ongoing vulnerability to government intervention (Marcus, 1989). They also help explain why so many Aboriginal people see welfare, education and health workers as dangerous and as agents of surveillance and control.

The assaults by government agents and policies, compounded by racism and poverty, and by high rates of imprisonment, unemployment and early death of Aboriginal men in particular, have reconstituted Aboriginal families. Aboriginal families are often extended and multi-generational, and many are female-headed and with a changing residence membership. Particular administration of welfare and definitions of women's roles pressured Aboriginal women to live separately from their men, often a condition of welfare support (Langton, 1981; Collmann, 1988).

Thus there are complex features lying behind representation of Aboriginal women as matriarchs (Pettman, 1991). They are more often heads of families and single parents than are other women in Australia. But representing responsibility as dominance disguises the pressures that they and their families experience (Larbalestier, 1980). It drastically over-estimates their capacity to protect either themselves or their loved ones against racism or poverty, and drastically under-estimates the costs of their holding families together against enormous odds.

Aboriginal families bore the brunt of conquest and miscegination through different governments' responses to the 'mixed-race problem'. While many 'mixed-race' children were absorbed into the mother's family, others were singled out by government agents substituting for the 'missing' white father, rupturing family relations and depriving mothers of their children. The process was uneven but remorseless, and compounds bitter arguments about who is and who is not Aboriginal. The national project was defended by the common process of declaring mixed-race children to be Aboriginal, or to be members of a specially constituted mixed category (Jacobs, 1986). Now many Aboriginal people reply in kind by arguing that anyone who has any Aboriginal 'blood' *is* Aboriginal (Keeffe, 1988:69), and Australia has moved away from officially recognising a mestizo category which is a buffer group in some colonial societies. Meanwhile there are many people who are still discovering their Aboriginal relations and heritage (Morgan, 1986; Keeffe, 1988).

ABORIGINAL WOMEN AND WORK

Aboriginal women share with many other Australian women experiences of poverty, welfare dependence, and primary responsibility for family care and provision. But the nature and cause of their poverty and the kinds of work available to them is distinct.

Aboriginal women have experienced work in some ways differently from other Australian women. Historically they often did what was not considered women's work; for example, stock work, fence building, rabbiting, and fruit picking, although poorer especially rural white women did 'men's work' too. Aboriginal women worked sometimes with and sometimes without their Aboriginal or non-Aboriginal menfolk (McGrath, 1987; Langford, 1988). But many Aboriginal women were also directed into domestic work, in a wide range of different situations and times—working as houseworkers on the stations where their kin lived close by, or in country towns, or in distant cities far from other Aboriginal people (Huggins, 1987/8). This last was largely the experience of Aboriginal girls seized from their families and trained specifically for domestic service in white-run missions and institutions like the Cootamundra Girls Home (Tucker, 1987; Ward, 1988; see also the film *Lousy Little Six Pence*).

Aboriginal women's experiences as domestic servants parallel those of black women in other racist and colonial situations, such as South Africa and the southern United States (Gaitskell 1982; Rollins 1985). Colonised class relations released some white women from women's work. Black women who were often characterised as unreliable or dirty mothers were responsible for home and child care for white women and their families. This often involved a hierarchy of domestic labour which correlated with colour—the 'darker' women were the domestics, the lighter child carers (Evans, 1982:13). All the women in domestic service were also vulnerable to sexual abuse by white men in the household. A 1934 report on Cherbourg mission in

Queensland suggested that 95 percent of Aboriginal girls and women sent into domestic service returned to have a child by a white father (Evans, 1982:18).

The relations between Aboriginal women and white women varied depending on time, place and the particular women involved. However the power relations were always unequal, and the mistress–servant relationship rarely encouraged or even allowed reciprocal or caring relations (Tucker, 1987; Ward, 1988; Morgan, 1986). But some Aboriginal women do recall with affection white children and occasionally white women for whom they cared and worked (Huggins, 1987/8). Some, like those of pastoral workers in McGrath's (1987) account, seem remarkably lacking in bitterness and anger. This raises questions about nostalgia and the politics of experience, and representations which go beyond degrading versions of the powerless as passive victims (see chapter 7).

Many Aboriginal women's 'close encounters' (Davenport in Moraga and Anzaldua, 1983) with white men in sexual relations and with white women and white men in domestic service have given them intimate information about their colonisers which most women and men of the dominant groups lack about their colonised Other (Watson, 1989:18; see also Stanley, 1990b:156—'We know too much about our betters, and they know very little about us').

ABORIGINAL WOMEN AND WHITE WOMEN

These encounters continue to inform Aboriginal women's views of white men and women and of racism today. Many Aboriginal women have had extensive experience of white women, whereas many white women come 'new' to contacts with Aboriginal women as teachers, health workers, community workers, or political allies. They are often surprised both by the generosity and acceptance they commonly meet and by the less frequent anger and resentment among Aboriginal women, who hold them responsible for dealing with the legacy of colonisation and ongoing racism. They may not know how to respond to accusations that they are complicit in colonial relations and in racism.

All non-Aboriginal women in Australia may be seen as beneficiaries or partakers in Aboriginal dispossession, even if they are recent arrivals or from backgrounds far removed from the dominant colonisers. White women are also positioned in a racist power structure where whiteness and English-speaking culture are socially significant and rewarded, and where being Aboriginal still often invokes a penalty. The experiences of the past include situations where individual white women and some particular unions, the Communist Party and some church groups did support Aboriginal women, and where most white women were never really sisters nor acted in defence of Aboriginal women's interests. This is why many Aboriginal women stress racism rather than sexism as their primary concern in exchanges with white women, observing that sexism neither led white men to bond with Aboriginal men against women, nor led white women to identify with and support Aboriginal women (Huggins, 1987).

Rereading colonial relations highlights unresolved issues of colonisation and racism, embedded within and structuring gender relations in Australia. White women in colonial relations often had power over Aboriginal women, and some power over Aboriginal men (Huggins 1987:78). But some white women had more power than others (cf Joseph, 1981; Palmer, 1983). At the same time both Aboriginal women and white women were subjected, although differentially, to patriarchal institutions and practices. Colonisation established a patriarchal racist and capitalist structure, through which social relations in contemporary Australia are still articulated and experienced.

White women are ambiguously placed in these relations, as Aboriginal women remind them when requiring that white feminists examine their own racism and ethnic location, before trying to develop ways of working together across racial and ethnic boundaries (Pettman, forthcoming, a).

Colonial relations are usually drawn in binary terms as whites against Aborigines, or more rarely as white women against Aboriginal women. 'White women' were, and are, a heterogeneous category, and some white women also had some power over other, especially poorer, white women. White women could be simultaneously oppressed and oppressors, or at least appear complicit in other women's oppression or exploitation. Meanwhile there were other women who are rendered invisible in the white:Aboriginal binary opposition, including for example Melanesian women and Chinese women who were also involved in complex local race politics (Saunders, 1982; Evans, 1975).

Today non-Aboriginal women can be seen as living off Aboriginal dispossession even if they have never met an Aboriginal person (and might ask themselves why this is so). Here there are complicated questions concerning complicity, collusion and innocence. If many non-Aboriginal women do not know what happened to Aboriginal people, and how dispossession and racism continue to damage them—are they still implicated? And what of the relations between

Aboriginal women and other minority women in Australia, the latter also often victims of vicious racism and sexism? What are the relations between Aboriginal women and ethnic minority women today?

Colonisation is part of Australia's present as well as its past. The colonial encounter in its unresolved and ongoing signification of race and its positioning of Aboriginal and non-Aboriginal women in very different ways continues to affect their relations with each other, and to provide major obstacles to the development of a decolonised, anti-racist and inclusive feminism.

3   Migration and incorporation

In 1947 Australia's population was only 7 million. By 1988 it was over 16 million, an increase due largely to the post-war immigration program. This program has been massive, and has drawn on increasingly varied sources of migrants, so that today Australia is second only to Israel in the numbers and range of its migrant population (Castles et al., 1988:1). In 1980 the total percentage of immigrant populations was 21.6 for Australia, 4.7 for the United States, 6.5 for Great Britain, and 15.2 for Canada (Collins, 1988: Table 1.2).

Women are frequently invisible within racial and ethnic categories, and 'migrant workers', for example, are spoken of as if they are men. There are few academic studies or government department policies which address the experiences or needs of migrant women (Eliadis, 1989:25, 37). Where they are made visible it is frequently in ways which reinforce their victim–problem status, as over-exploited workers or as over-controlled family members, for example. They are contained within the 'normalised absence/pathologised presence' couplet familiar in the representation of ethnic minority women elsewhere (Phoenix, 1985:51). They are also often represented in ways that imply that it is because they are Greek, or Muslim, or 'Asian' that they face the particular difficulties and dangers that they do. Thus it appears that cultural difference or race is the explanatory variable, obscuring other factors that help to locate women socially. These factors include women's experiences of the migration process, and of class, racism and sexism here, and their treatment by the Australian state.

Women in general occupy differential positions in racial and ethnic categories and in relation to both nation and state, compared to 'their' men (Yuval-Davis and Anthias, 1989). So we need to gender race, ethnicity and migration, to ask how migrant women's experiences and social interests may vary from those of migrant men; and how women's experiences differ within and between the various racial and ethnic categories into which they are placed, or place themselves.

This chapter seeks then to locate women within the migration process, and to identify the ways in which they are incorporated into 'Australia'; and to analyse the category 'migrant' or 'ethnic-minority women'.

IMMIGRATION AND POPULATION

Among other things, immigration has to do with population. Immigration and reproduction are two ways that the population, the nation and the labour force are remade. Nation-state controls on immigration are in part ways of controlling, restructuring and reshaping population growth, both of the state, and of particular racial or ethnic collectivities within it. Thus chapter 1 noted Australia's racially restrictive former immigration policies, aimed at keeping the nation white (Sherington, 1990). While these restrictions have been progressively lifted over the last two decades, debates over 'Asian' immigration and multiculturalism reveal that many people still read 'Australia' as white, and that race is still a part of the cultural politics of nationalism (Markus and Rickfels, 1985; Pettman, 1988b).

Historically, women's role as reproducers of citizens and workers has been complicated by their role as reproducers of members of particular racial and ethnic categories, so that some women rather than others have been exhorted to 'breed' (de Lepervanche, 1989:165). White English-speaking background women in particular have been constructed as 'breeders for Australia', with strong connections between eugenics and birth control in the early decades of this century (Bacchi, 1980). Historically too there has been lack of support to non-white families through restrictions on the immigration of non-white women (de Lepervanche, 1989) and on access to family welfare benefits. Assaults on reproduction rights of Aboriginal and other non-white women through, for example, forced sterilisation and the use of unsafe contraception like depo provera (de Lepervanche in Yuval-Davis and Anthias, 1989), continue. Today we still cannot say that all Australian women have equal rights, care and support with birthing or with the upbringing of their children.

SOURCES OF IMMIGRATION

Immigration into Australia reflects both Australian government policies determining who is approved to come here, and a variety of push-and-pull factors determining people's desire or need to migrate and reasons for choosing Australia (not necessarily their first choice).

Australian federal government controls the criteria for excluding, including or enticing different groups of potential immigrants (Collins in Bottomley and de Lepervanche, 1984:24; Jupp in Najman and Western, 1988). Before the Second World War the criteria were highly discriminatory on racial and country-of-origin grounds. After the war immigration programs reflected a steady widening of the racial and ethnic and/or country-of-origin net. Traumas in the war's Pacific theatre had underlined the urgency for a strong population in defence terms. Post-war recovery and the development of a modernised capitalist economy also required a substantial immigration program, both as labour for the enterprise, and to support an expanded domestic market (Castles et al., 1988).

As traditional, that is white and preferably English-speaking, sources of migration weakened, and with growing demands for labour to 'man' the new manufacturing and industrial sectors, the definition of who was assimilable gradually became less discriminatory on grounds of race or culture. The 'supply' factors also reflected economic difficulties or political troubles in source countries, so that some elements of Australia's migration program, especially concerning refugees, read rather like an atlas of troubles around the world.

Thus while Britain and Ireland remain the largest source of migrants, other major source countries have changed over time. About 170 000 displaced people came from Eastern Europe in the late 1940s (Kunz, 1988). Through the 1950s and early 1960s many migrants came from southern Europe, especially from Italy and Greece. In the 1960s migrants came increasingly from Turkey and through the 1970s from Lebanon. From the mid 1970s both migrants and refugees came from South-East Asia. Since then increasing numbers of migrants have also come from other Asian countries, and more recently from Latin America and Oceania. In 1989–90 the main source countries were Britain and Ireland, New Zealand, Vietnam, Hong Kong and Malaysia (Bureau of Immigration Research, 1991:37; see Table 3.1).

The impact of the immigration program on the ethnic composition of the Australian population has been dramatic. In 1947 only 9.8 percent of the population was born overseas. In 1988 21.8 per

Table 3.1 Settler arrivals—top ten source countries of birth, selected years, 1966–67 to 1989–90

Country of birth	1966–67 no.	%	Country of birth	1976–77 no.	%
UK/Ireland	75 510	54.4	UK/Ireland	19 220	27.1
Italy	12 890	9.3	Lebanon	12 190	17.2
Greece	9 830	7.1	New Zealand	4 840	6.8
Yugoslavia	7 550	5.4	Cyprus	2 770	3.9
Germany	3 410	2.5	Malaysia	1 770	2.5
New Zealand	2 750	2.0	Philippines	1 680	2.4
USA	2 340	1.7	Yugoslavia	1 650	2.3
Netherlands	1 870	1.3	Greece	1 530	2.2
Lebanon	1 720	1.2	Italy	1 320	1.9
India	1 650	1.2	USA	1 220	1.7
Sub-total	119 520	86.2	Sub-total	48 190	67.9
Other	19 160	13.8	Other	22 730	32.1
Total	**138 680**	**100.0**	**Total**	**70 920**	**100.0**

Country of birth	1987–88 no.	%	Country of birth	1989–90 no.	%
UK/Ireland	27 250	19.0	UK/Ireland	25 591	21.1
New Zealand	20 910	14.6	New Zealand	11 178	9.2
Philippines	10 430	7.3	Vietnam	11 156	9.2
Malaysia	6 270	4.4	Hong Kong	8 054	6.6
Vietnam	5 980	4.2	Malaysia	6 417	5.3
Hong Kong	5 580	3.9	China	6 124	5.0
China	4 430	3.1	Philippines	6 080	5.0
Lebanon	4 230	2.9	India	3 016	2.5
South Africa	3 790	2.6	Fiji	2 632	2.2
Yugoslavia	3 270	2.3	South Africa	2 424	2.0
Sub-total	92 140	64.2	Sub-total	82 672	68.2
Other	51 350	35.8	Other	38 605	31.8
Total	**143 490**	**100.0**	**Total**	**121 227**	**100.0**

Note: Figures rounded to the nearest ten for 1966-88.
Source: BIR 1991: 37

cent, that is over one in five Australians, were born overseas. In 1947 the percentage of overseas-born that came from Britain and Ireland was 72.7, in 1988 only 33.2. A further 32.3 percent came from other European countries, 18.5 from Asia (including the Middle-East), 8.7 from Oceania, 3.7 from Africa and the same from the Americas (Review 1989:22).

MIGRANT LABOUR AS CITIZENS

Many migrants, especially in the 1950s and 1960s, came from poorer and/or rural regions of southern Europe and the Middle-East. They came to an urbanised capitalist society, a parliamentary democracy with little overt communal conflict beyond the largely invisible Aboriginal domain. They came, often, to do the jobs that the Australian-born workers shunned. They were incorporated into the working class, but into different fractions from Australian-born workers (Collins, 1988). Their migration and incorporation into Australia was part of the internationalisation of labour, which saw millions of people migrate or travel to other countries to work (Castles et al., 1988:94; Bottomley, 1988:171).

What has been especially significant about post-war migration into Australia is that those sought for their labour were allowed—indeed expected—to settle here (Jupp, 1988:167). Australia rejected the guest-worker policy of some western European countries (Castles and Kosack, 1975), which accepted the labour but not the labourer or the labourer's family, although those guest workers and their families proved more settled than expected (Castles, 1984). Coming as settlers, migrants to Australia found citizenship relatively easy to attain, at least from the early 1970s, through a process referred to as 'naturalisation' (raising alarming suggestions about the personal as well as legal status of non-citizens). For many purposes, too, permanent residents and new citizens are entitled to welfare and other social rights, although there are some exceptions, including a longer residence requirement for the receipt of aged pensions for immigrants sponsored as aged parents (Price, 1989:45).

Australia's treatment of its migrant labour as settlers has given migrants access to legal and social rights denied to guest workers, which in turn has inhibited structural marginalisation of migrants as a permanent and legally distinct underclass in Australia. For these reasons Lever-Tracy and Quinlin (1988) reject arguments of those like Collins (1984, 1988) who represent migrant workers as an industrial reserve army in Australia. They point to migrants' citizenship rights, and to the central rather than peripheral role of migrant labour in the development and maintenance of local capitalism.

Rather, Australia has used certain regions and classes overseas as a pool of labour during its own labour shortage, underwriting its own growth in part by seeking workers whose reproduction and education costs have been borne by other often poorer countries. As local capitalism has been restructured, largely as a consequence of shifts in international capital, Australia has progressively lifted barriers to the migration from those regions and classes, seeking different and more skilled labour. Thus only 1.8 percent of those who migrated to Australia in 1989 were in unskilled occupations, making family reunion beyond spouses and dependent children almost impossible for older arrivals and those from poorer backgrounds. The family reunion program for siblings, for example, now requires a high economic skills and qualifications points score for entry.

This is not to say that citizenship is unproblematic in Australia. Many migrants choose not to become citizens. Interestingly, this is most common among those from Britain (Evans, 1988). Some are illegal immigrants who overstay temporary residence visas, with those from Britain doing so in largest numbers. However, as a percentage of overstayers those predominating in 1989–90 were from Lebanon, Tonga, Pakistan, Poland and the Philippines. China was formerly highly represented, but many Chinese students have now applied for permanent residence in Australia (Bureau of Immigration Research, 1991:51). Overstayers in effect become illegal immigrants, who become super-exploitable, for they lack the documentation or status for regular employment or for welfare entitlement, and are constantly in fear of detection, arrest and deportation (cf Sivanandan, 1989).

WOMEN AND MIGRATION

A further crucial consequence of a settler labour migration program is the core component of family reunion. Immigration was sought for labour (with a significant refugee and humanitarian component), and to support the reproduction and growth of both labour power and the local consumer market. The reproduction of the labour force required the presence of women in social and stereotypic roles. Thus women came to Australia largely as dependants, except occasionally when concern for unbalanced sex ratios was thought to place 'Australian' women at risk or encourage anti-social male migrant behaviour (stereotyping Italian men as fiery or violent for example); or when some women were sought as domestics, again within traditional family and female roles (de Lepervanche, 1989:164).

Some women did come alone (Arena in Scutt, 1987:32; DIEA 1987:14). However, most migrant women came and were treated as wives, fiancées, daughters and sometimes as mothers (Martin 1986:234). Migration was approved for the family unit, defined in terms of immediate nuclear family as parents and dependent children only, with dramatic effects on family structure and membership. The women were to care for and control the migrant men, service the current labour force, and reproduce and raise the future labour force. They were expected to do all this in strange circumstances, and without the traditional supports for their wife/mother/homemaker roles that many of them might have enjoyed had they remained at home (which is not to romanticise extended families or traditional kinship arrangements).

Dislocation and displacement—even where it also involves escape or adventure—is part of the migration experience. Even those women who came from Britain, with little language or public culture shift, lost kin, friends, local familiarity, and may not have left home willingly. For those women who came without English-language competence or from very different systems and roles the shock of the new was even more traumatic. The Australia they found was often very different from the one they had been led to expect from Australian government propaganda or relatives' brave or boasting letters home (Greek–Australian Women's Workshop, 1989:10). In the case of women from rural villages and a social world of intimates and familiars (even if not necessarily all loved, or even liked), coming to a chaotic inner city or desolate outer suburb, with neighbours speaking other languages and living other ways, was often profoundly disorientating. The more distant but still all-pervasive dominant system and dominant culture was frequently even less accessible or predictable. However, for some women the very strangeness, in some cases the aloneness and anonymity, and the new choices, were exciting and indeed liberating (Bottomley, 1984b:104; DIEA, 1987; Greek–Australian Women's Workshop, 1989).

In speaking of their experiences a group of older Greek migrant women who came to Australia in the 1950s and early 1960s expressed some of the contradictions involved.

> In migrating to Australia they were freer as wives and mothers in not having the constraints and control of in-laws and the village community. 'Our in-laws don't rule us. We talk more openly. In Greece we all lived under one roof, generations of us. The father-in-law was in charge there . . . ' (Greek–Australian Women's Workshop, 1989:22)

However, the women also recalled the last thirty years in Australia in terms of exploitation, exhaustion, anxiety, injustice and ill-health.

> The majority said they had gained economic comfort and a better future for their children. The price for that was loss of health and support structures provided by extended family. (Greek–Australian Women's Workshop 1989:25).

Indeed tiredness is a constant theme in migrant women's descriptions of their lives (Bottomley, in Bottomley and de Lepervanche, 1984: 119; Martin, 1986:116; Storer, 1975).

The demands and contradictions of migration and settlement were compounded for many by the desperate financial situation in which many new migrants found themselves. Many had borrowed extensively for fares and most now faced heavy costs of seeking housing. Many sought to bring out other family members or to send some money back regularly to support parents or to maintain obligations and standing in the home community. Migrant men often found themselves in low-income jobs or unemployed as the economy dipped, or as industrial accidents or ill-health took their toll. So in relative newness to the country, and at times of heaviest family responsibilities, many migrant women found themselves forced into the labour market (Martin, 1986:234). Thus married 'Mediterranean' women, stereotyped as contained at home and under closer patriarchal control than their Anglo-Australian sisters, were often in paid employment in larger comparative numbers than were Australian-born women (Bottomley, 1984b:2); and today married women who are recent refugees from South-East Asia are over-represented in the labour force (Price, 1989:47).

CONSTRUCTING THE CATEGORY 'MIGRANT WOMEN'

Before migrating, many women were members of families which identified with a religious or linguistic group, or particular region or sub-national group, rather than with their country-of-origin as such. In some cases, especially those of refugees, their status at home was one of a minority group, perhaps identified with a neighbouring country. Many had already experienced foreign occupation, civil wars, or serious ethnic and religious conflict, persecution or repression (Storer, 1985:5). Some also came from countries with strong left and/or feminist movements, and from personal experiences far removed from the confined and contained spaces that many Anglo-Australians imagined for them.

In Australia ethnic identity is often read as people's presumed country-of-origin or 'race', so that here a Calabrian becomes Italian, and a Tamil becomes Sri Lankan, or perhaps Asian. In some cases migrants are identified with the very regime or ethnic group they came here to escape.

Imposed categories frequently homogenise people, disguising the variety of their backgrounds, identities and social interests. Thus an 'Asian' woman may be a fifth generation Australian of Malay descent, or a recent Vietnamese refugee of Chinese background, an Indian-born economist, or a Filipino feminist.

Even where the category appears more specific, the differences within its boundaries may be vast. Thus Chinese people who have migrated to Australia in the last twenty years include 30 000 from Malaysia, 29 000 from Vietnam, 5000 from Indonesia, 2500 from New Guinea, 2000 from the Pacific Islands, and 1200 from Europe, as well as those from China itself, from Hong Kong, Taiwan and Singapore (Price, 1989:16). 'Greeks' include those born in Egypt, and those who were born in Greece are strongly divided in terms of class and region, and religion and politics (Bottomley, 1984:101, 105).

Each category is divided in terms of age and gender, and usually class, with differences in sexuality, ablement and so on also obscured. Political affiliation may be decisive. Hostel-eating and English-language class arrangements which, for example, put 'Spanish-speaking' migrants together without regard for whether they are escapees from Cuba or from post-coup Chile quickly reveal that ideology and past political struggles are often more salient than supposed ethnic identity (e.g., Langer, 1991). In class terms members of the same ethnic group may have conflicting interests and quite different lifestyles, and ethnic bosses may exploit 'their own' just as much as an outsider boss would.

One category that has become especially significant in recent decades is that of 'migrant'. While there may be some validity in recognising the significance of the migration process for all who are not Australian-born, 'migrant' usually has narrower connotations. Some overseas-born groups are presumed to be more migrant than others, and some are more likely to be identified by others primarily in terms of their 'migrantness'. Thus migrant is often a codeword for people from non-English-speaking backgrounds, whose cultures are then represented in ways that demonstrate what Morrissey calls 'migrantness as ideology' (in Bottomley and de Lepervanche, 1984:75).

Popular and academic representations of migrant women call up a range of images and associations, as the most exploited (in the labour market and at home) and most oppressed (at home) women in Australia, besides Aboriginal women. Here there are notions of multiple jeopardy (King, 1988:42). Migrant women are perceived as triply disadvantaged, being women, working class, and culturally different; or quadruply disadvantaged if they are also not white. From this representation it is often assumed that most recent migrants, especially those from Asia, are worst off, and that we can read much into simply knowing a woman's colour or country-of-origin. However, real life is much more complicated.

So it is necessary to scrutinise representations of migrant women that homogenise and essentialise them, to deconstruct the categories and locate different groups of women within wider structures and social relations (Stasilius, 1990).

DECONSTRUCTING THE CATEGORY 'MIGRANT WOMEN'

On closer examination 'migrant women' often refers to women from non-English-speaking backgrounds, especially those from southern Europe and Turkey, who came here in the 1950s and 60s, often from poor rural families. There are grounds for distinguishing broadly between these women and those from western Europe and Britain, because they did face quite different barriers to settlement, although they also shared some of the traumas and fears. Some generalisations can be made about their pre-migration situation, their incorporation into the labour market, their experience of the state, and of racism or cultural chauvinism, even while recognising the variety of experience and response among individual women. Many more recently arrived migrant women, for example from Asian countries, may also face racism, although mediated by class in various ways, but their experience of the labour market, for example, is often quite different from that of earlier arrivals. The exception here is refugee women, whose status signifies turmoil and danger before migrating, and whose resettlement here may be undermined by their fearfulness for and perhaps guilt concerning those left behind. The special conditions of their entry may leave them disadvantaged in terms of the labour market (Price, 1989), which currently requires far less unskilled and semi-skilled labour.

Thus some write 'migrant women' as signifying displacement and differential incorporation into Australian society. Others prefer to speak of 'ethnic-minority women', signifying their membership of groups outside the boundaries of public power in Australia (Tsolidis, 1986). Whatever the label the making and contesting of those boundaries is an exercise in power and politics, not something pertaining by virtue of birth or 'culture'.

Thus it is not enough to talk of 'migrant women', or even to identify them simply in terms of country-of-origin or ethnic group. The category 'migrant women' is generated within an international political economy, within terms of the shifting labour requirements of local and international capital. Women's different pre-migration identities and experiences, including ethnic, class and gender relations in their home countries, also help to place them as they enter Australian society and the labour market. Their reasons for migrating are important, as too is the timing of migration.

Timing of migration and settlement shapes migrant women's experiences. Australian migration policies shift over time and changing selection criteria determines who is allowed to come in. Economic conditions make it more or less difficult to get jobs, with those who come in times of high unemployment facing particular financial and social hardship. If they are conspicuously different, migrants may also be scapegoats for others' insecurities (Bottomley, 1984a). Thus the rising tide of racism since 1984 has made harassment and danger a day-to-day reality for many Asian and more recently Arab and Muslim women (see chapter 4). Australian government post-settlement policies shift too, as do popular perceptions about both migration and difference. In the last few years the rhetoric of a multicultural society has been accompanied by increased ethnic political mobilisation, and some administrative and funding support for ethnic provision and activity (Foster and Stockley, 1989).

Timing is also significant in determining whether migrants come to already established communities which can buffer and mediate between them and the wider society, and whether new migrants may already have kin here to ease the transition, and provide support for recently arrived women, especially those with children who also seek jobs outside the home.

WOMEN, MIGRATION AND LABOUR MARKET SEGMENTATION

The ways in which migrants are incorporated into the labour market load their choices and opportunities in almost every area of their lives.

Post-war migrants to Australia entered a country which was comparatively urbanised and industrialised, with a strong labour movement and considerable state involvement in the structure of wages and work (Mizstal, 1990:7). Their labour contributed centrally to the growth of capital and to both the expansion and the restructuring of the working class in Australia (de Lepervanche, 1984:172; Castles et al., 1988:25). They also entered a labour market segmented both in terms of ethnicity or country-of-origin (Collins, 1988; Stromback, 1988) and gender (Mumford, 1989).

Trade union and political party organisations are still overwhelmingly white, English speaking and male. Class relations, including the sexual division of labour, reflect a history of long and unequal struggle between capital and labour on the one hand, and between men and women workers on the other (Sharp and Broomhill, 1989:24). Migrants, both men and women, tend to be directed into particular parts of the labour force, so that the working class turns out to be fractured along axes of both gender and ethnicity.

The gender segmentation of the labour market means that women in general are concentrated in particular occupations, including those that may be seen as extensions of their mothering and nurturing roles like nursing, teaching and social work, although the powerful positions in these areas are more likely to be occupied by men (Game and Pringle, 1983; O'Donnell and Hall, 1988; Mumford, 1989). Women also face enormous obstacles to equality of opportunity through their treatment and often their responsibilities as wives, mothers and home workers. Multiple tasks claim a toll on many women, especially in the face of expensive, inadequate and often inappropriate child-care. Women are contained within the state–paid work–family labour nexus (cf Barrett, 1980; Stasilius 1989:29), reflected in women's labour force participation rate of 46.8 percent as against 73.5 percent for men, and in women's average income of $9850 per annum as against $17 300 for men (1986 figures, Price, 1989).

While some jobs are women's jobs, some are migrant women's jobs, or rather jobs of migrant women from particular class and country backgrounds. Migrant women often have the worst jobs. This doesn't mean, however, that all migrant women are in the worst jobs. Women from Britain, Ireland and most western European countries have occupational profiles similar to Australian-born women. Women from Turkey, Lebanon and more recent refugees from South-East Asia have the worst time, both in unemployment and the jobs they do get. Non-refugee women from Asian countries, who have only been eligible for migration since the early 1970s, are often more educationally qualified and get better jobs and better pay than do Australian-born women. This reflects Australia's shift from a labour shortage economy to a labour surplus one, with a consequent increase in economic skills necessary for entry, at the very time immigration selection was becoming non-discriminatory in terms of race and country-of-origin.

Price (1989) has provided us with a detailed profile of the labour market in terms of both ethnicity and gender, based on 1986 figures. Labour force participation rates for women vary from group to group, with recent arrival groups from south Asia, South-East Asia, Latin America, Africa and the Pacific over-represented. Married women who work in larger numbers come from two very different class locations. The first are the worst off groups, especially from Vietnam, while the second includes recent migrants from India, Sri Lanka and Malaysia, who are highly qualified and working in middle-class occupations. Thus the divided nature of the 'Asian women'

46

category becomes clear, with some women clustered at the top of the market, and others at the bottom.

Women from southern Europe except Yugoslavia, from the Middle-East and Indo-China have much lower than average qualifications. Women from a number of European countries have higher than average trade qualifications, while women from India, Sri Lanka, Malaysia, North America and Africa have relatively higher university qualifications.

The national average for unemployment for women was 9.6 percent in 1986. Women from eastern Europe, Latin America and the Pacific Islands had unemployment rates of between 12 and 20 percent. The worst off were women from the Middle-East with 21 percent and from Indo-China with 35 percent, reflecting recent arrival, low qualifications and lack of English. Women from particular countries with very high rates of unemployment included those from Turkey, Lebanon, Syria and Vietnam.

In terms of occupation women from southern Europe, the Middle-East (except Israel), and Indo-Chinese refugees were over-represented in general labouring jobs, like machine operators, or in textile or canning industries. Again, non-refugee women from Asian countries and from North America were over-represented in professional, administrative and managerial occupations, although with variation according to country-of-origin (see also DIEA, 1984). Income levels reflected qualifications and occupation profiles.

Some migrant women are employed in family businesses, where they may enjoy more familiar and congenial relations, and mothers may have more flexible working hours or support from other family members. Alternatively some women may be exploited without recourse to union or legal wage protection, and subject to 24-hours-a-day supervision. Some migrant women who show in the self-employed category are actually engaged in outwork, again beyond union support and in conditions that allow the worst abuses (Women Outworkers, 1986; Alcorso, 1987).

Thus the experiences of migrant women vary widely, although there are clear patterns in terms of country-of-origin, time of settlement, and refugee status. Those currently worst off are women from Turkey, most of whom have been here for some time, and those from Lebanon and recent refugees from Vietnam. Other women from Asian countries tend to be doing better than average, reflecting their class and education backgrounds in their countries-of-origin. This does not mean that recent arrivals from non-English-speaking backgrounds do not face difficulties in the labour market, however. They may find that their professional or trade qualifications are not recognised, and they may face frustration and downward social mobility (DIEA, 1987:18). They may also have primary child-care responsibilities, and have lost female kin support that they had at home. Those that are conspicuously different in language or appearance may also be subjected to both racist and sexist harassment, especially if they are labelled as Asian or Muslim (HEROC, 1991).

There is little information available about how migrant women experience work. One study done in 1975 is still often quoted, giving evidence of the dreadful working conditions, the dirty, tiring and boring work, the harassment by bosses and supervisors and occasionally by Australian-born co-workers, and the fear of dismissal that continues to silence the women (Storer, 1975). Ironically many of those women worked in the most vulnerable sectors of the economy, and may well have since lost their jobs as the capital that used to bring in migrant workers goes 'off shore' in search of ever cheaper labour and greater profits. A 1985 conference of migrant women identified three priorities to do with migrant women's work. These were health, safety and working conditions; access to language, education, training and retraining; and access to culturally appropriate child-care. It also catalogued poor working conditions, harassment, injury and ill-health, and lack of support through compensation claims and other procedures which might have increased migrant women's rights (DIEA, 1986).

There are also a few more specific studies, for example of Spanish-speaking women (DIEA, 1987), which reveals the wide variety of backgrounds and experiences of Spanish-speaking women in Australia, and the shift from professional, administrative and clerical jobs in the home countries, to service and manufacturing jobs here, where non-recognition of home qualifications and lack of English are keenly felt. It also documents the poor working conditions, shift work and lack of support from unions that many of the women experience.

A recent study of outworkers in Melbourne speaks to another development in local capital that has disproportionately affected migrant women. Outworkers are by definition in workplaces that are extremely difficult to supervise or organise. The working conditions are often appalling, ill-health and injury frequent, and the pay low and piecemeal. Outworkers are often already victims of industrial injury or accident, and/or are primarily responsible for child-care. They are especially vulnerable to sexual harassment from bosses and isolation, anxiety and exhaustion are chronic (Women Outworkers, 1986; Alcorso, 1987). Most recent and racialised migrants like the

Vietnamese are especially vulnerable to exploitation as outworkers (Lam Thi Cuc, 1989).

Migrant women in the workforce have been commodified (cf Ng, 1987) in part through the construction of the category and the response to stereotypes of those who are placed in the category. Thus migrant women are represented as passive, used to patriarchal control, less politicised and more malleable and exploitable than 'Australian' women.

> The (migrant) women are better suited to these jobs. If they were more intelligent or educated they would go round the bend. But this sort of person is suited to the job . . . these women are naturally submissive . . . they will do whatever you tell them (Personnel manager quoted in Martin, 1984:118).

Employers and career advisers act on these stereotypes, and help direct certain women into certain jobs, and pass them over for others. This is the sexist or gendered version of 'migrantness'.

It may not only be the bosses and supervisors who hold racist and sexist views of migrant women. Trade unions have long acted to protect the interests of certain groups of workers, especially of white English-speaking men, with some honourable exceptions (for example the Australian Council of Trade Unions has had a strong policy in support of migrants rights and against racism for some years). The under-representation of both women and migrants, usually posited as alternative categories, is even more noticeable in the case of migrant women. Explanations for this offered by union officials often reproduce victim–problem images of migrant women, and blame them for their lack of participation and influence (Gale, 1989:6).

Gale has analysed a large trade union in New South Wales by asking both 'migrant' and 'Australian' women about their perceptions of union politics and organisation. She examined dominant explanations for women's low participation in union affairs. These cited women's lack of interest in the union, the opposition of their menfolk to their participation, and their view of the union as men's business. Gale found that most women were interested in and relatively well informed about the union, and that neither Australian nor migrant women saw their partners as opposing their participation. Nine-tenths of migrant women interviewed and over half of Australian women believed that women would be better than men at getting better conditions, but some still said they preferred a male union representative on the grounds that union leaders and employers took men more seriously.

The top three priorities for both Australian and migrant women were education and retraining (although access to English language classes was of particular concern to migrant women); harassment on the job; and leave to care for sick children. Both groups feared discrimination if they spoke out or became active in union affairs, reasonably so, as there were many instances cited of women given less overtime and more work, and being subject to unpleasantness for speaking about their grievances. This again underlines the need to provide support for politically active women (Gale, 1989:13; see also Hargraves, 1982:158).

All the women recognised the need for encouragement and support through informal networks of women. Those women who were active in the union generally had fewer home and child responsibilities, and/or more supportive partners. So in many ways gender was more significant than cultural background in shaping the women's perceptions and experiences. However, there are also studies which reveal discrimination and hostility towards migrant women on the part of some 'Australian' women co-workers. So again it depends on which aspects of identity and which social interests are salient in each situation, recognising both the specificity of different women's experiences, and also the things they share.

It is the articulation of private households with wage labour and the state that affects women, especially here, migrant women mothers in paid employment (cf Stasilius, 1989:29). Many of the worries and dangers the women face are to do with anxieties about children (Bottomley, 1984:7; Greek–Australian Women's Workshop, 1989:20):

> It is nice and easy for working mothers in Turkey. Here it worries me all the time (Turkish woman).

> Here he does not understand. We are always expected to help with bringing in the money. He expects me to do it here, but he doesn't understand about the children and how tired it makes us all (Sicilian woman). (Martin, 1984:11)

In home countries there was often more support and more security even within gender relations that were seen as oppressive by women. As many migrants continue to feel loss and nostalgia for home, and in the face of exhaustion and exploitation and harassment here, it is the hope of a better and safer future for their children that will ultimately make it all worthwhile (e.g., DIEA, 1987:13, 34). This helps explain the high expectations that many migrant parents have for their children's education, and the pressures that some children of migrants feel (Tsolidis, 1986). This is aggravated by the ways that the state through its provision of welfare, health, education and so on sets gendered expectations, and makes biological mothers solely responsible for the welfare of their children (Martin, 1986:236).

> The way of bringing up your children in Turkey is better. There you are helped by the school, your friends, your relatives, your neighbours. Here no-one does the same . . . it is only the mother and it is bad for the child (Turkish woman).

> It is all the mother here . . . if someone else helps then they say it is wrong (Greek woman). (Martin, 1984:116)

Migrant mothers are not alone in their concern about children, of course. Inadequate child-care and the tiredness that comes from multiple tasking and primary and frequently unsupported parenting takes its toll of many mothers. And migrant women share with Aboriginal women the heated gaze of the state upon them, and the intervention that determines who can and cannot live together (Martin, 1986:239; de Lepervanche, 1989).

Thus we can identify a range of factors that show women have multiple identities and associations beyond their ethnicity and race, and indeed they experience these in complex interaction.

MIGRATION, CULTURE AND SEXUAL POLITICS

Culturalism—assuming characteristics and explanations located within people's presumed culture—informs representations of migrant women. This is especially so in terms of sexual politics and gender roles, both within particular communities and within the wider society. Women do experience migration, incorporation into the economy and as citizens and state subjects differently from men. Women come from particular sets of gender relations in their home country, although there may be contradictory pressures and demands between them, especially if they had minority status in their country-of-origin. Gender roles may already have been unsettled by shifts to an urban centre, or by political unrest or exile.

The gender relations of the new country intrude even before migration, in definition of the family, for example, and in the selection of the male migrant as the worker (usually). It becomes ever more pronounced through resettlement and negotiation through a range of social, welfare, economic and other arrangements which are clearly gender-specific (if not always acknowledged as such). In the stress of the new surroundings and the loss of familiar roles and sanctions, some men may react by becoming more jealous of their domestic authority, and more fearful of their own capacity to protect and provide for their family (Martin, 1986:238; de Lepervanche,

51

1988:50). Thus migration may heighten danger to women (Bottomley, 1984:6). It may also reinforce conservative values as some migrants cling to a remembered way long after it has changed radically at home. It is quite a common experience for young women brought up here with fairly strict notions of what it is to be a 'good girl' (Pallotta-Chiarolli, 1989) to visit 'home' and discover that female aunts and cousins there enjoy greater freedom. This process can have rather unexpected consequences. For example, in the early 1980s of all marriages in Greece 25 percent were arranged; in Australia 73 percent of Greek marriages were arranged (Bottomley, 1984:6).

Thus country-of-origin or ethnic group cannot be used to predict fixed attributes, interests or identities. Yet ethnic labels are not only imposed from the outside; nor are they used only instrumentally to organise the group and make claims against the state. Ethnic identity can also be a powerful form of affiliation and association, although this is likely to be more pertinent in particular situations. So it is necessary to ask questions about identity and community, and about where women are, and how they see themselves, in relation to racial and ethnic categories.

IS 'MIGRANTNESS' HEREDITARY?

Women labelled as 'migrant women' or as 'women of non-English-speaking background' may not necessarily be migrants themselves, but may be second or even third generation Australians. This raises questions about when migrants cease to be migrants. Some may achieve this in their lifetimes, especially if they are in colour and culture close to the dominant groups. Others like the Germans and the Dutch do not organise (although some may socialise) as 'ethnics' (Price, 1989). Are some ethnic groups more inclined to identity maintenance, or to associate on grounds of ethnicity or country-of-origin?

An interesting issue here is that of intermarriage, and the transgressing of community boundaries. The rate of ethnic intermarriage, while very different for different groups, is high overall in Australia, and raises questions about where the children of these marriages place themselves or are placed by others. Factors that influence the rate of intermarriage include the migration effect of a frequent predominance of men over women, the small size of some communities which do not provide enough marriage partners, and cultural and religious constraints, which vary from group to group (Price, 1989:18). Migrants from Britain, New Zealand, Germany and France marry out at a high rate, while Italian, Greek and Lebanese migrants marry out much more slowly. Of marriages of men born in Greece to women born in Australia 42 percent were to second generation Greek women, and 37 percent of marriages between Greek-born women and Australian-born men were to second generation Greek men. Over half of the children born in Australia where one or both parents are non-English-speaking-background migrants were of mixed ethnicity. There is a high outmarriage for the second generation; for example, 72 percent of Maltese men and 70 percent of Maltese women married out; for Italians the figures were 53 percent and 47 percent; for Greeks 44 percent and 36 percent; and for Lebanese (mainly Christian) 51 percent and 38 percent. Here religion is a key. Italian Catholics may marry Maltese or Polish or Irish Catholics, while the Greek Orthodox religion reinforces inmarriage (Price, 1989).

Thus in some houses the shared language may be English and in others there will be several languages used. Some children may prefer to identify simply as 'Australian', especially in teenage years when other kinds of identification may be more salient. Here again are dangers of those forms of multiculturalism which presume a pre-eminent ethnic identity when being a female or a heavy-metal band member may be rather more important.

4 Racism and sexism

How do we go about tracing the interconnections between racism and sexism, and analysing the ways minority women experience racism; and the ways that different women experience sexism? Racism and sexism, even where connected, do not operate alone, but articulate and are articulated through structures of power in society. Yet it seems especially difficult to theorise or represent multiple or simultaneous oppression (Broom in Jennett and Stewart, 1987).

Both category politics and much academic writing focus on one oppression at a time, analysing Aboriginal or migrant or women's inequality, often in terms of a binary opposition (Meekosha and Pettman, forthcoming). Thus there are Aborigines versus the whites, migrants or ethnic minorities versus 'Australians', and women versus men. This model of alternative oppressions renders minority women invisible once again (Pettman, 1991) as signalled in the title of American black feminist *All the Women are White, All the Blacks are Men, But Some of Us are Brave*, (Hull et al., 1982).

Other representations of oppression posit a primary and generative base from which all follows. Thus some feminists argue patriarchy as the determining oppression for women, although the more inclusive of them will recognise the changing nature of patriarchy over time and place, and may thus seek to include minority women's experiences. Others may argue the primacy of class, or of race, again seen as singly generative.

A further model of oppression recognises that people have multiple identities, but allows for a particular oppression as primary in particular situations. Thus racism may be recognised as the primary oppression facing Aboriginal women today. This still segments and gives priority to certain oppressions. Or there may be an attempt to hyphenate oppressions, to take account of sex and class, or of race and sex.

It seems especially difficult to develop multidimensional models of oppression. One such attempt is an additive model, which argues that race + class + gender is the black woman's triple jeopardy; or race + class + gender + cultural difference is quadruple jeopardy; and so on. While recognising the multifaceted nature of both identity and oppression, this model still does not allow for the dynamic interaction and mutually constitutive relationships of the different facets or dimensions (King, 1988). Aboriginal women, for example, experience sexism in some ways differently from other Australian women, and racism in some ways differently from Aboriginal men; and they also experience sexism and racism differently according to their class and job, dependence on welfare, age, disability, sexuality and so on.

This chapter begins with the construction of racism and of sexism in Australia, and then looks at the interconnections of race, cultural difference, class and gender in some aspects of the lives of Aboriginal women and ethnic-minority women, and asks how these differ from the experiences of dominant-group women. It highlights the sexual division of labour, the social construction of racialised gender categories and different representations of femininity and the family, and sites of difference and danger for women.

RACISM

Racism as a focus of academic writings in Australia has been largely the province of historians (e.g., Markus, Curthoys) and anthropologists (e.g. Cowlishaw, Morris), although some sociologists (e.g., Bottomley) and more rarely political scientists (e.g., Tatz, Jennett) have also addressed the issue. Many other academics prefer to talk about 'race' or cultural difference than about racism (Pettman, 1984, 1988c).

Racism is multifaceted. It is commonly used to refer to individual attitudes and behaviour directed against those who are identified on the basis of their presumed race or country-of-origin. These may range from vicious abuse or physical violence, to sharing widespread stereotypes about 'others' which are inaccurate or derogatory, and avoiding or treating people on the basis of these stereotypes. Much that is written about such racism is concerned with the bigot, the pathological personality, or those who have been socialised into a racist culture. This 'prejudice model' urges tolerance and education to overcome misinformation, along with anti-discriminatory legislation and peer pressure to contain bigots.

The prejudice model drastically underestimates the politics and power of racism. It is not simply a matter of bad, mad or misinformed (or even stupid) individuals. Rather, racism is an ideology and a whole set of social relations which are historically generated and materially based, and which reinforce or deny rights and social interests. The particular structure of race power in a society locates everyone, those who are privileged as well as those who are penalised by their socially allocated race. Racism in this understanding is both a discourse—language, images and explanations about race and cultural difference—and material relations between people who are socially constructed as different (Hall, 1980, 1988a; Brown, 1986a, 1986b).

Ideology reflects, rationalises and helps organise particular social interests. Racist ideologies provide a vocabulary about race and cultural difference, and understandings about who 'we' are and what is normal (Pettman, 1988b). It is powerful in its common-sense understanding, which functions to naturalise differences and inequalities, disguising their political and contingent nature (Hall, 1978; Lawrence, 1982; Bannerji, 1987).

As noted in chapter 1 the language around 'race' has changed dramatically over time, from the heathen fall from grace, through nineteenth-century scientism of social Darwinism, to contemporary representations of the New Right, coded more in terms of difference than inferiority, and of socio-biologists who assert the primary claim of kin and closure against others as 'natural' (Banton, 1987a; de Lepervanche, 1984).

Some contemporary discourses around 'race' are culturalist, but are still racist in their effects (de Lepervanche, 1980; Brown, 1986a; Cowlishaw, 1986). They are based on deterministic notions of culture, which constitute 'the other' who is not 'us' in essentialist ways. They construct categories that exclude or entrap whole groups of people, and construct differences in value or entitlement in society. These are expressed through assertions like 'they take our jobs', or that special provision for Aboriginal people or recent migrants is 'reverse racism' (Markus and Rickfels, 1985; Cowlishaw, 1990a).

Racist discourses provide a pool and fuel for individuals' views of difference and ways of identifying. But people are also actively engaged in negotiating their own meanings, drawing on or reacting against dominant representations in language and the media, and also on localised discourses among peers and family members. Racist discourses are constantly being remade, in ways that are often highly creative and contradictory (Gundara, 1988; Cohen and Bains, 1988; Ward in Kovel, 1988).

There is a close and mutually constitutive relationship between racist discourses and practices (Brown, 1986b:394–96; Hall, 1980:334). Racism is reproduced through a range of individual practices and interchanges between people in different locations, and through institutionalised arrangements located within structures of domination and subordination.

Institutional racism offers another perspective on racism (Mason, 1982; Williams, 1987). This concept points to the reproduction of systematic patterns of social inequality correlating with race, ethnicity and country-of-origin. These patterns are revealed in terms of different groups' location within the labour market and in unemployment profiles, and in the gross over-representation of Aboriginal girls and boys in the juvenile justice and child welfare system, and of Aboriginal women and men in police custody or prison (29 percent of all men in custodial cases in Australia are Aboriginal, and 50 percent of the women).

Institutional racism addresses the fact that simply treating racism as due to ignorance or individual pathology does not affect social outcomes. It also suggests ways of identifying racism in the absence of conscious or intended behaviour. It draws attention to the operations of particular institutions and organisations, and provides clues about how racism is reproduced. It facilitates a recognition of structured social inequality, and enables people to turn cases into issues by locating examples of individuals' experiences of discrimination within a wider social context (Sivanandan, 1983).

Institutional racism shifts attention from individual feelings and actions to the distribution of social resources. 'The critical sets of relationships which decide who gets what, take place in the institutional settings of education, employment agencies, welfare agencies, trade unions and politics' (Brown, 1986a:183). So patterns of Aboriginal deprivation can be tracked through the workings of government departments and agencies, for example, housing, health, education and the law.

In the past institutional racism was often based on legal discrimination, such as excluding Aboriginal people from citizenship (Markus in de Lepervanche and Bottomley, 1988). Now it more often operates unofficially, indeed often against official rhetoric and current government policies.

Institutions validate rules, roles and certain understandings about entitlements which are often seen as fair or universal, but which actually reflect and protect dominant social interests—through, for example, understandings about who is a good parent, a reliable tenant or borrower, or the best applicant for the job. But these rules are not applied mechanistically or deterministically. They are activated by bureaucrats, social workers, receptionists and so on, whose own perceptions, priorities and values are fused with cultural meanings that speak of their own personal histories and social location. Within particular constraints and in their own ways, they 'do their job' (Brown, 1986b:387–88).

Institutional racism means that each of us who is in a position to give or withhold a service, a hearing or information can help people or else make them pay. Tackling institutional racism requires examining workplaces and work practices, including those based on culturalist expectations and misinformation (Pettman, forthcoming, b). It also highlights the significance of race and 'culture' in determining access to the institutions and to their resources.

Institutional racism segments racism into a number of sites, so that strategies may be developed to identify and combat it in particular places (e.g., Toomelah Report, 1988). There are often links across departmental or organisational boundaries, so combating institutional racism requires an inter-agency approach (HEROC, 1991). There are also other less formal places of danger, like the streets and public transport, where racism is often experienced. Here it is necessary to ask who experiences racism, and where. This will reveal different sites, including those where government agents may be active. Different groups experience racism differently. Policing is a key concern for Aboriginal people, but recently-arrived migrants may be more concerned about immigration entry restrictions and the availability of English-language classes and of interpreters.

Thus racism is multidimensional, dynamic, and constituted and experienced through interactions with other forms of social inequality. As suggested in chapter 1, it may be more useful to talk about racisms than racism. But whatever the form, racism is always about power—about constituting and treating others as 'different' for the purpose of excluding, exploiting or containing them. The power may be only local and contingent. The working-class youths whose social or economic insecurity calls for scapegoats, or whose macho mates harass Vietnamese youth, may be relatively powerless themselves, but on the street and in numbers they have some semblance of power.

Racism is also a relationship. It is not 'they' or their difference or their numbers which is the problem, but those who are in a position to make others pay. Racism requires people who 'do' racism as much as it does people who 'get done' (Brittan and Maynard, 1984; Brown, 1986b:388). White is as essential an ingredient as black in racist exchanges where white is the dominant political colour (Ward in Kovel, 1988).

Who experiences racism? The National Inquiry into Racist Violence (HEROC, 1991) defined racist violence widely and provided evidence covering racist abuse, harassment and discrimination, as well as physical attack. The Inquiry identified Aboriginal people, people from non-English-speaking backgrounds, especially those seen as Asian or Muslim, and anti-racist activists as those most likely to experience attack.

Descriptions of victims of racism are frequently ungendered (de Lepervanche, 1989:166), and yet it seems likely that women in some ways experience racism differently from men. There is also often no reference to age, no enquiry into how older people, children, teenagers and young adults experience racism. Evidence from Britain suggests that the primary victims and perpetrators of racist violence are teenagers and young people, and overwhelmingly male, a pattern which appears true in Australia. The National Inquiry into Violence identifies young men between 18 and 30 as the main victims and offenders in non-fatal assaults generally (AIC, 1990). The National Inquiry into Racist Violence identifies white, English-speaking-background boys and young men as the main perpetrators of racist violence, along with and often used by racist organisations (HEROC, 1991). Again the links between violence and masculinity—or particular constructions of masculinity—need investigating (cf Morgen in Hanmer and Maynard, 1987).

It is necessary to ask what racism is and how it is reproduced, who experiences what kinds of racism, what sites are especially dangerous, and for whom, in order to develop strategies and arguments against it, while also supporting and empowering those who experience it.

RACISM AND SEXISM

An analysis of racist stereotypes and language soon reveals a gendered racism, with particular stereotypes of Aboriginal women or Muslim women or Italian women, for example. Indeed representations of different cultures often rest on representations of different femininities and family roles, which are also keys to the ways many define their own cultures (Yuval-Davis and Anthias, 1989). Women may also experience racism in different forms and sites from men (Carby, 1982; Parmar, 1982; Pettman, 1991). Women from different racial and ethnic backgrounds may also experience sexism differently, in terms of representations of a tradition from which they came or to which they may still belong; of community mores and expectations where they now live; and of the dominant society, whose institutions and social relations are structured in terms of gender.

Racism and sexism are often talked of as if they are alternative, and comparable, kinds of oppression. The racism/sexism analogy has been widely used by feminists and others, but often in a way that talks of women *and* blacks, or compares the status of women to slavery, again representing them as alternative designations. Here black women are invisible within both the ungendered 'race' and the apparently white 'women' category (Howard, 1989; Pettman, 1991). This is especially devastating for those black women whose foremothers experienced slavery or colonisation, and whose own lives as women are damaged by racism and by the poverty and violence associated with it. The racism/sexism analogy can also be used to call up a presumed equivalence of oppressions, and some bonding between white women and black men, again leaving black women on the outside (Burgmann, 1984; Wallace, 1978).

Sexism, like racism, is often spoken of in terms of individual attitudes and behaviour, for example, individual men regard women as powerless or as sex objects, or act in discriminatory or violent ways towards them. These attitudes and behaviours tap into widely spread images and myths about men and women, about masculinity and femininity, that both inform and reflect relations between the sexes.

Sexism as an ideology operates in some ways like racism, in that it constitutes differences in power and entitlement as natural, based supposedly on obvious biological differences. Naturalising difference disguises the power and politics involved in constructing gender categories and in representations of gender relations.

Gender, like race, is a social construct. A lot of ideological work, backed by a lot of power, goes into reproducing gender relations. Dominant representations are also resisted and subverted—by individual women and sometimes by individual men, and by political mobilisation by feminists.

Sexist ideologies construct particular notions of masculinity and femininity, which shape and constrain women's roles and women's choices. The ideology of motherhood and the idealised nuclear family are frequently represented as natural and other family forms or women's roles as deviant. Representations of femininity as passive, dependent and accepting underscore men's rights to women's unpaid labour and to sexual services. They deny the possibility of rape within marriage, and encourage assumptions in the administration of social security that a woman having sexual relations with a man is or should be supported by him. Dominant notions of masculinity reinforce a man's rights as head of household, including to control his family, which he may take to include the right to use violence against them.

Sexist ideology determines what it is to be a 'wife', a 'mother', and even more alarmingly a 'housewife'. Its meanings are coded in language that says she is 'not working' if she is not currently in the paid workforce (Waring, 1988). As the family is constructed ideologically with the husband/father as breadwinner, women's paid work is seen as secondary and conditional. Thus notions of femininity and ideologies around motherhood underpin the systematic devaluation of women's labour, while leaving men free to pursue a job, to be parents (while often not parenting), and to enjoy the comforts of a home while choosing what if any labour they will put into it. Thus sexist ideology constitutes, legitimises and reproduces relations of domination, subordination and exploitation through women's sexuality, through the sexual division of labour at home and in the labour market, and through women's interactions with the state.

This division of labour and structured inequality between the sexes is reinforced by the division between public and private domains, with women relegated largely to the latter and away from places of public power and validation. The public domain is usually occupied by men who are white, English-speaking, middle class and above, middle aged and above, and at least publicly heterosexual. Women are excluded from the social, as the individual who inhabits the social world of politics and power is male (Pateman, 1988). Male power is incorporated into state structures (Franzway, 1990; Connell, 1990). The state acts on gendered subjects, directing its attention to women as women over a range of activities, and also determining policies which, while ignoring gender, disproportionately affect women (see chapter 5).

Gender is a feature of social relations and public power where women are absent as much as where they are included or contained. Yet the association of public with male, and the naturalising of men's rule so that it appears normal, means that men's spaces are frequently represented as ungendered or neutral (Walby, 1988:223). Thus gender is coded to mean women, as race is coded to mean black, or at least not-white. The norm is defined through the creation of the 'other' (de Beauvoir, 1970; Said, 1978; Trinh, 1989). Yet the significance of public spaces and political power as men's, and the construction of dominant masculinity, is central to state and international dealings and determinations (Enloe, 1989).

This structure of male domination in both its ideological and material dimensions is frequently referred to as patriarchy. While there is currently a lively debate within feminism about the nature, meaning and bases of patriarchy (Walby, 1989, 1990) the concept does draw attention to a structure of power which systematically benefits men and penalises women, although the particular shape of the relations varies over time and place. These relations are also mediated by class and by race and cultural difference. Here it may be useful to talk about sexisms, recognising that both the ideology and the material forms vary from society to society, and indeed within particular societies.

Some would prefer to limit the use of the concept patriarchy to the rule of the fathers over the younger men as well as over women and children. In this sense 'traditional' cultures, including a number of migrant cultures in Australia, are often represented as patriarchal, or as excessively so compared with the supposedly more open and equitable gender relations of the dominant society.

Pateman (1988) suggests that modern male-dominated society is better described as fraternal, while Waters (1989) suggests the label 'viriarchy' to describe contemporary western society, characterised by rule by adult males, and gender relations that systematically devalue, discriminate against or damage women. Talking of masculine or masculinist domination also draws attention to social construction and power relations, rather than to essentialised notions of 'men' as powerful/evil and 'women' as victims/good. The debate about where individual men are in patriarchy, for example, gay men and/or men who support feminist causes, is heated (see Moi, 1989; Marcus, 1988; Stone, 1989; Connell, 1990).

While men as a category have power over women as a category, and most men benefit from their access to women's labour and bodies, not all men are equally powerful. The structure of power in a class society loads choices, resources and rewards heavily against those men who are poor. It is doubly loaded against those men who are black or members of ethnic minority groups as well.

Black feminists have challenged 'white' and falsely universalised notions of patriarchy by pointing out that the bonding of the fathers or of the brothers has been at the expense of both women and of non-dominant group men. Thus concepts of patriarchy or capitalist patriarchy still obscure crucial dimensions of public power. Joseph (1981:101) speaks of a capitalist white supremacist patriarchy, and Carby (1982:218) and Parmar (1982:258) of racist patriarchy (see also Huggins, 1987). In such a patriarchy or fraternity, the positions of white women and black men are highly problematic.

Masculinity also requires reassessing in terms of racist patriarchy.

Thus Staples describes black masculinity in the United States as a subordinated masculinity, in which black men are denied the public power and economic opportunities to fulfil their 'male' role. Some men may then seek to exercise the only power they have—physical and sexual power over 'their' women and children (Mercer, 1986).

THE SEXUAL DIVISION OF LABOUR

Here it is necessary to look at institutionalised social practices through which sexism is reproduced. They are as diverse—and often the same—as those reproducing racism. The remainder of this chapter will look especially at women's work in the family and the labour market, at constructions of women's sexuality and femininity, and at issues of safety and danger. Later chapters will pursue different women's experiences of the state, welfare and education.

Women's work differs systematically from men's (Hartsock, 1983). Clearly women bear children, but there is no necessary extension that those who bear them have primary responsibility for rearing them. It is even less clear why women should keep house for men. On the whole, men still enjoy access to women's unpaid labour as domestic labourers, who provide child-care and house and husband-maintenance as well as sexual services. Women are also often unpaid or underpaid community carers, largely invisible and relegated to work that is publicly under-valued and contained.

Sexist ideology rests on and reinforces a particular material base. Barrett points to the double shift that women in western societies do as unpaid domestic labour and poorly-paid wage labour, in the interests both of capital and of men (1980:255). Here again the nexus between the individual household, wage labour and the state is crucial in reproducing gender relations (Stasilius, 1990). Women's work both produces and reproduces the labour force, physically through childbirth and child rearing, and socially through servicing the current labour force at drastically reduced costs to capitalism and the state, and to individual men.

Thus like whites in racism, men in sexism benefit from their social location within the relatively powerful and privileged group, through controlling and disproportionately benefiting from women's labour. Women are in turn penalised within the labour market and largely confined to secondary jobs, and must juggle their paid jobs with other physically and emotionally demanding unpaid jobs.

Women's paid work is frequently an extension of mothering and nurturing and being 'good with their hands', or good in managing human relationships. Women are concentrated in jobs to do with teaching, health care, restaurant and personal service, welfare and so on (Mumford, 1989). The labour market is segmented along gender lines, and the average wage for women remains well below that for men (Mumford, 1989:37), although women generally are now more highly educated, more women are in paid employment, and women's earnings have risen somewhat compared with men's (Daly, 1990). Still, women working in women's jobs often have male bosses, and rarely find that conditions of employment are geared towards or even make allowances for those many women with domestic responsibilities as well (Pringle, 1990:214). The workplace and work practices continue to be structured in terms of gender relations as well as capitalist–class relations (Game and Pringle, 1983; Pringle, 1988).

The labour market is structured around class and around race and country-of-origin (see chapter 3). Many women from non-English-speaking backgrounds, for example, have a white woman boss or supervisor (cf Rich, 1980; Hooks, 1984:49). Some white women are relieved of much of their own domestic or childcare work by paying other women, who are frequently from a different class and/or cultural background from their own (Huggins, 1987/8). This can be especially problematic for those feminists who are dependent on such support to do their perhaps women-related jobs, or attend conferences and meetings for women's liberation (cf Hooks, 1984; Gaitskell, 1982). But while class separates, it may also provide common interests and connections. Those women who do share class position and workplace may have much in common across race and ethnic category boundaries (Gale, 1989).

The search for commonalities and differences among women inform current debates within feminism about what exactly can be assumed or built on the category 'woman'. There are many shared interests among women as women, in experiences of multiple tasking and as carers, of gendered notions of work and home, of sexual harassment and sexual violence, and in many of their dealings with the state; but there are differences in many of these areas too.

WOMEN AND THE FAMILY

Women's increasing participation in the paid workforce has shifted the boundary between public and private (Sassoon, 1987:23), although those feminists who represent this shift as recent ignore the experiences of many poor, rural, Aboriginal and migrant women who have always 'worked'. White feminist writings on women's dependency can render minority women invisible yet again, by ignoring their frequently disproportionate responsibility for their own and their family's upkeep—while also relieving some white women of their own childrearing and domestic labour (Carby, 1982; Gaitskell, 1982; Huggins, 1987/8).

Black feminist critiques of 'white' feminism often centre on feminist representations of the family. Thus Hazel Carby began her agenda-setting chapter 'White Woman Listen: Black feminism and the boundaries of sisterhood' by calling on white feminists in Britain to reconsider three concepts central to feminist theory which were problematic in their application to black women's lives: the family, patriarchy and reproduction (1982:214). She and other black British women point to the existence of racially shaped gender stereotypes which characterise black families and black women in quite specific ways. Thus 'Asian' families are represented as excessively patriarchal and 'traditional', while Afro-Caribbean families are characterised as damaged and deviant, suffering from a lack rather than an excess of culture. Here, explanations often evoke the cycle of poverty, and loss of culture due to slavery or colonisation.

In both these rather different representations, family forms and women's roles within families and communities were seen as stemming from the culture or nature of those families and communities, rather than from their location within wider structures of power and subordination. In turn, these families and communities are blamed for what are seen as their problems, including low educational achievement and behaviour problems of black children and youth (Carby, 1982), and over-protection and control of daughters in the traditional Asian family (Amos and Parmar, 1984).

Representations of the black family in Britain and North America are in some ways similar to representations of Aboriginal families in Australia (Pettman, 1991). While women are frequently presumed to be dependents of men, Aboriginal women are often heads of households, responsible for the financial as well as the emotional survival of their families as primary kin-keepers (Lewis, 1987). Where they are welfare dependent, they are subject to state surveillance and intervention concerning their sexual relationships, household membership, and control of children, who are disproportionately taken into 'care'. Where they do find paid work it is frequently in the worst-paid and most vulnerable sectors, including domestic service. Against appalling odds, they find themselves portrayed as survivors who act as power-gatherers in times of crisis (Ryan, 1986a:41), or as 'black matriarchs', as women who are dominant, who are part of the problem. In this latter representation they are berated for their very survival and capacity to cope. They can then be blamed for their children's problems, for youth's delinquency, for emasculating 'their' men, and for usurping male roles in the family. The high physical and emotional costs of their coping are ignored (Larbalestier, 1980), and so too is their frequent vulnerability to violence, including from male kin (Bell J., 1986:71; Langton, 1990).

The black matriarch construction is both racist and sexist. Masculinity is associated with property, patriarchy and authority. Black and Aboriginal men are blamed for failing to be providers and heads of households, while black and Aboriginal women are blamed precisely for being providers and heads of households (Pettman, 1991).

Aboriginal anthropologist Langton has criticised white studies of urban Aboriginal families and communities which represent them as damaged and deviant, the product of poverty and 'loss of culture'. She raises

> the possibility of the matrifocal family as an accepted or perhaps even desired family form for Aboriginal women and children arising out of particular social conditions, that is those in which Aboriginal men are unable to reside permanently with wives and children because of itinerant labour patterns, unemployment, imprisonment, regulations pertaining to social security benefits for supporting mothers and so on. (1981:18)

She continues

> The anomie and signs of marginality that have been observed in poor, urban Aboriginal populations may be responses to racism, the denial of housing and services, the insensitive intrusion of social workers, the image of the poor, both black and white, as criminal, the diminution of particularly male roles where Aboriginal men are forced into menial employment positions, or worse into unemployment, and the range of half truths and myths about 'part-Aborigines'. (1981:18–19)

Collmann has documented the experiences of Aboriginal 'fringe-dwellers' in their interactions with, and resistance to, welfare authorities. Especially before 1967, welfare agents could legally restrict Aboriginal people's movements, and they intervened extensively in Aboriginal families, often by removing their children from them (Edwards and Read, 1989). Aboriginal men usually had to move to jobs, and welfare regulations made it impossible for Aboriginal women both to accompany their husbands and be seen as good mothers (Collmann, 1988).

Studies of contemporary Aboriginal families confirm the ongoing vulnerability of those families to welfare intervention, especially with respect to the placement of Aboriginal children in 'care' (Tomlinson, 1986; Wundersitz, 1990). Moreover, in the face of high unemployment or sporadic, seasonal or unreliable employment for Aboriginal men, Aboriginal women may be better off financially as single mothers on supporting-parent pensions. Thus while Aboriginal family forms do exhibit cultural characteristics, including attachments to a home place and to extended kin, they also reflect the effects of mutual support in the face of generations of state intervention and ongoing poverty and racism.

Aboriginal women may experience family forms and roles in some ways differently from ethnic-minority women. Those women from non-English-speaking backgrounds are often represented as 'traditional' and under the control of zealously patriarchal men, again in ways similar to representations of Asian and/or Muslim women in Britain. Like those women, they are often forced into the labour market at the time of greatest responsibility for children, and in jobs that are hazardous and vulnerable (Martin, 1986:241). Their experiences in the labour market in turn affect their families and their own roles as wives and mothers. They may find themselves caught between competing representations of these roles, associated with their places-of-origin, their community here, and the gender relations of the dominant society (e.g., Pallotta-Chiarolli, 1989:49).

Here it is necessary to separate out ideological representations of women's roles in pre-migration countries and communities and changing social relations there (remembering that many migrants came from minority status in their countries-of-origin), and to analyse the effects of migration and subsequent incorporation into Australian society and economy on family structure and roles. Aboriginal women and ethnic-minority women have reminded white feminists that their families have often been the only place of comfort and source of validation for them (Martin, 1986). They also point to the problematic nature of attacks on 'the family' as the source of women's oppression, when minority families are already under attack from a racist state.

There are difficulties, too, of analysing both cultural difference/s and racism in their construction of black and ethnic minority families. Thus Barrett and McIntosh (1985) responded to black British feminist critiques of their work on 'the family' by acknowledging that their work had 'spoken from an unacknowledged but ethnically specific position' and had ignored the different experiences of ethnic-minority women and families (1985:30). Bhavnani and Coulson (1986) responded to this self-critique by accusing Barrett and McIntosh of culturalism—recognising the very different experiences of the family of minority women, but doing so in ways that stress cultural difference as explanation. Thus they still fail to understand the powerful and generative effects of racism, and the on-going significance of a structure of race and class power that cuts across, even while constituting, gender. Other ethnic-minority feminists have joined the debate by arguing that both racism and cultural differences are crucial. Thus Yuval-Davis and Anthias recognise the key role that racism plays in locating families in relation to the state and the labour market, but argue that ethnicity is also a central dimension of gender. They criticise the binary opposition of 'black' and 'white' feminism as leaving Jewish, Greek-Cypriot and other ethnic-minority women 'politically unaccounted for' (1983).

These exchanges have resonances in Australia, where 'the family' is highly problematic. The family is declared in crisis, as divorce rates are high and the numbers of single parents and other non-conventional family forms increase. But the family is especially problematic for those women whose family forms and roles are already pathologised.

Martin (1986) writes of Australian radical immigrant critiques of Anglo-feminist accounts: 'while they agree that the family is the site of female oppression, it is an extraordinarily ambiguous and contradictory site', especially when divided families are often imposed on them unwillingly through migration or entry restrictions, and where the family may be the only familiar and affirming place many migrant women know.

> Radical immigrant women are not arguing for the sanctity of family life—indeed their political experience and activities point to the reverse. What they are saying is that modes of domination and exploitation in our society may be structured in such a way that the family is the only sphere of validation for many women, the only base of opposition from and within which they can act. They point to the privileged status of a range of Anglo feminist demands (especially round the family) whose tenor silences their desire for something else (e.g., family reunion and consolidation, anxieties about children). (Martin, 1986:245)

Aboriginal women and ethnic-minority women attempt to validate and celebrate their families, and to make them less vulnerable to intervention by various agents of the state. Here too women often represent themselves as carers of the community, as responsible for safeguarding both their families and their communities—a political project which is part of a social health program (e.g. *Women's Business*, 1986). And yet many Aboriginal and ethnic-minority families, like other families, are not safe places, especially for women and children. Much of the danger stems precisely from experiences of racism, migration, poverty, dislocation, that undermines the families and their usual or former support structures. Naming these dangers, devising strategies to support at-risk families, and seeking resources for action is especially difficult when those families are already stigmatised as deviant and dangerous, and subject to unwelcome attention from state agencies.

Chapter 2 noted the construction of black male sexuality in colonisation and racism (Carby, 1986; Mercer, 1986). While black women are represented as deviant and in some ways dominant, representations of black men are contradictory. They are seen as 'emasculated' in that 'their' women are often breadwinners and heads of households, but they are also seen as excessively masculine in their physicalness and even violence (Phoenix, 1985). Thus talking about domestic violence or rape within Aboriginal communities or families may appear to reinforce racist stereotypes and provide evidence for those who argue for racist explanations of social problems. Further, they may provide excuses or enticement to police or other state agents to intervene in families and communities which are already under seige from the state (Bryan, 1985:27).

WOMEN AND DANGER

Here we enter troubling terrain, as we ask questions about where women are safe and where they are in danger; and why it is that women of so many backgrounds are least safe in their own homes, and most at risk from the very men who claim to love them.

Many feminists, especially radical feminists, would argue that the root of male dominance is male violence, no matter how sophisticated and subtle are the other ideologies and social practices that underpin gender relations. Notions of women as property and as dependents whose bodies and services are somehow bought through men's breadwinning combine with particular constructions of masculinity, and with men's insecurity about and dependence on women to provide them with children. Compulsory heterosexuality (Rich, 1986:23) forms the basis for maintaining men's access to women's bodies, for children, and for unpaid domestic, including sexual, services.

Certainly there is now a wide awareness of the extent and terror of men's violence against women (Hanmer and Maynard, 1987:3), and the fact that women are most likely to experience violence at the hands of men they know, and especially those they live or lived with. Here feminism has had an impact in determining what is seen to be a social problem. Stranger-danger is still there, but domestic violence such as rape, child sexual abuse, physical abuse and neglect are now on the public agenda (McIntosh, 1990).

The interaction of class with racism and sexism has given us representations of some families as being particularly dangerous to their members. Here are debates about poverty and abuse, for example, and of working-class violence (Vinson, 1989). Yet we know that poor families are subject to more surveillance by state agents and are more likely to be reported and have files held on them. As Aboriginal families and some migrant and especially refugee families are over-represented in the poverty and stress figures they may be expected to reveal a higher profile in terms of family violence. They are also more visible and more likely to be labelled as criminal. So raising issues to do with domestic violence or child abuse within these families and communities is fraught with dangers.

Figures for violence within a number of Aboriginal communities are horrific (Tatz, 1990). Aboriginal people are ten times more likely than other Australians to be murder victims (AIC, 1990). Other forms of violence including serious assault, child abuse and self-mutilation are also common. More Aboriginal women have died in domestic violence in Queensland and the Northern Territory over the last ten years than all Aboriginal deaths in custody over that period, and in two Aboriginal communities alone more women have been killed in family violence than all Aboriginal deaths in custody in Queensland (the *Australian*, 27 June 1990; Atkinson, 1990). Some Aboriginal people are reluctant to discuss femicide (Langton, 1990) in open forum, when ongoing racism encourages a reading which appears to confirm Aboriginal men as savage (cf Walker, 1982; Marshment, 1983; Mercer, 1986; Mama, 1989). Others seek to find a way to speak by situating the figures in the damage of colonisation, racism and poverty, while also asserting that understanding the damage can never mean condoning the violence. Thus the Report into Aboriginal Child Poverty locates violence towards children in terms of community and family trauma through colonisation and ongoing racism (Choo, 1990; Greer, 1989).

Some attempts to place the violence within its historical and structural context can appear to condone or at least lessen the crime. This was highlighted by the dramatic trial of an Aboriginal man, Alwyn Peter, for the murder of his girlfriend, and his successful defence through evidence of community dislocation and chaos, and his own history of self-mutilation (Wilson, 1982; see also the film *State of Shock*). A similar defence recently resulted in only short terms of imprisonment of two Aboriginal men after they were found guilty of raping a young Aboriginal woman. A leading Aboriginal woman worker against domestic violence bitterly contested the judgement as trivialising Aboriginal women's experiences of domestic violence and rape (Atkinson, the *Canberra Times*, December, 1990).

Many Aboriginal women, and others, are organising against the violence, and building support for victims while also tackling the wider questions of how to build a safe and secure community. Aboriginal women are naming domestic violence, sexual assault and child abuse as of urgent concern to them (*Women's Business*, 1986; *Aboriginal Health Worker*, 1989). A 1990 New South Wales statewide conference of Aboriginal women called for specific conferences on these dangers (*Womanspeak*, September/October, 1990). The delegates also expressed concern that the Aboriginal Legal Aid Service does not represent Aboriginal women in cases of domestic violence because of its policy of not defending Aborigines against Aborigines. (Note a recent decision by a conference of British Asian lawyers to represent Asian women victims of domestic violence free of charge, as well as all victims of racist violence, *New Society*, 5 May 1988.)

Apparent disregard of Aboriginal women's efforts was part of the motivation for strong reaction from a number of Aboriginal women to an article by a white woman anthropologist claiming to break the silence on the question of intra-racial rape within Aboriginal communities (Bell and Nelson, 1989). This also raised complex ethical and political questions about who owns the problem and who is authorised to speak publicly about violence and conflict among Aboriginal people (see chapter 7).

These conflicts raise the issue of family in situations where large family groupings are pushed together in cramped and stressful living conditions, and the boundaries around family or household are less clear-cut. They also raise questions to do with speaking rights, with audience, and about who owns or should own the problem. Sometimes recognising Aboriginal demands for control of Aboriginal health and community programs can be a way of dumping the problem back on 'them' while not providing Aboriginal people with the resources or the support to cope in the long run or to provide essential protection in the short run.

There is some evidence to suggest that the stress, family dislocation and trauma of migration and especially of refugee experience increases violence in families (Storer, 1985; Kahan-Guidi and Weiss, 1989). Some men, in the face of change and financial difficulty, and as their wives go into the labour market and take on new responsibilities, may respond by attacking those women. In many communities domestic violence may be seen as a private matter, or trivialised in ways still common in the dominant culture.

Women in ethnic-minority communities are keenly aware of the strains on their communities, and the dangers of attracting the attention of the state to them. Some have organised and named the dangers in families, and have offered their experiences at conferences on domestic violence or child protection. Victoria now has a Refuge Ethnic Workers Project, which supports victims of domestic violence and provides community language, education and information services to refuge and mainstream domestic workers. In New South Wales, half of the Immigrant Women's Speakout Grant-in-Aid welfare workers' clients in 1989 were family conflict victims (*Speakout*, 1989). A recent Australia-wide survey of ethnic-minority women revealed that 81 percent believed domestic violence to be a serious problem within their community (*Canberra Times*, 21 April 1990).

In these situations feminists of whatever background who have worked and talked to get domestic violence and child abuse on the agenda contribute to a politics where other women, whether they call themselves feminist or not, are more strongly placed in raising these issues within their own communities. Now there is a language, an understanding, a set of concepts and some strategies that may be tried out (Mohideen, 1990/91:11; Langton, 1989), and both Aboriginal women and ethnic-minority women organised within the Commonwealth Office of the Status of Women 'Break the Silence' public education campaign. There are also some resources, though often minimal, around which to organise and make claim. Sometimes the existence of a policy or program or the possibility of funds becomes the basis for action in itself (cf Sassoon, 1987:26).

SEXUALITY AND DANGER

The reality and the fear of violence informs many women's lives and reduces their choices, so that they become their own police, limiting their own mobility and claims lest they 'provoke' men (Hanmer and Maynard, 1987; Scutt, 1980). The main danger is at home, but different public places are out of bounds to many women, and others like public transport or the streets are perceived and negotiated as threatening. This is especially so for the many women for whom sexual danger is compounded by racism. Here again class mediates by permitting some women a car and a working life which avoids or reduces public danger, although it never really goes away. There is always the possibility of a flat tyre or a disturbing confrontation in the car park.

The interplay of racism and sexism generate racialised stereotypes that portray different versions of femininity and sexuality. Thus Aboriginal women may be portrayed as loose and easy, and Asian women as sexually exotic, passive and used to male domination (Pettman, 1991). Such representations make these women more visible, and allow some men to deny responsibility or to resort to the usual blame-the-victim strategies. They can also mean that quite young women have to face systematic intrusions, innuendos and approaches in public places, and that their mothers and others who care for them experience a chronic indirect assault and fearfulness on their account which can permeate their lives.

Representations of 'Asian' women in Australia are associated with one dimension of the internationalisation of labour, through the tourist and marriage sex trade. There is a political economy of sex (cf Rubin, 1975:157). Many women in Asian countries have felt the disruptive and impoverishing effects of colonisation and of capitalist 'development', which drives them into the exploited offshore economic zones, attractive to international capital as supposedly more pliant and certainly less paid and less union-protected labour; or into prostitution, servicing tourists or service personnel, as in the huge American bases in the Philippines, for example (Enloe, 1990).

In Australia a particular category in the sex trade has become increasingly visible—that of the Filipino bride (de Lepervanche, 1989:174; Masian, 1990). Seventy percent of Filipino women in Australia are married to non-Filipinos (Masian, 1990:182). Some women may look to marriage with Australian men as a way out of poverty through access both to his personal wealth and to the lucky country. Here again are contradictions, and examples of agency. In some cases Australian men seek pliant, passive and sexually exotic wives and may express anger and violence against those women if they show any signs of independence, or indeed so much as speak to other people. Even women friends may be seen as threatening, lest they inform the newly-arrived wives of their rights, including to social services. There have been scandals lately, including violence against some women, and marriage contracts (which have no legal status) forbidding any contact with others (Philippines Resource Centre, 1990). In other cases the trade seems more equal, as women sponsor relatives for migration to Australia or as husbands financially assist those still in the Philippines. The very high numbers of older parents living with Filipino women in Australia suggests that the picture of the isolated victim is only one part of the picture (Price, 1989).

Another part is the many Filipinas in Australia who are highly educated and independent, and those who are in freely-chosen marriages, who bitterly resent being labelled as mail-order brides (Masian, 1990:183; *Canberra Times*, 2 November 1990). So it is necessary to unravel both the ideological constructions and the material pressures which may position some women in ways that seem to confirm racist-sexist representations of them, while recognising the agency and the contradictions at work that are rarely visible to outsiders.

Women who have been raped or suffered domestic violence are often reluctant to report these crimes, as they may be trivialised or treated as private problems, or met with suggestions that the woman somehow 'asked for it' (Scutt, 1980). Until recently there have been few supports for women victims of violence, especially when they knew the perpetrator. Those who did go to the police often had to contend with suspicion, not being taken seriously, interrogations about relations or experiences that were not relevant to the attack, or feeling that the whole event has been taken out of their hands, so they are pressured to agree to action that they may not want, or whose consequences they may fear. These dangers are compounded for Aboriginal women, for whom the police themselves are often a source of danger and violence (HEROC, 1991); and for many migrant women, especially those who have suffered at the hands of state agents in their home countries or during migration or flight, or who may find their migration status and right to be here questioned.

Many women who experience violence still lack access to support. The price of 'protection' may be that women act as victims who are deserving of help, which further disempowers women and reinforces social controls against them (Mikhailovich, 1990). Poorer women and those from stigmatised groups, especially those whose own sexuality is represented as deviant, are in an even worse position. While now there are rape crisis centres, women's health centres and feminist groups to support and work with victims, they are frequently desperately lacking resources and overstretched. They are also often simply unavailable to many women, like those who live in rural areas. Sexist ideologies, including homophobic ones, reinforce sexual and social domination of men over women. For example, myths about feminists tell other women that refuges are controlled by white middle-class lesbians who will demand complicity in return for support. Divide and rule tactics are powerful, as they are when black feminists and especially black lesbians are told by those who disapprove of their work for women's safe places that they have 'left the race' (cf Smith, 1983:xxix).

Here too are issues to do with the race politics of different feminisms and the sexism of different communities. There are many white women in the women's refuge movement, for example, who, while not necessarily middle class and not monolithic in their positions regarding sexuality, have yet to work through issues to do with the social and sexual significance of whiteness and of their own ethnic location. However, many women working in refuges either come from minority backgrounds themselves and/or have done a lot of thinking and talking with women from different backgrounds about how to make their own work and politics more inclusive. Aboriginal women and ethnic-minority women working against domestic violence, often with other women, bitterly resent some members of their own communities representing their work or in many cases their feminism as something derived from or only relevant to white feminists.

All women in relationships with Aboriginal or ethnic minority men may experience family and community politics and evocations of a 'tradition' and of community mores that are patriarchal, but take significantly different forms from dominant patriarchy. No set of gender relations is homogenous, uncontested, nor unaffected by the others. Thus particular constructions of femininity and notions of shame may be used to try to keep domestic violence as an issue within the community or the family—itself perhaps a way of silencing women about it. They may also be used to prevent women from seeking support or taking action even when the attacker was from outside the community. On the other hand, stereotyping 'Australian' girls as sexually promiscuous and disrespectful, compared with 'good' Greek or Italian girls, discounts girls' friendships across the boundaries, and the variety of relations they have with their families as they each negotiate their own definition of their young womanhood (Greek–Australian Women's Workshop, 1989; Pallotta-Chiarolli, 1989).

WOMEN AND COMMUNITY

'Woman' as a social category is problematic (Alcoff, 1988; de Lauretis, 1988). Like categories defined in terms of race or country-of-origin, 'women' can speak to powerful associations, emotions and roles. Women do experience male and public power in particular ways, although these experiences are also mediated by class, race and ethnicity, along with age and disability, for example. Gender is a highly significant social fact, and women are frequently represented and treated as mothers and as dependents, whether or not they are. Women also frequently experience work and living as multiple and unpaid or under-paid workers. Women have a keen interest in the provision of services, support and safety for themselves, and for their own or others' children.

The category 'women' is a social construction that may disguise the range of women's interests as mothers or not, as wives or not, and their location in terms of different class, race and ethnic associations and identities. Women live in a range of household forms or live alone. They are heterosexual, lesbian or celibate; able or disabled; and of different ages and stages in the life cycle. They are green or pink or red or conservative or disinterested politically, or belong to different religions. Many women and men live alone or in group or friendship households that we are not used to calling families. New extended families growing out of separation, remarriage and blending do not have appropriate kin terms, while children may live in several different kinds of households as they grow up. Each household form contains the possibility of congeniality and safety, or of exploitation or danger.

Individuals do matter too, as the nurturing and loving father, the willing co-parent, the abusive mother and the generous ex-wife support or subvert particular relationships. Here too negotiations proceed between the generations as well as between individuals within particular communities. These negotiations are contained within or press against the gender relations of the dominant society and its institutions, and often involve exchanges within marriages and other relationships which cross race and ethnic boundaries.

The feminist project requires developing a language that recognises the variety in both household form and women's experiences within each. It means reappropriating the reified 'family' that the New Right claims to itself, or that some anti-feminists speak to; recognising that many women who do not live within the idealised nuclear family do spend much time and energy within families too.

Other kinds of exclusion also happen within language and analogy, for example, when calling up notions of family or community associated with caring and safety, while the politics and power relations involved are so complex. Using maternal or familial language and recognising and valuing women's traditional caring roles is affirming, but may converge with the language and associations of patriarchy, and reinforce boundaries that keep women out of public power and choice. These representations may also idealise motherhood in ways that exclude those who are not mothers or who cannot or chose not to become mothers. Likewise, pursuing a radical feminist separatism that calls for women to 'evacuate motherhood' denies women's links with their own mothers, and for many with their own sons (Saunders, 1989:47). Similarly giving up on men may deny many women's loving attachments, including those to their sons.

The task then is to analyse families and women's experiences in them, developing images of what feminist mothering looks like, and what kinds of gender relations and household organisation can work for women, for children, and for men who are prepared to or can be persuaded to give away the upper hand. A more inclusive feminism does mean the right to choose—whether or not to have children, to live with a man, or with anybody, the right to say no as well as the right to say yes. It also means enabling those choices through women's equitable access to the resources necessary to sustain these choices.

The possibility of a community of women, or communities of women, must begin with a recognition of the differences among and between women, including situations of unequal power and exploitative relations. But privileging difference can disguise shared interests and undermine the possibility of friendship, alliances and working relations. Many women do work closely across the boundaries in social and family networks, at work and in politics, although both the boundaries and the ways of crossing them are under-theorised in Australian feminism. So the specificity and variety of women's experiences must be recognised within the context of power relations in which gender, class, race and ethnicity are all constitutive. Gender relations themselves are never static or fixed, but are highly political and highly contested sexual politics.

5   Experiences of the state

How far is there life 'beyond the gaze of the state'? (Taylor, 1989:23). 'It is impossible today to think of an area of society or of people's lives where politics and state policy don't have an impact' (Sassoon, 1987:23). The state penetrates every aspect of social relations through its management of the labour market, the provision of state services and the increasingly complex legislative and administrative complexes. The state is heavily implicated in the constitution and reproduction of social relations that underpin power structures, social relations of class, gender, race and cultural difference. Yet the state is also the target of much political organisation and claim by women, Aboriginal people, and migrant and ethnic organisations. Many of those seeking support of the state regard it with ambivalence, suspicion or downright hostility.

This chapter will examine the problematic nature of the state's relations with women, and especially with minority women. Women depend on the state more than men do. The state in turn treats different women differently (Williams, 1987:15). How do women in general and Aboriginal women and ethnic-minority women in particular experience and respond to the state? How amenable is the state as an instrument of anti-racist, anti-sexist and social justice action in support of women's and minority interests? This chapter looks at women, citizenship and social rights, and women and welfare. It analyses the growth of Aboriginal affairs, ethnic affairs and equal opportunity as state activities; and the role of women as state workers, femocrats, and those who work in Aboriginal and ethnic areas. It concludes by identifying different discourses, practices and possible strategies for anti-sexism and anti-racism within, through and against the state.

THE STATE IN AUSTRALIA

The state goes beyond apparatuses of the military and bureaucracy associated with the administration of a legal entity known as the nation state. The state includes a range of institutions and services, like education, health and social welfare.

In Australia state intervention dates from the 1890s, in terms of the regulation of the labour market and the beginnings of state welfare (Head, 1989:35). The political mobilisation of labour led to compulsory arbitration, wages awards, old-age pensions and so on, conceived of as rights of workers rather than as social needs of citizens. Preoccupation centred on working conditions, wages and industrial relations, with welfare seen only in terms of a safety net (Castles, 1985:87; Jakubowicz, 1989:15).

In the political science literature the debate proceeds about whether the state is inherently meshed with a particular class or ideology (Head, 1989:17). The state itself is not monolithic or deterministic. The state is a site of struggle between different interests, which themselves are linked into structures of power and processes of political mobilisation in the public domain. It also has interests of its own.

The state in Australia is a capitalist state, and it acts to protect the long-term interests of capital and to maintain its own legitimacy. It is centrally implicated and involved in the reproduction of social relations in, for example, the labour market—which is not to deny that the interests of particular capitalists or their managers may conflict at any point in time.

The state thus involves a series of engagements, decisions, norms and rules which represent the outcome of past and present struggles and trading among them. A class settlement between capital and labour maintains capitalist relations but also secures a welfare base, won in part by labour struggles, and in part by the state compensating for the more brutal and disruptive aspects of capitalism (cf Offe, 1982). The modern state is thus a complex administrative and highly interventionist state (Yeatman, 1990:169). The state is also *ad hoc*, residual and contradictory, in places disconnected and fragmented, although structured overall in terms of societal power relations and politics.

The state is also patriarchal, or perhaps more correctly, fraternal (Pateman, 1988; Randall, 1988:14). Feminist contests about the links between men's power in society and men's power in the state include differences among those labelled marxist or socialist feminists and radical or cultural feminists (Randall, 1988). The former analyse the links between capitalism and patriarchy, for example between the labour market, women's domestic labour and the construction of the family (e.g., Barrett, Hartmann, Eisenstein, Curthoys). The latter focus in different ways on sex power as primary (e.g., Brownmiller, Daly, MacKinnon, Scutt, Thompson). Here the state is seen as complicit in perpetuating men's violence against women, and central to the exploitation of women's sexuality as well as of their labour. Thus MacKinnon (1983) looks at the law and its treatment of women, and argues that neither the endemic violence, which is over-whelmingly men against women or girls, nor the legal and social constructs of rape, for example, in which 'consent' becomes a matter of the man's perception, can be explained solely or primarily in terms of a political economy.

There is ongoing contestation among feminists over the nature of the state and the various relationships between women, feminists and state. These have crucial implications for strategy and the possibility of feminists using the state for liberation, despite its implication in the subordination of women.

The capitalist and patriarchal or fraternal state is also a racist state (Joseph, 1981). The state constructs the nation and determines access to and entitlements associated with citizenship. As we have seen, the structure of power in Australia is dominated by those who are white, English speaking, male, middle class and above, middle aged and above. All men are positioned positively and all women negatively in their capacities to exploit gender assets, but many men are negatively positioned in terms of access to capital skills and other assets, and majority women are positioned negatively on sexual dimensions (Yeatman, 1990:69).

Given that the state is heavily implicated in the day to day man-agement and reproduction of power relations, what are the limits, possibilities and obligations of state intervention and appropriate forms of state action in terms of social justice?

CITIZENSHIP AND SOCIAL RIGHTS

Citizenship is a legal status defining both nationality and entitlement to certain legal and social rights (Barbalet, 1988). Citizenship is ambi-guous for women who are frequently constructed as dependants, as passive citizens, objects, clients and consumers of policies, rather than as individual citizens (Fraser, 1987:97; Shaver, 1990:95). Their citizenship was also long subverted by women's loss of individual rights through marriage, needing their husband's signature for pass-port or loan applications for example, and by their treatment as 'wife' rather than subject. Pateman (1988) points to the contract of fraternal citizenship as incorporating the sexual contract which established men's sex right to women. In this sense women were not simply overlooked or even excluded from the polity; rather the polity was constructed on their exclusion and control.

Citizenship is also militarised through its association with the capacity and willingness to bear arms. The Australian armed forces were exempted from the Sex Discrimination Act in 1984, which some saw as continuing to exclude women from full citizenship (Sullivan in Watson, 1990:180). In May 1990 the Ministry of Defence announced that women would now be eligible for combat-related positions, but still not for combat itself (cf Enloe, 1988). This 'protection' of women does not secure their safety in wars, where they are often victims of the fighting and where rape is frequently used as a weapon of war. Nor are women safe within the nation, as the epidemic nature of domestic and sexual violence against women and children, especially female children, attests.

Women were neglected and confined within the private and domestic sphere long after they acquired political and legal rights, including the right to vote. In this situation Pringle and Watson argue that 'What feminists are confronted with is not a state that represents "men's interests" as against women's, but a government conducted as if men's interests are the only ones that exist' (in Watson, 1990:234). Yet even in their invisibility, they were and are subject to heightened control, in a mix of denial and imposition.

Citizenship is also highly problematic for Aboriginal people, who were long formally excluded from it and subject to a particular and inferior legal status 'outside the nation: inside the state' (Beckett, 1988b). A 'bewildering array' of statuses contained Aboriginal people within a range of definitions constructed for the purpose of controlling, managing and 'protecting' them (McCorquodale, 1986). The brief assimilation phase officially recognised Aborigines as full citizens with entitlements, to be treated like other Australians, as individual citizens with the same hopes and the same fears (Bennett, 1989). Almost immediately afterwards Aboriginal people set up the 1972 'tent embassy' and declared themselves foreigners in their own land. Since then, assimilation has been replaced by a recognition of Aboriginality and a special collective relationship of Aboriginal people with the state (Beckett, 1988b). There is tension here between the moves towards non-discrimination on grounds of race and the parallel recognition of special claim, as there is between notions of Aboriginal self-determination and autonomy and the presumed universality of citizenship.

Citizenship is also ambiguous for migrants, with earlier restrictions on citizenship for non-white, non-English-speaking background people and continued limits on eligibility, and continuing constructions of 'Australians' as white and English speaking (Pettman, 1988b). It is unclear when a migrant ceases to be a migrant and accepted in their claim to rights within and loyalty to their adopted country. Expressions like 'they take our jobs' and debates about their economic contributions are often about whether migrants have earned social rights or are unfair competition, depriving Australians of resources (Jakubowicz, 1989:18). They also raise issues about the bases for recognising special entitlement or special needs, in this case due to migration, refugee status or language or cultural difficulties in negotiating social and economic life here.

Notions of citizenship as entitlement to legal rights are often part of the liberal tradition against government, including rights to political participation. What rights do people have as citizens? What rights should they have? Issues to do with citizenship and equality are strongly contested. Thus Harris seeks to ground the welfare state in rights that individuals have as members of a political community, the community of the nation state. Here welfare is conceived as the institutionalised recognition of social solidarity (Harris, 1987). Arguments for collective social provision for those who cannot cope or for dependants are issues to do with needs and rights and citizenship. But the shift from liberal to social democratic arguments in terms of representation and the welfare state also reflect a class settlement, which may defend capitalism and its state and re-establish hegemony in the face of increasing worker or other organisation and claim.

Citizenship is at one level a set of inclusion/exclusion practices, an exercise of social power in determining which individuals, groups and categories have what rights (Taylor, 1989:20). Citizenship here can also be used as part of a conservative nationalist discourse to deny belongingness and entitlement to many, including in Australia those migrants and Aboriginal people whose labour (and land in the case of Aborigines) help to sustain the lifestyle of those who close against them (Pettman, 1988b).

Here Yeatman identifies the absence of an Australian discourse on citizenship in terms of social citizenship and social rights (Yeatman, 1990:116, 129). Is it possible to have a radical purchase on citizenship? (Taylor, 1989:29; Croft and Beresford, 1989:5; Hall and Held, 1989). To talk, for example, of citizenship as full and equal participation in the political life of the whole community? (Hindess, 1990:114). To argue also for access to the social conditions necessary for individual development, including social and economic rights and control of resources for challenging the structures and ideational representation of power through which so many are currently excluded or marginalised? Does citizenship also entail certain social rights which may be necessary to effect participation—for example, minimum education, literacy in the dominant language, access to information to allow participation? (See Turner, 1990:189, on the notion of active citizenship.)

Majority-group women have enjoyed legal political equality for some time, and Aboriginal women and ethnic minority women have achieved formal equality in recent decades. Yet women continue to experience subordination and exclusion from a wide range of social and industrial rights. What is the connection between beneficiary status and participation and social rights? (Shaver, 1990:93). There are issues here about the nature of the claim and of dependence, about discourses of rights as against welfare, about nationality, citizenship and entitlement, and also about the ways in which groups and categories are constituted for the particular attention of the state in terms of categorical claims.

There are fierce contests about the meaning, desirability and bases of equal treatment, equality of opportunity and special entitlement, for example, where particular groups have particular problems that arise from their social history and location. Notions of justice or fairness are often played out in a conflict between support for universal provision (which may well not be universal) and autonomy or particular claims; a re-run in some ways of the equality/difference debates of early feminism (Caine, et al. 1988; Curthoys, 1989). Some anti-discrimination and equal opportunity policies aim for equal human rights for all. At the same time there is increasing recognition of differences, special needs or minority groups for the purposes of entitlements, often constructed as social problems, which can run against this grain (Fulcher, 1989:7). There are clear links between categorical construction and legal and ideological entitlement within the welfare state (Shaver, 1990:100).

WOMEN AND THE STATE

What are women's relations with state processes, and what are their experiences of the state? What is the state's role in reproducing gender relations, including the sexual division of labour and particular construction of the family and of women as dependants? (Franzway, et al. 1990; Watson, 1990; Yeatman, 1990).

Many policies and programs are 'gender neutral' in that they do not specify women's experiences or social interests, even where women are differentially affected by them. It is difficult to develop an appropriate language and to make women visible. But the state itself is centrally implicated in the construction of gender relations, and is a target of mobilisation and claim in gender politics. It is also itself gendered, both in its reproduction of a sexual division of labour, and in the ways that the state is constituted through, among other things, gendered power (Connell, 1990).

Women occupy various statuses in relation to the state. Women are citizens, permanent residents or potential migrants. Women are workers, including often as employees of the state, or unpaid workers in the family and community. Women are clients and consumers of welfare. Women are members of particular racial, ethnic or other category groups which are targeted by the state, or which mobilise to make claims against the state. Women are defined as social problems or as minorities with special needs requiring special state attention, whether it be as white women, as Aboriginal women, or as ethnic-minority women. For some purposes women are treated in accordance with their race or ethnic category, in others according to their gender or other social designations.

Women are also related politically in struggles against or as claimants of the state, again perhaps as women, or as community members, peace activists, trade union officials, and so on.

WOMEN AND WELFARE

The welfare state is often presumed to be either neutral and universal, or redistributive and benevolent. Its welfare functions are variously interpreted, from humanising and thereby stabilising capitalism, through a class compromise reflecting left and worker mobilisation, to a progressive political project expanding social rights (Offe, 1982:13). It is likely that each of these is an aspect of its development in Australia. Since the Second World War it has been widely presumed that the state would be responsible for collective minimum provision, and that it would continue to compensate for the machinations of the labour market—a presumption that is now in doubt in the new welfare wars.

Hindess (1990) draws attention to the contradictions between assumptions of citizenship and entitlement based on supposedly independent individuals in a shared political community, and the constitution of large numbers of people as dependants of the state (or of many women as dependants of their husbands). In addition redistribution through tax and welfare is usually within classes rather than between them. There is also a construction through welfare of the distinction between the deserving and the undeserving poor (Jakubowicz, 1989:14), the latter often women and young people of both sexes. The welfare state is especially intrusive against those who are dependent on social security, and uses powerful combinations of surveillance, information-gathering and monitoring regarding family form, sexual relations and so on against them.

Nevertheless the availability of certain benefits to women like the supporting-parents' pension (also available to the far fewer single fathers) is positive. So, too, is the funding of women's refuges, health centres, child-care centres and so on, even though that funding may be conditional and inadequate. Thus the welfare state is involved both in women's subordination and control, and in crucial and at times liberatory provision for women. At the same time the recognition of new categories and claims by the state has expanded the area of the political, and the state's effect on areas of living formerly considered private (Sassoon, 1987:22; Yeatman, 1990:171).

There are now, prompted largely by feminist demands and women organising, a wide range of state services in support of women, even though they remain under-funded and politically vulnerable. One theoretical representation of these changes is in terms of a shift from private patriarchy to public patriarchy (Brown, 1981; Walby, 1990; Shaver, 1990), as more and more women and children become dependent on the state rather than on a particular male. Again, as when talking about so many women now 'working', i.e., in paid employment, these changed circumstances apply mainly to white and often middle-class women.

Women are central in and to the welfare state. While they play small roles in policy making, it is overwhelmingly women who spend time negotiating welfare services as clients, low-paid workers and unpaid carers (Dale and Foster, 1986:ix). Women are the main users of welfare as consumers of health, social security benefits, and so on. Seventy-seven percent of all social welfare clients in Australia are women (Mayberry, 1987). They are also often employees of the state, from highly-paid femocrats to office cleaners, including many women whose work as service deliverers often brings them into unequal relations with other women. They are also unpaid carers in families and communities whose work takes pressure off mainstream services or compensates for their inadequacies (Croft, 1986:23). They are intermediaries with the state on behalf of their children and other family members (Dale and Foster, 1986:60; Sassoon, 1987:209). Many women are also involved as women and often as feminists in political struggles over welfare. Here Hurtado represents feminists of colour in the United States as training to be urban guerrillas by doing battle every day with agencies of the state (quoted in de Shazer, 1990:351).

Women are also attended to or seek attention from the state in a variety of other roles and social identities. Women are overwhelmingly the victims of rape and domestic violence; and the large majority of the aged, outworkers and custodial parents, for example. Women, especially as single parents, are disproportionately affected by the increase of poverty (Cass, 1988). They are also differentially affected by the current restructuring of the labour market. Any cutbacks in welfare and other state services thus affect women particularly, as one of the 'disposable minorities'.

The welfare state constructs women as dependants according to its gender script (Shaver, 1990). The state constructs gender power relations, including through its control of women's sexuality (Pringle and Watson, 1990:235). The state has its own ways of interpreting women's needs and positioning women as subjects (Fraser, 1987:93), as dependents and clients in need of the state's protection.

Part of the construction of femininity and the family involves women as carers of children, the elderly, the ill and disabled, as well as of men (Waemes in Sassoon, 1987:208). Women are located within cycles of caring—often just when they think the children have left home, or that they made it through without having any, an elderly parent is widowed or falls, and a new care relationship begins. Women's roles as care-givers jeopardise their participation in the labour market, and frequently require time out of the labour market for which they later pay. Which is not to deny that some women have no wish to be in it.

'Community care' is often a code for women's unpaid or underpaid work, reducing the costs of social reproduction to the state, and both humanising and filling gaps in state provision. The care relationship is also often unequal and can be isolating and exploitative, locking women as carers and cared for into a relationship which is privatised and unsupported. There are hints of violence directed by some carers at their more difficult or resented charges, or of conflicts that build up between the two—and some of the cared for become expert in games that make it unclear who is the keeper of whom (Croft, 1986:23). Alternatively many women prefer care by other women, preferably those they know and love, and prefer home care to institutionalisation, and for good reason. The task then is to identify how carers and cared for can best be supported; and how those women who cannot or choose not to 'care' can be assisted in their decision.

Even where women are in reasonably secure, unionised and

rewarded work, it is often an extension of their caring role, as nurses, teachers or social workers, for example, or less securely as community workers with Aboriginal or ethnic-community organisations. Again there is the familiar sexual division of labour, for the administrators and power brokers are usually men (cf Dale and Foster, 1986:60; Waemes in Sassoon, 1987:208). Those men are also usually from particular, and dominant, race and ethnic backgrounds.

MINORITY WOMEN AND WELFARE

The state deals differently with different women (Williams, 1987:15). It is constitutive in the social construction of 'women' and of minority women. Its provision is not universal or equally available. This may occur through the guise of universal provision, but the underlying assumptions and operations are often loaded culturally or in terms of class—in definitions of the family, for example. This loading is subverted or reinforced by those working in the state, whose views of their own job and of worthy clients, parents or patients influence the quality of care or access to information or services available to different women.

Many minority women experience the state in the person of a white woman, as health worker or social worker, for example (Sassoon, 1987:28; Hooks, 1984; Rich, 1980). What are the possibilities for a feminist and anti-racist project, then, when issues of power and difference place service deliverers in ambiguous or contradictory relations with their clients, and when the structures and policies within which they must work are rarely those on which they themselves have much influence? (Wise in Stanley, 1990).

This raises issues to do with institutional racism in service provision, and the crucial role of gatekeepers in the institutions (Brown, 1986; Pettman, 1988d; Toomelah Report, 1988). Meanwhile those women who are constituted as different by the state face a combination of discrimination, neglect, and unwelcome attention. Aboriginal women, visible migrant women, and women in non-traditional families and relationships find they are the objects of particular treatment, often through provision of welfare and the stipulation and policing of various conditions for eligibility and entitlement.

State control and the difficulties facing minority women in gaining access to welfare or alternatively escaping from welfare intervention have been the catalyst and focus for political mobilisation, for example, Aboriginal struggles around education, health and the legal system. The state responds to some of these struggles by funding along category lines, or to others by declaring, although not necessarily implementing, access or equity plans. One effect has been that while Aboriginal women and ethnic minority women are eligible for many benefits and services as women, there is now also some provision available to them as race or ethnic-category members. This provision too is often inadequate, inappropriate and at times unknown to those who are eligible; or else the difficulties of 'fronting' discourage many women from applying. And where provision is designated, as it often is, for women, or Aborigines, or ethnic-community members, minority women again may fall between the category and allocative cracks.

ABORIGINES AND THE STATE

Aboriginal women often identify themselves and are identified as Aboriginal first and women second. Their relationship with the state is often as Aborigines, but their everyday relations with the state are also as mothers and carers in family and community roles. Aboriginal people have an intense and frequently damaging relationship with the state, which many regard with suspicion—both in terms of its policing and legal system, and in terms of its welfare functions, including education. At the same time Aboriginal people are especially dependent on state funding, state service provision and state legislation for their status and rights.

Aboriginal Affairs is a significant part of government (Beckett, 1989:127). Aborigines are indigenous, dispossessed people who pose acute problems for the settler state. Clearing the land, securing white capitalist title and in some areas facilitating the exploitation of Aboriginal labour involved the ideological and legal construction of Aborigines as Other. Their separate and inferior legal status facilitated exclusion, confinement and control as a separate class subject to special laws and special administration. This collection of measures amounted to an extraordinarily diverse range of legislation.

McCorquodale (1986:8) has identified some 67 different classifications or definitions of Aboriginal people arising over the last 200 years. Legislation permeated and disrupted every aspect of life for Aborigines, even those whose geographic remoteness or economic self-sufficiency provided them with some protection. They too could in a single moment be reduced to institutionalisation (Tatz, 1979; Markus, 1990).

Beckett notes that Aborigines have always been seen as a problem for the state, for which it was expected to find a solution, especially once the 'dying race solution' failed to eventuate. The resultant 'welfare colonialism' saw controlled administration and tolerance for a lower standard of living and level of state provision than for other Australians (Beckett, 1988b).

In the 1960s and early 1970s international attention and Aboriginal protest highlighted continuing Aboriginal poverty and stress against a backdrop of the enormous boom in Australia (Bennett, 1989). Confrontations with mining companies led to embarrassing attention to unresolved issues regarding Aborigines and land, Aboriginal economy and social security. Neither ordinary welfare nor the daily operations of the labour market were capable of coping with the severity of Aboriginal disadvantage and disorganisation, or of incorporating them into the wider society (Beckett, 1988b).

Since then a vast range of Aboriginal provision and administration has been set up under various labels, including self-determination and self-management, and including limited land rights (Jennett, 1983:90). Why would capitalist nation–states recognise difference and go to the lengths of creating non-capitalist forms of land holding? (Peterson, 1985:85). There are powerful arguments for land rights as compensatory justice and as securing for Aboriginal people a resource base to support self-determination. Land rights legislation has had the positive effect of allowing access for some Aboriginal groups to their own land and a degree of security, and it is of powerful symbolic and political significance as a recognition of prior ownership. But land rights legislation is a contradictory development. Thus Peterson sees it as another form of welfare colonisation, interpreting land rights and by extension Aboriginal affairs as a welfare measure, not as a social justice measure, nor compensation for dispossession (Peterson, 1985:97).

Even as a welfare measure it is highly problematic. Land rights are racially based rights which are seen by many whites as reverse racism. Yet they can help to perpetuate disadvantage. Here Aboriginality and self-determination may render poverty 'cultural', while taking pressure off mainstream services and leaving Aborigines responsible for their own continued poverty and distress.

Managing the Aboriginal problem has led to a degree of structural pluralism (Jennett, 1987:58), as Aborigines are locked into 'highly segregated and specialised institutions' (Howard, 1982a:89). These include a secondary welfare state based on race (Shaver, 1990), although many Aborigines also or only receive ordinary social security benefits. This secondary racialised state is a complex administrative structure which included a separate Department of Aboriginal Affairs, now replaced by the Aboriginal and Torres Strait Islander Commission, and a range of Aboriginal desks, units and sections in other state and federal government departments. There is also significant government funding for many Aboriginal organisations and programs (Perkins, 1986; Peterson, 1985:145), including Aboriginal medical services, legal aid centres, and so on. These organisations are often kept chronically short of funds (Langton calls it 'drip-feeding'), and funding is used as a method of surveillance and control (Howard, 1982b:85). Aboriginal people frequently find themselves without resources, and conceive of their own right to funding as compensatory, where they and not the state should determine how the money is spent. Thus they appeal to the state for more funds and support, while simultaneously demanding self-determination, autonomy and to be left alone.

Aboriginal people are not alone in being recognised as a special category for government administration and funding, even though some critics speak as though they are (see e.g., Cowlishaw, 1990a, contrasting Aboriginal study grants and isolated students' benefits, which usually go to graziers' children).

The state acts to co-opt people in an attempt to administer them, only to find that its own associations or creations become the focus of mobilisation and criticism, revealed in the troublesome history of the National Aboriginal Consultative Committee (Weaver, 1983). The federal Labor government created the national Aboriginal body to give policy advice and later dissolved it in the face of its increasing politicisation and radical demands. The state nurtures political forces which it then has to contend with (Beckett, 1988b:3. See also MacDonald, 1988:35).

Indigenous politics, like ethnic politics and feminist politics, are frequently articulated in the political arena, directed especially towards the state, which responds through a combination of coercion, co-option, concession and control in its attempt to contain and manage the demands (Pearson, 1988:177). With regard to indigenous people, there are parallels between Australia and New Zealand and North America, where governments may utilise formerly tribal or communal identities or associations for administration or service delivery (Pearson, 1988; Cornell, 1988; Enloe, 1981). Through the process of institutionalising people and social identities it changes them. Governments are also part of a complex process by which individual people or communities become supra-tribal or pan-national, defining themselves and being administered as a people or race or even nation. In this process of ethnogenesis (Jones and Hill-Burnett, 1982) they become Aborigines, Maoris or Native Americans. Then government programs and specifically designated agencies or departments themselves become a focus for political mobilisation and claim (Beckett, 1988b; Enloe, 1981). This process also created an Aboriginal bureaucratic elite, embedded within and heavily dependent on the state (Howard, 1982b:94; Peterson, 1985), sometimes referred to by critics as coconuts or Kooricrats (Keeffe, 1988:75).

In the process of managing Aboriginal affairs Australian governments acquire huge powers to intervene, monitor and research Aboriginal people's ordinary lives (Beckett, 1989:121). Marcus (1989) reviews the extraordinarily detailed information about Aboriginal families and individuals held on various departmental and other files and so available to the state. There are so many Aboriginal people in hospitals, 'care', custody and jail, and who are recipients of welfare. Aboriginal people are over-researched, usually by academics or consultants with no accountability to them (Huggins, 1990). Yet such researchers are involved in the process of constituting knowledge about them, about Aboriginality, in terms of cultural traits like kin, sharing and extended families, or of cycle-of-poverty explanations that constitute them as social problems or according to a cultural deficit model. Such constructions of their problems lead to further welfare management and control models for Aboriginal affairs.

Aboriginal people themselves may constitute their claims on very different bases, arguing, for example, for rights not charity, and constructing themselves as a fourth-world people, rather than as a special needs category or as a group of welfare clients. But in the current political climate it is difficult to keep Aboriginal issues on the political agenda. Many non-Aboriginal Australians seem to be suffering from 'compassion-fatigue' (cf *Asian Migration* Editorial, 1989), and often regard even minimal Aboriginal rights as unfair privileges (Jennett, 1987:277; Cowlishaw, 1990a). So state sponsored discourses of special need must also be utilised, even while other Aboriginal discourses seek to change the terms of the debate.

Within these debates Aboriginal women are frequently active but rarely visible. Many of the accounts of Aboriginal affairs ignore gender. Yet Aboriginal women are very active and heavily responsible in families, communities and in Aboriginal organisations. They are central in many local campaigns and strategies, for health, in schools, for their children's security, and in wider mobilisations like the Committee to Defend Black Rights, which led to the Royal Commission into Aboriginal Deaths in Custody (Boyle, 1987).

Aboriginal women's articulation of their experiences, social interests and needs are often deliberately subsumed under a concern to address the primary reality of Aboriginality and Aboriginal status in confrontation with the state. They stress their shared interest with

Aboriginal men against the racism that devastates them all. But Aboriginal women have also criticised the domination of Aboriginal affairs by men, both Aboriginal and white (Gale, 1983:165, 173; Mundine, 1990).

Political negotiations and consultations, especially at state and federal level, are often between Aboriginal men and white male bureaucrats. Aboriginal men have stronger representation within government structures, often at the expense of women. Aboriginal women have been especially concerned at ways in which their exclusion from political negotiations and consultations have led to failure to recognise their rights as landholders and cultural authorities, and as community managers and teachers (Gale, 1983).

Aboriginal women are on the whole better educated and better employed than Aboriginal men (Burgmann, 1984; Sawer, 1990), but Aboriginal women have particular difficulties gaining voice in Aboriginal affairs. Thus the Department of Aboriginal Affairs (DAA) long resisted Aboriginal women's call for a task force to investigate their needs. It was not until 1983 that the first and only national consultation with Aboriginal women got under way. That consultation involved visits to 200 Aboriginal communities and drew up a wide-ranging report. It received almost no publicity, and languished in the Office of the Status of Women for years, although Aboriginal women's organising did lead to the formation of an Aboriginal women's unit in the DAA in 1984. The unit was upgraded to an office in 1986 (Sawer, 1990).

Women's Business (1986) is especially revealing for perceptions of the state and of Aboriginal women responding as users of government services, whether part of general welfare provision or specifically targeted towards Aboriginal people. Aboriginal women construct themselves as claimants with entitlements through indigenous status and dispossession as well as through social need.

Housing was the most discussed issue, with health, education, employment, child-support, protective services and land rights all major concerns. Women's desire for more, better and especially culturally appropriate services were framed by their concern to be independent of welfare and able to determine and control their own lives. Land rights was and remains a symbolic claim for a resource and power base which would permit self-determination.

Aboriginal women's organising has been hampered by the variety of situations and backgrounds in which they live, and the urgency of survival and immediate family and community demands. It has also been subverted by the poverty, poor education and weak resource base of so many. However, some strategic moments have strength-ened Aboriginal women's networks and helped generate more know-ledge about women's issues. These moments include conferences that have brought Aboriginal women together, including an Adelaide con-ference in 1980 where Aboriginal women from very different cultural and socio-economic situations talked together and discovered that many of their experiences and needs were similar or at least mutually understandable (Gale, 1983). In 1990 the first statewide Aboriginal women's conference in New South Wales was held, dealing with a range of concerns, including Aboriginal Legal Aid services not repre-senting women in domestic violence cases due to its policy of not defending Aborigines against Aborigines, mainstreaming appropriate education for Aborigines, and Aboriginal roles in government (*Womanspeak*, 1990).

Hundreds of Aboriginal women also attended the first inter-national indigenous women's conference held in Adelaide in 1989, as a result of Aboriginal women's involvement in both the Nairobi women's conference and internationally organised indigenous forums (Huggins, 1990). At this conference some Torres Strait Islander women, long tired of being subsumed and rendered invisible within the 'Aboriginal' category, and asserting different social identities and interests, stated that they, too, were international delegates at the conference, and not 'Australian Aborigines'. Also at the conference more 'traditional' women and some older urban Aboriginal women urged solidarity with non-indigenous women, while a number of younger and/or more radical Aboriginal women wished to secure a safe space for Aboriginal women to talk and learn together without the continual presence of 'white' women (Huggins, 1990:114).

MIGRANTS, ETHNICITY AND THE STATE

Migrant women and women of non-English-speaking backgrounds have been classified and treated as migrants or ethnics first, and women second.

Migrants are subjected to a state-managed and directed selection process as a condition of entry into Australia. Immigration policy is currently one of the most controversial areas of Australian politics with competing notions of economic management and of nation, citizenship and social rights and in terms of family reunion policies. The latter are especially contested between those migrants whose attempts to sponsor relations and reunite their families come up against both official definitions of the (nuclear) family, and immigra-tion opponents who think there are too many of 'them' here already.

There are contests too between members of different ethnic groups, as some older-established groups fear that increasing the refugee component may reduce places available in those categories of concern to them.

There are several rather different though often confused aspects of state management in this area. The selection, migration and initial settlement process is in some ways separate from the nature of incorporation of migrants into Australian society, including into the labour market, which in turn generates particular needs, for example, for English language training or for child-care. There is also a wider area of need, and the related constitution of a special interest or minority group, variously defined as ethnic or of non-English-speaking backgrounds. These designations speak not so much of the migration experience, which many English-speaking-background people have also come through, but of the state's response to difference and its management of problems and politics defined around culture. These target groups or categories may relate to a specific community or a specific language group, or more often be constituted as 'ethnic', which usually refers to those who are neither Aboriginal nor of English-speaking-background. They are defined for the purposes of managing demands, meeting needs and providing services. These may include the needs of those who are second or occasionally third-generation Australians.

Like Aborigines, the large numbers of non-English-speaking background migrants admitted during the 1950s and 1960s were expected to assimilate (Jupp, 1988). So state responsibility for and attention to them was restricted initially to the short-term post arrival phase. The rediscovery of poverty in the late 1960s, recognition of ethnic-minority migrants as among the most vulnerable groups, and the mobilisation of ethnic rights claims led to their constitution as a social problem for which the state sought particular education and welfare solutions (Martin, 1978). These solutions were typically directed at 'them', as if it was their culture, lack of English or appropriate education that was the problem, rather than their mode of incorporation into or exploitation within society.

Migrants were often marginalised within or excluded from particular aspects of political life and administrative provision. Their difficulties were compounded for those women who were also forced into the labour market at the time of heavy responsibility for children. Meanwhile the state had an interest in creating malleable citizens and exploitable workers, including domestic and community workers who were usually women.

The large-scale immigration program and especially its diverse sources confronted the Australian state with a major challenge to manage the differences and hold everything together. The long boom and the constitution of Australia as the lucky country that had done migrants a favour by admitting them disguised the structural location of many of the migrants. This location became increasingly apparent and vulnerable in the face of the recession and consequent restructuring of the economy, hitting hard precisely those industries where migrant women and men were concentrated.

As the economic crisis mounted there was a danger of conflict between different groups of workers, especially as some 'Australian' workers were mobilising around the familiar 'migrants as unfair competition' discourse. Alternatively the crisis presented the possibility for a radical critique of capitalism and an alliance of workers across their segmented workplaces and factions in the working class (e.g., Lever-Tracy in Bottomley and de Lepervanche, 1984).

Migrants were often seen as a conservative influence in trade unions, although there is little evidence for this general reading (Lever-Tracy and Quinlin, 1988). Many migrants were also often exhausted by settlement difficulties, and some refugees especially wanted anonymity. But there were also many workers who were radical, who came from socialist, marxist or feminist traditions, traditions marginal to Australian labour and union politics.

Several crises came together in pressure for a new terms-of-settlement trade off with ethnic-minority migrants and their children. This trade-off came to be known as multiculturalism (Jakubowicz, 1989:21; Hampel, 1989). While partly a strategy for managing intergroup relations and accommodating the ethnic middle class, it also formed the framework for identifying categories of people with special needs which were not currently being met through mainstream welfare provision. Women usually remained invisible within multiculturalism, and culture and country-of-origin were privileged as explanations above gender (de Lepervanche, 1989:174).

Multiculturalism itself remains politically controversial, and there are competing discourses around what multiculturalism is. The early influence of the ethnic-rights movement and of Labor social democracy and optimism fuelled and financed by the boom were already coming to an end in 1975, along with the Whitlam government. The subsequent Fraser conservative government did not abandon multiculturalism, but de-politicised it into a welfare and management strategy, resting on a model of culturally appropriate services (Foster and Stockley, 1989; Hampel, 1989). It incorporated the male ethnic elite as cultural brokers, and exploited 'ethnic' women as home and community carers, volunteers and poorly paid grant-in-aid workers (Jakubowicz, 1989).

Since 1983 the Hawke government has reworked multiculturalism yet again (Foster and Stockley, 1988, 1989). Multiculturalism appeared under assault with a new emphasis in federal and some state governments on mainstreaming, formulated through a series of access-and-equity plans in a range of departments (Sheldrake, 1989). Ethnic communities' mobilisation in the face of these changes and of tightening and increasingly discriminatory (in class terms) migrant entry procedures forced a partial rethink after 1986 (Castles, 1990:16), and the 1989 announcement of a National Agenda on Multiculturalism towards a new accommodation (Jakubowicz, 1989; Jupp, 1989).

The National Agenda identified three strands of multiculturalism: cultural identity, social justice and economic efficiency. It also entailed explicit limits on multiculturalism: that all Australians accept the basic institutions of Australian society, including parliament, the law and the English language; that the right to express one's own culture and beliefs involves a reciprocal recognition of others' rights; and that all Australians have an overriding commitment to Australia (*Focus*, 1989:5). Such an elaboration appeared to confirm multiculturalism as an ideology to incorporate migrants and cultural differences with minimal change to dominant institutions and practices (Jakubowicz, 1984, 1989).

The current stress on access and equity in mainstream services and departments puts the whole ethnospecific area under attack (Jupp, 1989b:17). Provision and policy formulations of multiculturalism have often been ad hoc and contradictory (Jakubowicz, 1989). However, they have involved the recognition of specific need and certain categories like the ethnic aged, or migrant women workers, as a way of targeting groups and recognising particular entitlement, in a strange mix of inadequate provision, surveillance and control (Jakubowicz, 1989:15).

State attention is largely on 'them'. Culturalism takes its toll in representations of ethnic communities as extended families and safe communal ghettos with mothers and daughters at home to care for everyone. Representations then have material effects by justifying lack of specific provision for the ethnic aged. Yet many ethnic aged have no family, or children who are unwilling or unable to care for them at home. Seitz (1989) identifies care of the elderly along with the effects of award restructuring as the two major areas of concern for non-English-speaking background women. Both add to pressures on women.

The difficulties for the ethnic aged are compounded by the constitution of the aged as childlike, dependent and sexless, again jeopardising their citizenship and their claims as individuals. There are also groups of ethnic aged who are now being identified as subject to post-trauma stress disorder, who are former victims of torture, concentration camps, forced labour, repatriation and refugee experiences, for whom aging and removal to an alien institution are especially frightening (Hanen and Williams, 1989). Likewise some aging migrant women who have always cared for ill or disabled family members are now fearful of what happens to those members in the event of their own death or increasing fragility.

Migrant women are frequently marginalised in both women's and ethnic affairs. Migrant women's issues have only become public in the 1980s, thanks to migrant women's groups' mobilising. Again, conferences have provided for strategic interventions. The first national Speakout migrant women's conference was held in 1982. A 1984 conference on migrant women's issues was organised by the Women's Desk of the Department of Immigration and Ethnic Affairs (DIEA, 1986), which continues to monitor and report on migrant women's issues, and is involved in the new Commonwealth/states Council on Non-English-Speaking Background Women's issues (DILGEA, 1990:102–04).

In 1986 the Association of Non-English-Speaking Background Women of Australia (ANESBWA) was established. There are also various regional and particular ethnic women's groups, and the Federation of Ethnic Communities Councils now has a women's network.

In 1987 the Office of Multicultural Affairs, located in the federal Department of Prime Minister and Cabinet, appointed a taskforce to enquire into the needs of women of non-English-speaking background. Their report identified 15 percent of Australian women as being from non-English-speaking backgrounds (Eliadis, 1988:5). They described the politics of immigrant women's issues and the progress or more often lack of progress in access and equity plans and programs of various government departments, usually revealing the familiar pattern of invisibility or marginality.

Their overview identified several barriers to state responses to the needs of non-English-speaking background women. Different definitions confuse the nature of the group, named sometimes as migrant women, and sometimes as non-English-speaking background women. Confusion over who is responsible for women of non-English-speaking backgrounds led to their falling between the 'women' and 'ethnicity' categories. A concentration of services for and attention to immigration and settlement also often obscures the needs of second and third-generation women of non-English-speaking backgrounds (Eliadis, 1988:25).

The report resisted reducing non-English-speaking background women to a 'special-needs group', which it saw as encouraging a deficit model and effectively marginalising women. The report called for recognising the women as a significant component of the population entitled to rights within mainstream servicing, while also seeking ethno-specific services. There appeared to be a contradiction then in its assertion that women from non-English-speaking backgrounds are 'a special and specific group in the community' (Eliadis, 1988:37), although this may be understood as stating that ethnic men can't speak for them. The report called for participation, consultation, cultural sensitivity and appropriateness of services, for accessible information and for supply of adequate and appropriate resources. It also called for participation of women in policy making, program design and service delivery.

Despite the report's critique of mainstream departments' policies, and perhaps because of the policy options articulation process, non-English-speaking background women are again constituted primarily as clients and users of government services, although there is a weaker discourse about participation and social rights. Racism, including institutional racism, is not itself an object of analysis or claim, nor is the role of the state interrogated in its constituting gender relations and cultural relations in ways that effectively marginalise, contain and exploit women from non-English-speaking backgrounds.

There is further evidence too of the ways in which government policies and processes themselves, and especially the creation of particular programs to service special needs, become the focus for political mobilisation and further organisation along category grounds. In some cases government employees set up organisations where none appeared to exist, and these organisations themselves could then become claimants against the state (Jakubowicz, 1989:24).

Yet women from non-English-speaking backgrounds, and especially from particular groups within that category, do have specific needs that are not being met within state policies and provisions. They are often among the poorest and less politically organised, and may not be willing or able to face bureaucratic gatekeepers who appear hostile or uninformed about their needs. They also have a range of specific needs, for example, regarding their labour market positioning. Thus many women who do shift work find child care either unavailable or inappropriate (Yeatman, 1988).

FEMOCRATS AND STATE

Australian feminists have addressed their claims strongly to and against the state, and a number now work within the bureaucracy. Sawer claims significant victories for feminism through the state, including a range of women's services, equal opportunity provisions (often coded or read to mean 'women') and the women's budget processes. As a result she suggests 'feminist theory has lagged behind feminist practice' (1989), although the recent publication of several studies partly ameliorates this position (Franzway et al., 1989; Sawer, 1990; Yeatman, 1990; Watson, 1990).

Feminists began to enter the state in the Whitlam years of the early 1970s as part of Labor's social democratic reformist impulse and recognition of new constituencies to be accommodated (Dowse in Broom, 1984; Ryan in Watson, 1990). These were also the beginning years of Aboriginal and ethnic affairs as significant areas of administration and recruitment. The Hawke Labor government passed the Sex Discrimination Act in 1984, and the Affirmative Action Act in 1986 boosted moves towards equality in some areas and aspects of employment, which were added to again in 1989 (Radford, 1990; Sawer, 1990; Simms and Stone in Jennett and Stewart, 1990). Some states also instituted equal employment opportunity policies which provided some opportunities for some women (Eisenstein in Watson, 1990:89). These initiatives were usually marginal and so were easily downgraded or removed with changes of minister or government.

'Femocrat' usually refers to those women who identify as feminists and who are identified in the upper levels of government with special women's or equal opportunity offices, units or programs, although individual feminists in mainstream departments or areas may also be included. There is much ambivalence towards femocrats, including from many feminists. 'Femocrat' is often a term of abuse, implying compromise with or even pleasure in incorporation, complicity in use of the language of economic rationalism, the practice of professionalism, and a cosy relationship with the men at the top (Watson, 1990:2–4).

There are issues here to do with the relations between femocrats and feminists outside the bureaucracy, be they in academia, the helping professions and/or grassroots or community feminist organisations, and between femocrats and other women. Femocrats may feel themselves caught between the organisational and political demands of bureaucratic work and loyalty to their constituency of women, especially in the face of current cuts to welfare and support areas. They are under heavy pressure to demonstrate competence and skill in terms which appear useful to their male colleagues, but their use of the language may show their understanding and manipulation of the culture of their work rather than the betrayal of feminism (Sawer, 1989:13; cf Mueller and Newton, 1986:5).

Sawer identifies the dilemmas facing femocrats as including the language of economic rationalism and managerialism, fundamentally hostile to women's experiences; problems of surviving hierarchy and masculine values; and conflicts of loyalties. She asks how feminists can work in government without being co-opted or sacked, or without losing one's friends in the women's movement, one's family or one's self (Sawer, 1989:15).

Femocrats may suffer divided loyalties not only between the organisation and their constituencies, but also in the face of divide-and-rule tactics and competition against potential allies for scarce funding. They confront complex issues of accountability and the double load when they are recruited to service special-interest groups in terms of equal opportunity, Aboriginal affairs or ethnic affairs, perceived as in some ways apart from the mainstream. Here again are the politics of representation, asking who can speak for the 'community', and indeed who is constituted as a community for political and administrative purposes (cf Caine and Yuval-Davis, 1990). Territoriality and threats to competence or the right to speak are thus legion.

How is feminist knowledge translated into policy language? How do women's own knowledge and experiences become information articulating state agencies? (Mueller and Newton, 1986:5). This has to do with the state's willingness to allow entry of feminists into some parts of the policy-making process (Yeatman, 1990:70), and how it constitutes women's issues and characteristics for political purposes. Here the state may disaggregate claims and reconstitute the different claimants as 'special needs', which can then be targeted in ways that allow for their containment (Barnsley, 1988:18; cf Mueller and Newton, 1986:5).

WORKING IN AND AGAINST THE STATE

There are many dilemmas in working in and against the state. The existence of special units or areas may take pressure off the mainstream to change or become more inclusive. Or feminist agendas may be co-opted, and their objectives institutionalised in such a way that they are turned against the very people they were supposed to empower. The state's response may entail dangers of marginalisation and entrapment, but it may be possible for feminists to use even a small space. There are also the frustrations and weariness of being a token, and being cited as evidence that something is being done. Representation may only be effective if there is a critical mass—remembering Alice Walker's wise words 'Never be the only one, except, possibly, in your home' (1984:279). These dilemmas apply particularly to women working in women's equal opportunity, Aboriginal or ethnic affairs areas.

The current elaboration of access and equity debates can disguise a distinction between the two parts (Sheldrake, 1989). Access refers to people's rights to services and their capacity and willingness to use those services. Equity often refers to equal opportunity, and to issues of who is or is not employed in the institutions. Frequently a connection is presumed, as if more women/Aboriginal women/ethnic-minority women as deliverers of services will automatically improve those services, as they know better the needs and culture of 'their' constituency, and will be more approachable and 'positive'. It can also be suggested that just 'having them around' will (in some vague way) help sensitise dominant-group colleagues (cf Stubbs, 1985). Yet if the minority workers are isolated within an unreconstructed system, if they are viewed as token and their qualifications for the job seen as second rate, they may be domesticated or neutralised.

There are lively debates in Britain currently concerning ethnic or race relations units that may throw light on the situation in Australia (Pettman, 1988c), including the authorising uses of 'token blacks' whose endorsement gives moral sanction to state or agency action, even where it faces severe community opposition (Bhatt, 1986). Here Stubbs asks what difference does the appointment of black social workers make? (1985:18). And what is the possible role of radical workers in and against the state? What are the possibilities for a radical project within the state, (Hearn, 1982) for a feminist project? Debates concerning the social control functions of social welfare (Dale and Foster, 1986:chapter 5), critical scrutiny of the 'troubled persons professions' (Gusfield, 1989:431), and of increasing emphasis on certification of workers suggest this to be unlikely. How can people work within but aim to change state provision or administration, within a hierarchical and rule-bound structure, within a culture that is both formally and informally racist and sexist, where they are dominated by a political discourse of economic rationalism, managerialism and professionalism which constructs its clients as target groups or as isolated families and individuals? (Fraser, 1987; Fulcher, 1989).

Because the state is a variety of sites, agents, practices and interests which may be seen as erratic and disconnected, it may provide spaces in which intervention can be effective (Randall, 1988: 237–39). There are a number of state workers who do small miracles and many who make a difference in the lives of ordinary people. There are also occasions when state intervention in families may be both necessary and desirable, for the protection of children or women who are in real danger (Wise in Stanley, 1990:236). But feminist and radical minority workers within the state intervene against the grain, and there are often penalties for unsettling or subversive activities which may neutralise or eliminate those who try to change things. It is hardly likely that the state will willingly subsidise revolution (Bryan, 1985:175). However, the demonstration of a serious threat to its workings may generate support for many education, welfare and community development activities, seen most dramatically in the riots in Britain and the sudden surge of state funding to anti-racist and black community activities. One black British feminist publication notes 'Political mobilisation has come to be seen as a subsidised activity' (Bryan, 1985:28), analysing dilemmas facing 'ethnic workers' who accept state funding for much-needed services and facilities, which come with increasing state audit and direction.

Bhatt is critical of the category politics of the British left Labour and black crisis managers in their 'long march through the institutions' (1986:47), who both naturalise the categories and set against each other in a competition for recognition and funds. The creation of a professional layer of black managers recruited in the name of consultation actually intensifies surveillance. Through their increasing dependence on the state for their livelihood and their status they act as managers and 'funded leaders' of their self-defined 'communities'. 'They replace as well as represent the people' (see Pettman, 1988c:24–33).

In Australia too since the early 1970s a whole range of women's, Aboriginal and ethnic community organisations are dependent on government funding. This dependence raises crucial political and tactical questions about the radicalness, representativeness and effectiveness of both state workers and state subsidised community work.

The class and bureaucratic position of category-representing state workers frequently depends on the political mobilisation and energy of different women, among them feminists from various backgrounds, and Aboriginal and ethnic-minority women who may not call themselves feminist. Yet the category worker is caught between the interests and demands of the constituency and the expectations and pressures of their bureaucratised work. They play complex and multiple roles, including as representative, advocate and state agent (Caine and Yuval-Davis, 1988). Strategies and mechanisms are needed to overcome the almost chronic isolation and alienation of many category workers. But current moves against a discourse of social justice and democracy and in favour of one of rationalism and professionalism undermines the legitimacy of the category claims and renders category state workers particularly vulnerable (Yeatman, 1990:161).

Both hegemonic moves to contain claims and the politics of the constituencies beyond the state raise fascinating and often painful questions about representativeness and responsibility, appropriation and powerlessness, the political resources of the communities, and the relationships between those who work in and outside the state. They also raise again the question of the possibility of using the state for anti-racist and/or anti-sexist projects.

Yet the state is not monolithic. It is a major employer, especially in those areas or services in day-to-day contact with women, ethnic minorities and poor people. State support may make the difference between living tolerably, or being able to leave a violent spouse, or not. Again housing officers, social security desk staff and so on may function as gatekeepers defending the rights of the taxpayers against the claimants, often replaying old distinctions between the deserving and the undeserving poor, the latter seen as being somehow responsible for their fate, or with lesser entitlement by virtue of their status as single mothers or migrants, for example.

ANTI-RACISM, ANTI-SEXISM AND THE STATE

Different formulations of the state—as a site of struggle, as structured power relations or as contradictory spaces, for example—each have different implications for strategy, and make different assessments about possible points and kinds of intervention towards institutional change.

Different players in the state may be in conflict with one another or at least have different understandings about what the problem is and how it might be addressed. Here discourses play a strategic role, and the state may also be represented in terms of discursive formations. Discourses 'explain' problems and make available possible solutions to them. Thus constituting special needs or culturally appropriate services allows for some provision, but may also allow the state to appropriate category claims and energies. Social rights and participation is a stronger discourse, but it is currently overshadowed by the dominant discourse of economic rationalism, which reconstitutes us from a polity or society to an economy or marketplace, in which the minorities are again rendered invisible or deviant. Yet the very state that now talks of disengagement, of privatisation and de-regulation which will cost politically weaker groups dearly, also intensifies its gaze upon them and incorporates them into ever more policed and bureaucratised entanglements.

The state, however conceptualised, is heavily implicated in reproducing and reconstituting class, gender, race and cultural difference, but not in any predetermined, mechanical or uniform way. There are countless engagements in tension, struggles fought out within different aspects of the state, lack of fit, misrepresentation (not always deliberate), revenge and altruism. There is a complex play between 'the state' and the wider political arena, which in turn redefines groups and relations previously 'private', expanding the definition and scope of the political, often in ways that catch the attention of the state.

The mobilisation of the new social movements and the state's moves to manage both claims and newly visible difference undermined the older hegemony and its falsely universalising metanarrative. Yet the state reformulates both claim and difference in ways that contain them and protect the centre. It constitutes special needs in ways that disaggregate potential allies against the state (Meekosha and Pettman, 1991).

A category discourse subverts the stronger and more inclusive social rights discourse. Further distraction and re-centring is facilitated through a discourse of professionalism and expert management, of rationalisation and cost efficiency which depersonalises and depoliticises state activities. Yet policy pronouncements and provision in terms of the now-weaker discourse of special needs, and the weaker still discourse of social justice, have generated some progressive responses, put some forms of social difference on the political agenda and allowed for contesting some meanings. This has involved resistance to the discursive closure so often practised by the state and by dominant groups against rights claimants.

The politics of discourse requires a re-politicisation of the contest, and an inclusive agenda that recognises but is not contained within difference. It means contesting (even while selectively using) category discourse, but especially contesting the elitist and exclusivist discourse that silences most people, and reduces them in welfare terms to roles of clients and of cases (Fraser, 1987:97, 100). Thus Fulcher

(1989) examines the professionalism of welfare services and the interests of government and of welfare workers, and then analyses policy in terms of political struggles. She identifies the role of discourse as both tactic and theory, and urges an alternative discourse of social justice against the currently predominant discourse of economic rationalism (Fulcher, 1989:10. See also Yeatman, 1990). Radical and feminist welfare discourse seeks to re-politicise welfare within a language and practice of solidarity and social rights (Croft, 1986; Wise in Stanley, 1990).

This contest also means analysing the institutions and examining the power brokers, instead of the current preference for researching the 'needy' (Jakubowicz and Meekosha, 1989). It means examining the functions of departments, for example, rather than the problems or shortcomings of their actual or presumed clients. It means shifting the language beyond welfare to rights, and beyond culture to politics. It means historicising and politicising social relations within the structures of power, including race power, sex power and class power, in which the state in all its various forms and interests is itself constituted, even while it actively reproduces and reconstitutes relations of difference.

6 Dealing with difference

Dominant discourses constitute certain social forms which naturalise gender, race and culture. Through this process the powerful become the norm. Dominant definitions of the subject of the state involve discourses which simultaneously universalise and individualise, and so render difference invisible; or else constitute it as Other in ways that exclude, contain and entrap those others (Bannerji, 1987; Fabian, 1983; Said, 1978). The Other has various identities, including woman and native (Trinh, 1989). Here sex, race and culture become markers and also apparent explanations of difference and inequality.

Sites of difference are sites of power (Barrett and McIntosh, 1985). But identity and difference are not only imposed. Identities are also sources of opposition and resistance, mobilised in the name of different political projects. Groups constituted as Other organise in resistance in different ways. They may deny the validity of boundaries or of categories that entrap them, as, for example, Aborigines did when they rejected ward status and categories like 'mixed race'. They may demand entry into the nation as equals, as Aboriginal people did in the 1930s, demanding the right to vote, and entry to 'white' schools. Others, or the same people at different times, may seize the category that has been used to contain them, invert it, and infuse it with positive meanings (cf Gilroy, 1987:66; Keesing, 1989:27), as Aboriginal people have done in recent decades, or as cultural feminists do when they honour the 'natural' and nurturing qualities represented as being part of womanhood. Shared experience of being labelled and treated as Other may give a basis for affiliation and a collective interest in mobilising in support of particular claims against the state, or against others within the society. This

is not only an ideological contest, for there are material consequences and distinct social interests involved here.

Especially since the late 1960s, with the rise of the new social
movements, difference and subordinate status have become a basis
for mobilisation and claim (Meekosha and Pettman 1991). Thus
people in categories which were previously excluded, marginalised or
exploited, like women, Aborigines, and lesbians, mobilised as new
political constituencies. This mobilisation frequently deployed the
language of community to refer to commonalities or perceived
common interests, and to authorise claims by giving them the backing of numbers (Caine and Yuval-Davis, 1990).

As noted in chapter 5, governments seek to respond to difference
in an attempt to manage and contain it, especially when it has
mobilised politically. They may also utilise the category and make
certain concessions and provisions while reformulating the claims. In
so doing categories are further reified and homogenised, and their
members are involved in complex relations with the state. Culture
and community then become part of the language of politics in a
contest over representation of difference and what it should mean
politically, and over who can speak for whom (Mercer, 1988; Spivac,
1988; Grossberg, 1989). This chapter focuses on the politics constituting culture, community, identity and difference, and on the politics of representation and of voice. It begins with an examination of
Aboriginality and the cultural politics of colonisation, and then of
multiculturalism and the construction of ethnic cultures and communities, and of the immigration debate and its implications for the
community of the nation. It raises issues of culture, community and
identity to ask what is identity for? and concludes with reference to
current debates within feminism about identity and difference.

ABORIGINALITY

Constructing Aborigines as Other involves both difference and distance (Muecke, 1982:103). Aborigines have been confined within
categories that facilitated and legitimised their dispossession and
their subsequent management by the state and its agents. Through
this century anthropology in particular determined how Aborigines
were perceived both by governments and by other Australians.
Cowlishaw (1990b) documents the ascendancy of a particular
anthropology in close and unexamined relationship with the state
and the colonial project. That anthropology was informed by a cultural development model, which took as unproblematic the superior-
ity of white imperial civilisation and the inevitability of Aboriginal

demise, if not physically then culturally, a belief that persisted into the 1960s (Mulvaney, 1986).

Anthropology depicted as Aboriginal and paid special attention to those who were also 'full blood', 'traditional' and living in remote areas in what Cowlishaw identifies as an Aboriginalist discourse (1986), and Tatz labels reconstructionist anthropology (1982:10). It often assumed that the disruption and the diminution of 'Aboriginal blood' in the more settled parts of south-eastern Australia was accompanied by a parallel loss of culture (Langton, 1981; Cowlishaw, 1986; Creamer in Beckett, 1988a:45). Anthropologists here colluded with a definition of culture as primordial, static and innocent, and essentially pre-colonial. So they contributed to and reflected popular common sense views of those Aboriginal people in settled Australia as somehow less or not Aboriginal. Those people could still be stigmatised and discriminated against, but this was compounded by their representation as inauthentic (Beckett, 1988a:6).

Until recently Aborigines, as the object of anthropology, did not have a voice in public or academic discourse. Lately Aboriginal voices have challenged 'authoritative experts' and popular representations and definitions, and asserted their own Aboriginality. There is often little connection between the representations of academia and Aboriginal perceptions of their own roles and histories, a point Hamilton makes with reference to recent Aboriginal women's auto-biographies (1986). This may reflect, in part, the different shape and purposes of private and public ethnicity (Beckett, 1988a:4), and the question of who the different writers are writing for (see chapter 7).

Forms of Aboriginality are imposed on Aborigines from the out-side, often equating Aboriginality with 'tradition' in what Rowse calls 'the European's spiritualising gaze' (1988:271). This representation is often racialised through its association with colour or blood. It is popularised through notions of Aboriginal art in its gallery and tourist uses (Willis and Fry, 1988/9). It is also given legislative and political content through, for example, the Northern Territory land rights requirements. 'The ironies and contradictions of Aboriginal peoples being denied rights they believe are culturally legitimate on the grounds that they do not fit an anthropological model have chilling implications' (Keesing, 1989:34; see also Bell, 1986).

Aboriginality is chosen as well as imposed, through a complex interplay with the state (Beckett, 1988b). Aboriginality can be seen as a form of ethnogenesis (Jones and Hill-Burnett, 1982), a mobilised political identity contesting both imposed categories and forms of discrimination and exclusion on the basis of those categories.

Aboriginality here is a claim of Aboriginal people to name themselves, to say who is Aboriginal and what that should mean (Hollinsworth, 1991).

'The construction and use of an ideology of Aboriginality is a specific attempt by Aborigines to regain and retain control over both things and ideas' (Keeffe, 1988:67). It rests on an assertion of commonality among Aborigines even in very diverse social, economic and cultural circumstances, on the basis of common descent, shared cultural identity, a sense of otherness, created in part through the shared experience of dispossession, of racism and of being labelled and treated as Aboriginal. Its bedrock is a common claim as descendants and legitimate inheritors of the original owner occupiers of Australia.

This claim has been met with scepticism by many other Australians and shows the contingent nature of identity. Thus some who are quick to label people or problems as Aboriginal may deny that an urban and/or radical Aboriginal spokesperson is 'really' Aboriginal (Chase, 1981:23). They may tolerate or collude in discrimination against Aboriginal people, while also objecting to 'reverse racism' if any positive advantages or even compensatory provision of services occurs, arguing belatedly that Aborigines are Australians and all Australians should be treated the same (Cowlishaw, 1988; 1990a).

Keeffe (1988) identifies two somewhat different and at times contradictory aspects of Aboriginality: Aboriginality-as-persistence and Aboriginality-as-resistance. Aboriginality-as-persistence speaks of a unique identity, a fixed body of cultural knowledge which is genetically transmitted, stretching back over tens of thousands of years to secure a continuity of culture. This form is given academic representation in an elaborate exercise to identify 'Aboriginality' (Coombs et al., 1983). Aboriginality here is defined in terms of a number of values:

> [These values] are the gist of Aboriginal culture, rarely grasped by outsiders; they have persisted over time and events; they still provide the principal means whereby Aborigines choose to accept or reject changes which may affect them. Indeed their particular synthesis is Aboriginality and what is distinctive about it. Those values are:
> 1. survival—spiritual as well as physical;
> 2. social, cultural and spiritual identification with the land;
> 3. a respect for the inherent dignity of a human being;
> 4. self control;
> 5. harmony in social relationships;
> 6. reciprocity.

These are expressed in the importance Aborigines attach to:

7. observing kin obligations;
8. pooling resources;
9. competence in social roles and performance;
10. shared experience as a component in group identity;
11. social knowledge; transmitted by traditional processes;
12. conformity and continuity; including the maintenance of individual and group identity; but modified by
13. respect for individuality and differences and a capacity for innovation and improvisation—the potential in all things. (Coombs et al., 1983:12-13; see also academic exchanges between Tatz, Theile, Rowse and others over Aboriginality in Mankind, 1984-85; Hollinsworth, 1991)

Aboriginality-as-persistence in such representations is highly problematic in its reproduction of the same boundaries and sense of essence that racists use against Aborigines, and in its coincidence with notions of Aboriginal culture as pertaining to tradition, to 'before'. In these circumstances some Aboriginal people can be made to feel inadequate, somehow less than Aboriginal, because of their unfamiliarity with traditional culture; or they might turn against their more quarrelsome, money-grabbing or uncaring relatives who blatantly fail to live up to notions of Aboriginal community. People who cannot recognise the idealised Aboriginal family or community in their own can also become further embittered by what has apparently been destroyed by colonisation and state control.

There is also a contradiction between presumed inherited culture and a number of Aboriginal people needing to be taught or helped to learn what that culture is. Thus those many Aborigines who were taken away from their families and brought up in white families or institutions, and others who lived in disrupted and marginalised families, may now seek to recover their Aboriginal identity and cultural heritage (Morgan, 1987; Edwards and Read, 1989). In the process of retrieval, culture may become externalised, objectified, reified: something, for example, taught to Aboriginal children in community awareness camps (Keeffe, 1988:69).

Recovery is central to and related to survival in much Aboriginal writing (Ryan, 1986; Thomas, 1988). 'Culture' can be reclaimed or relearnt as part of oppositional politics and the politics of identity. Here culture is a political resource, negotiated through struggle and used for resistance against the dominant culture (Cowlishaw, 1988; Morris, 1990).

Aboriginality-as-resistance is altogether more politicised, symbolised in the Aboriginal flag and colours, in the celebration of survival and in land rights and sovereignty claims (Keeffe, 1988:71). It is this reading of Aboriginality which the state seeks to subvert through its endorsement of Aboriginality-as-persistence and its rendering of Aborigines into yet another culture or ethnic group, albeit one with a particular status through its association with carefully worded 'prior ownership'.

Here recognition of difference may lead to containment and to the ethnicisation of Aboriginal people. Again the state reformulates claims and incorporates claimants into state political processes in an attempt to manage them. Rowse asks 'How is "Aborigine" constructed as a subject position in Australian politics?' (in *Mankind*, 1985:45). Von Sturmer suggests that

> if the language of assimilation actively concealed a discourse around the proletarisation of Aborigines, the language of self-determination may be discovered as concealing a discourse aimed at delivering them inextricably into the corporate state, either directly by recruiting Aborigines qua Aborigines into the bureaucracy, or by means of a more indirect process, namely by the creation of 'Aboriginal' organisations which are required or demanded or are invited to participate in government decision-making. (in *Mankind*, 1985:48)

There is a highly complex interplay between Aboriginal people and the state, as the state seeks to incorporate and manage 'the Aboriginal problem'. Some Aboriginal people are rewarded in their performance of certain aspects of Aboriginality by access to jobs, services and perhaps to land, while they also seek to use or subvert those spaces or hearings. The state seeks to control them through its manipulation of ideology and expressions of some kinds of difference, and Aboriginal people in turn use this opportunity to articulate a sense of difference as part of an oppositional politics. Thus the state tries both to encourage expression of difference and to control it (Morris in Beckett, 1988a:64).

The use of culture or race as an explanation and construction of a naturalised difference can be politically reactionary, or at least politically problematic. Yet it can also be mobilised as Aboriginality-in-resistance, as a resource in making claim. The issue becomes how to maintain a contingent and strategic confidence in Aboriginality (Rowse in *Mankind*, 1985:45), to affirm where before there was neglect and contempt, and to empower those whose defeat and damage has at times seemed almost total, while not colluding in the ongoing entrapment and marginalisation of Aboriginal people.

Aboriginality may be a double-edged sword. The markers of this mobilised identity draw on notions of tradition and culture that may cement and reify designation along 'race' lines. Biological determinism has often been used against Aboriginal people and there is obviously a danger in talking as if race is a socially valid or natural identity, especially in a situation of unequal social relations where difference is still used against people. Aborigines speaking of an essence, of something intrinsically Aboriginal or Other, can thus appear to confirm the boundaries and assumptions of otherness and of common sense racism, and unintentionally reinforce culturalist explanations of Aboriginal poverty and damage.

Likewise the language of 'blood' and heredity mobilised in some Aboriginal discourses may privilege descent even where individuals may have grown up rejecting or ignorant of their Aboriginal culture or kin. While Aboriginality is here given positive valuing, it is essentialised and deterministically associated with 'blood' in ways similar to racist discourse, although Aboriginal people usually lack the public power that makes dominant-group racism effective.

While 'blood' may be a metaphor rather than a statement about genetics and heredity (Beckett, 1988a:6), it is again part of the reversals and negations of 'race' politics (cf Hall, 1980:342). Earlier, white fathers often denied paternity (and not only of Aboriginal children), and 'mixed-race' children were absorbed back into the Aboriginal mother's family and community, with her husband often the social father. In this case 'mixed-race' children were culturally and socially Aboriginal, although that claim was contested by the racist state, and such children were always vulnerable to that state taking the children and asserting a highly ambivalent public paternity, even where the actual 'white father' was two or three generations back. If Aboriginality is now constituted at least partly through blood, taken so far sometimes as to assert that a single drop of Aboriginal blood makes for Aboriginality (Keeffe, 1988:69), what then becomes of the white blood (Bell, J. 1986; Cowlishaw, 1986:12), or of notions of self-identification? Again convergence with racist folk genetics are politically troublesome (cf Gilroy, 1987:65).

There are parallels between the construction of culture and tradition in Aboriginality and in other fourth-world and post-colonial nationalisms, and with the politics of ethnicity (Cornell, 1988; Pearson, 1988; *Anthropology Today*, 1990; Hanson, 1990). These ethnic identities for claim are new identities produced in the context of anti-colonial struggles or post-colonial nation building. They illustrate the political uses of tradition and the processes involved in its production (cf Hall in Framework 36, 1990: 69, 80). There is also cross-fertilisation of ideas and language as Aboriginal people talk with other indigenous people and racialised minorities in international forums (Keesing, 1989:30; Moody, 1988).

Aboriginality may thus be conceptualised as a mobilised political

112

identity, and as a colonial nationalism. It is not a remnant of primordial past or tradition, but rather a political project pursuing Aboriginal status and entitlement within the Australian nation state (Tonkinson in Howard, 1989:136–38). Here Aboriginality involves the choosing of cultural markers for identity maintenance and foreclosing against others. In the process an Aboriginal identity speaks to and in opposition to the dominant culture. It is a counter-hegemonic discourse, positioned within colonial and racialised structures and social relations (Jennett, 1987).

Aboriginal people may call themselves 'the first Australians', although this may also be a settler-state reading to give continuity and incorporate Aborigines within Australia as the first of many immigrants, rather than as an indigenous people (Morris in Beckett, 1988a:64). Aboriginal people use Aboriginality as indigenous status and claim, beyond cultural difference or the experience of racism. Here Aboriginal people deny that they are another ethnic group, or part of a multicultural project, even while asserting their cultural difference and rights to culturally appropriate provision and services in ways that appear to place them in alliance with ethnic minorities in Australia. There is within Aboriginal literature and conversation a profound sense of being Aboriginal, of otherness, positioned within a history of European domination and their own dispossession (Amiss in Beckett, 1988a:132).

Constructions of Aboriginality often draw on representations of traditional culture, including anthropological representations. Thus some Aboriginal people speak of at least 40 000 years (the current conventional academic dating of Aboriginal occupation of Australia, although some critics doubt that those early people could accurately be named 'Aboriginal'). Other Aboriginal people say 'for ever' as in 'Aboriginal land—always was, always will be' (*Land Rights News* motto). Again, some Aboriginal people speak of themselves as part of the oldest living culture on earth. These are clearly affirming and celebratory associations, contesting racist representations of Aboriginal people as primitive, uncultured and somehow transitory; but they are also being used to authorise current political claims against a very recent and immigrant state.

Like third and other fourth-world nationalisms, Aboriginality also speaks as a critique of western imperial and capitalist society, drawing on western discourses of loss of innocence. Thus Aborigines assert as Aboriginal values spirituality against white materialism; caring and sharing against white individualism; extended kin against isolated selfishness and affiliation; and custodial attention to place and land against white exploitation and degradation of the environment (Pettman, 1988a). Here Aboriginal values are idealised and acquire their particular significance as part of a political and counter-hegemonic discourse which makes sense only in the context of colonisation and the politics of anti-colonisation. Thus Aboriginality joins post-colonial nationalisms in a critique of modernity and of civilisation which is informed by and talks to the west's critique of itself, and the recent growth of the ecological movement, for example (Keesing, 1989). In the process Aborigines and whites are reified and homogenised, and many linkages between the two are disguised or denied.

This is not to deny that there are Aboriginal cultural practices beyond the ideological construction of identity in the political arena. There are many Aboriginal people who speak their own languages and live on or in communication with their own home places. Most Aboriginal people's social relations, while radically altered and penetrated by the state and the capitalist political economy, are still quite different from those of other Australians (Langton, 1981; Jordan in Beckett, 1988a). Aboriginal people who live on the fringes of country towns or in older Aboriginal settlements or ex-reserves have often maintained a degree of separateness and difference, informed by earlier practices and places as well as in response to constant harassment and institutionalisation (Langton, 1988; Cowlishaw, 1988).

Aboriginal communities long embedded in cities still often live in families and social relations different from their neighbours. Their families are often matrifocal, extended and with shifting membership. Women's experiences within these families are substantially different from those of many other Australian women. On the whole they have children earlier, have more children, have more children who die, are more likely to be ill and/or welfare dependent, and experience more frequent conflicts with state institutions, including the police. They are thereby constantly aware of the consequences of their being labelled and treated as 'Aboriginal' (Langton, 1981).

Increasing numbers of Aboriginal people live in single family homes and may only be in contact with other Aboriginal people socially or occasionally, while living lifestyles similar to their non-Aboriginal neighbours. Nevertheless they may still have a strong ideological and emotional investment in an Aboriginal identity, as an intrinsic part of who they are and how they define themselves.

Many Aboriginal people also live in families or relationships with non-Aboriginal people, but the understanding commonly is that the child of an Aboriginal parent and a non-Aboriginal parent is Aboriginal. Still, as elsewhere, individuals make choices about when and how to identify. Thus in a school where there are few Aboriginal peers and supports, and especially where staff or other students make Aborigines pay, some children may not identify as Aboriginal, although they may do so happily enough at home or socially. In other circumstances an Aboriginal child with a white mother may be ambiguously placed after a marriage or relationship breakup, if that mother does not have her own friendship or other links with Aboriginal people. Thus the Victorian Aboriginal Child Care Association has suggested that in the event of a custody conflict, an Aboriginal child should go to the Aboriginal parent, so as to maintain their membership of the Aboriginal community, and their access to strategies and support against racism that are available within the community (1990; cf Gilroy, 1987:65, labelling as ethnic absolutism some British black demands that black children only be adopted by or fostered to black families).

Here definitions of identity do matter, beyond their crucial significance in terms of personal identity and political mobilisation. Identity is also important in determining entitlement, and in the state's administration and delivery of services.

Some of those identities and practices which are currently identified as Aboriginal are not traditional nor politically instrumental so much as oppositional. They are generated in relation to and opposition to the state and dominant society. Thus Cowlishaw describes ways that many Aborigines in a north-western New South Wales town resist, subvert or defy dominant white values. These ways in turn become a trigger to white hostility, which itself reinforces the oppositional nature of Aboriginal culture (Cowlishaw, 1988).

Sivanandan (1982, 1983), Gilroy (1987) and Hall (1988b) identify a culture of resistance as part of a black-in-Britain identity. This culture is forged in struggles in the inner city, through common experience of being labelled black and/or migrant, and being marginalised in the labour market and welfare state, while also being subject to harassment and interference by police and other agents of the state. Black areas and black people become problems and victims, and black youth in particular are criminalised (Gilroy, 1987; Solomos, 1988). These shared political experiences frame but do not dilute

the extraordinary diversity of subjective experiences and cultural identities which compose the category 'black'; that is, the recognition that 'black' is essentially a politically and culturally *constructed* category, which cannot be grounded in a set of fixed trans-cultural or transcendental racial categories and which therefore has no guarantees in Nature. (Hall, 1988b:28)

While Aboriginal people are often represented as living in remote areas or fringe communities in country towns, the inner city is constitutive for them too. Redfern, Glebe, Fitzroy, Port Adelaide and other inner city areas are labelled as 'Aboriginal' in ways that criminalise places as well as people. Here Aboriginal people, and especially young people, are mobilised around defending social space against policing and other intrusions of agents of the colonial and racist state (Cunneen, 1990a; Carrington, 1990; Wundersitz, 1990). As in Britain, policing becomes a flashpoint (Cunneen, 1990b).

While images of resistance in the inner city are often of Aboriginal men and boys against the police, Aboriginal women are the ones who are represented as being the survivors, as more resilient and somehow less damaged than Aboriginal men (Hamilton, 1986). Almost all the Aborigines who have died in police custody or jail have been men, despite the very high rate of Aboriginal women in jail. But many Aboriginal women also experience stress, and some are engaged in very self-destructive behaviour, or have their capacity to provide safe parenting for their children questioned (Larbalestier, 1980; Ryan, 1986a). The costs of resistance are often enormous.

Oppositional culture may be romanticised, but the costs of colonisation, racism, depression and poverty are horrific. Heavy drinking and fighting, especially where not according to ritualised codes and constraining social mechanisms (Gilbert, 1977; Langton, 1988), take their toll. It is necessary to ask which forms of opposition are liberatory, and who pays for the damage and conflict, so often turned in against kin or self (Bell, J. 1986; Langton, 1990).

Still the notion of oppositional culture is an important corrective to representations of Aboriginal people as always victims, as locked in the hold of primordial time. Aboriginal people become agents, resisting even after generations of abuse, violence, exclusion and management. Here culture is something dynamic, made in and through living, and 'the community' is a part of that living. Culture is re-politicised, forged in relation to the power and the politics of the state. But agency must be re-placed within the context of the grossly unequal power relations of colonisation and racism (Thomas, 1990:141), and the power of the culture of dominance to position indigenous and ethnic minorities recognised (cf Khan in Howard, 1982:198).

Culture then is not a fixed or bounded entity, although in places in the Northern Territory, for example, the Aboriginal domain and the white domain are physically quite separate and frequently antagonistic. But everywhere some individuals are ambiguously placed and may move across the boundaries, depending on their behaviour, their job and their current allegiances (Cowlishaw, 1988). Aboriginal people in defensive as well as affiliative communities may be angered by 'coconuts' or others whose loyalties they question, but there is still social penalty in being Aboriginal. Earlier some Aboriginal individuals and families sought exemption or assimilation to reduce the cost, and to try to protect themselves and their children from the discrimination and state intervention that constantly threatened them. Those who did so now find that they are rewarded for identifying as Aboriginal (Cowlishaw in Beckett, 1988a:103).

Particular ways of categorising and counting people have implications for self-identification (Jordan, 1985). People's readiness to identify as Aboriginal depends on the categories and criteria available, and also on the social and political consequences of identification. Political mobilisation and affirmation, and increased provision and funding offer encouragement and support to identify as Aboriginal. Thus in the 1986 census 277 645 people were identified as Aboriginal—a 42 percent increase from the 1981 census (ABS, 1989). Those who refused or were not able to 'pass' may be bitter towards those who have expressed a choice, especially when for some 'passing' gave some access to dominant cultural capital, later helping them to get jobs within Aboriginal affairs. Which is not to deny that some Aborigines, like other people, go where there is a good chance and a comparatively easy life regardless: Aborigines are not inevitably non-materialist and primarily concerned with kin, caring and sharing.

MULTICULTURALISM AND ETHNICITY

Multiculturalism and ethnicity represent other public constructions of culture, largely in terms of the cultures of people from non-English-speaking backgrounds. These people were originally expected to merge with the dominant culture, but since the mid-1970s the new immigrants have been granted rights to 'maintain' cultural identity. The related model of Australia suggests a multiplicity of cultures co-existing in what on closer examination reveals itself as a highly problematic relationship (Hampel, 1989).

New social categories generated through immigration, resettlement, migrant claim and state response involve complex contests around culture. Culture and ethnic community often refer to presumed country-of-origin, to race and/or to religion. The categories are wider and more ambiguous than the traditional or locality associations of the home country. They may bear little resemblance to cultural practices where people came from.

Since the early 1970s the state has been active in the construction of both ethnicity and multiculturalism, having to manage difference and inter-group relations and to contain claim (Jakubowicz, 1989; Foster and Stockley, 1989).

The late 1960s ethnic rights movement was an explicit response to exclusion or unequal incorporation into the labour market, and to racism and uncertain social rights. This movement elicited some response within the Whitlam government's social democratic reformism from 1972 to 1975. Recognising disadvantage caused by migration, lack of cultural capital and institutional discrimination helped locate the problem outside migrants and their culture. The 1975 Race Discrimination Act was premised on an equality model which denied the social validity of difference.

After 1975 the Fraser Liberal–National government redefined ethnicity in terms of cultural differences, and culture again became explanation. Responsibility for problems were hoisted back onto communities (Morrissey in Bottomley and de Lepervanche, 1984; Jakubowicz, 1989) and often onto individual women. The accompanying construction of multiculturalism was a contradictory confirmation of social cohesion, cultural diversity and equality (Hampel, 1989). This formulation saw 'culture' as everyday practices and as an essence or given. It suggested a plurality of cultures, apparently both separate and co-existing. Yet where there was conflict between the 'migrant' cultures and the dominant culture and its institutions, the latter clearly presided. But the high rate of intermarriage, individual mobility across ethnic boundaries and the shifting politics within those boundaries over time and place means that categories represented as fixed and immutable are constantly changing.

The dominant construction of multiculturalism is thus itself a form of culturalism, a depoliticisation of culture that has the effect of denying both agency and structure. Again it locates 'culture' in 'the past', as tradition. Yet migration is often a rupture, a displacement; and return is always to a different place. Migration also engages with processes of industrialisation, urbanisation and a commodified system, reducing the space where cultural practices could be maintained (Kalantzis, 1990) and confusing relations between ideology and material practices. Some cultural practices are ideologically reproduced in the new place, outside the social relations that generated them. Thus arranged marriages no longer 'make sense' in terms of economic and labour needs, but are maintained within particular families and communities by men and perhaps by older women whose authority is already under threat in the new country (Bottomley, 1984; Humphrey in Bottomley and de Lepervanche, 1984).

Ethnicity, like multiculturalism, came to Australia in the 1970s. It is an ambiguous concept, with radical possibilities in mobilisation for rights against racism, discrimination, exclusion or exploitation. In this sense ethnicity is a modern, post-migration political identity and process. It speaks both to exile and to minority status in the new place (Pellizzi in Guidieri and Pellizzi, 1988). But its use as a political resource need not necessarily be radical. It also involves the incorporation of ethnic claims and ethnic brokers into the state in ways that are highly contradictory and at times politically demobilising. In all its tendencies, ethnicity is another player in the politics of difference and involves the ambivalent relationship of special interest groups and the state in ways similar to Aboriginality.

'Culture' is highly political in its representation and reinforcement of structures of power, including gendered power both within and between communities. The authorised spokespersons usually turn out to be spokesmen, who can use their political resources, access, a public voice or hearing, or funding to shore up particular relations or interests in the name of the community.

There are issues here to do with the role of women, and the still hardly visible feminist critique of multiculturalism (Martin, 1986). It is unclear where women are in public representations of multiculturalism as the family of nations (de Lepervanche, 1989), and where gender is within cultures and communities that are constituted as homogenous.

There is also the question of the impact on women within these communities of culturalist and conservative representations which either render women invisible or locate sex roles and male domination in tradition. Some suggest that state-supported multiculturalism has led to increasing sexism or fundamentalism through its toleration of cultural differences. This position is argued by Weldon in Britain, in reaction to the growth of Muslim fundamentalism signalled by and through 'the Rushdie Affair' (Jones, 1990; Spivac, 1990). It is argued through a very different politics by the group Women against Fundamentalism that it is not the pluralism or tolerance of multiculturalism that is complicit with fundamentalism (of any kind), but the particular essentialist and ungendered representation of culture which authorises as spokesmen older and more established conservative men, and the failure to recognise that communities are subject to unequal power and contests for control from both within and without (Connolly, 1991). This debate is also played out on a smaller stage in Britain and in Australia through tensions involved in implementing education policies of anti-sexism and multiculturalism. This is especially likely where a de-politicised and static notion of culture is employed, giving apparent authority to stereotypic or 'traditional' sex roles.

There are conflicts between fundamentalisms—Christian, Jewish or Muslim—and the liberal secular project of the contemporary nation state. Multiculturalism speaks to the validity and attractiveness of certain kinds of difference, of more than one way, while some community leaders brook no such liberalism or multi-vocality.

Muslim fundamentalism and other forms of cultural 'revival' are not a return to tradition, nor the more public demonstration of what some people have done at home or in the mosque all along. Rather they are the redefinition and mobilisation of a politicised, post-immigrant, post-colonial identity—ironically the kind of identity which Rushdie explores in *The Satanic Verses*. Islam in migration can become another counter-hegemonic discourse, a signifier of cultural difference where 'culture' is used as a political resource.

Again the uses of a politically mobilised identity are various and contradictory. Speaking of Britain, where Muslim fundamentalism is stronger and more visible than in Australia, Parekh writes:

> The Mullahs, as well as the so-called progressive Muslim leaders who act as brokers between the state and their community, have a good deal to gain by encouraging their followers to define themselves primarily in religious terms. This is one way they can retain their power base and attract money from British and international sources. (in Bhabha and Parekh, 1989:24)

But this mobilised identity is not simply imposed on other Muslims. Parekh goes on to point out that

> a group that feels besieged and afraid of losing its past in exchange for a nebulous future, under pressure from an inhospitable society and increasingly alienated, feel forced to define themselves, to say to others and even to themselves, who they are, what constitutes their identity or claim to distinction . . . In the process its history, traditions, memories, even geography get badly mutilated: clearly evident in the Muslim self-definition in Britain. (in Bhabha and Parekh, 1989:25)

Nationalism in the west is largely a secularised project, although some seek to associate it with their version of Christianity. Yet religion is central to a number of communities, and implicated in community conflicts, including between groups whose shared country-of-origin leads many other Australians to label them as belonging to the same community. Some also suffer from racist discrimination and abuse on account of their religion—currently especially so for Muslim Australians—but the Race Discrimination Act does not include religion as a ground for action (HEROC, 1991).

For many women from ethnic minorities, and for many Aboriginal and majority women, religious practice and affiliation are crucial. White/western feminism is largely a secular project, although religion is another dimension of difference among women and among feminists.

While Aboriginality and ethnicity are both different aspects of mobilised and modern political identities, there are fundamental differences between them. Aboriginality speaks to a very different political project, as a nationalism directed against a colonial state with capitalist and imperial impulse. Both Aboriginality and ethnicity, however, address the same state. Aboriginality and multiculturalism, the latter even in its most domestic and de-politicised form, still make visible difference and speak to a variety of cultures. Both then represent a significant symbolic break with the official representations of a homogenous Australia and with assimilationist policies of the recent past. Neither in most of their public readings attend explicitly to gender, although they may identify 'women' as a special needs group in their negotiations with the state.

CULTURE AND DIFFERENCE

Multiculturalism is supposed to be about all of us, although many Aboriginal people and dominant-group members deny this suggestion. Multiculturalism is inevitably associated with immigration, the process which led to its adoption as government policy in Australia. The immigration debate which has festered on several occasions in the 1980s is part of the politics of discourse and the crisis of the nation state and nationalism. It raises many questions about race, culture and difference, coded in terms of the ethnic mix, social cohesion, 'our' culture and so on (Markus and Rickfels, 1985; Cahill, 1988).

Difference is often represented as immutable and as dangerous. Here the Other is constructed, through and against whom dominant groups define themselves (de Beauvoir, 1970; Said, 1978; Bannerji, 1987). This is a highly contested and currently visible reconstitution or defence of the national political project, with particular notions of community, of belonging, of who 'we' are and who threatens us (Pettman, 1988b).

Again, 'culture' is something people 'have', and some of us have a better kind than others. Alternatively some people have more of it than others. Some Aboriginal people and some migrants are seen to have 'lost' theirs; and some other migrants from non-modern/non-western cultures are seen to have too much. People's primary identities in this debate are represented as cultural—as Aboriginal, migrant, or Australian. In yet another schema for representing culture, dominant culture becomes invisible through the normative presence of whiteness and maleness. Visibility then becomes a feature of difference, again defined as difference from the norm. In each of these representations women and sexual politics are usually invisible, although interrogating construction of cultural difference soon reveals race and gender differences.

Cultural practices are marked by and lived through particular gender relations, sex roles, notions of the family and particular constructions of masculinity and femininity in ways different from 'others'. Yet at the same time many discussions around culture, multiculturalism, Aboriginal rights and the nation often appear as ungendered, prompting the question: where are the women in these processes?

The 'culture' which the New Right and privilege defends is, among other things, to do with 'the family' and a defence of particular sex roles and sex power. The cultural politics of the New Right is a politics of nostalgia. It is also an example of hegemonic reactionism, as the apparent legitimacy given to difference in terms of recognition of Aboriginality or multiculturalism or women's equality threatens the dominant groups. They impute a power to difference which is often largely in their imagination, but do recognise the critical ideological work that goes into constructing difference and maintaining boundaries and privileges. The New Right aims its attacks at sites of knowledge-making and meaning-making, for example schools, tertiary institutions and the media, and to the terms of the discourse, recognising the power of the political construction of meaning and of the boundaries. They recognise too the radical restructuring of Australia which would indeed become necessary were even the most ambivalent political projects around anti-discrimination, equal opportunity, multiculturalism and Aboriginal self-determination actually be taken seriously.

THE COMMUNITY AND REPRESENTATION

The notion of community is problematic (Meekosha and Pettman, 1991). In the politics of nostalgia it means small settled localities of the same kinds of people, the ideal *gemeinschaft*. It has also meant mateship in Australian labour history, where the working class was distinctly male and English speaking. Nowadays 'the community' can mean the nation, as in the Australian community, so beloved by newspaper columnists and letter writers. Alternatively, community can mean everyone who was previously or is still excluded from public power (Caine and Yuval-Davis, 1990). 'Community groups' are often alternative or oppositional designations or special interest groups. Thus Aborigines, migrants and women are almost by definition excluded from power. 'Community' can also be a term for a 'target group', identified for government management of difference and provision of services.

Community and category claims are part of 'the struggle to come into representation' (Hall, 1988b), which involves naming oneself, recognising shared experiences of oppression or exploitation, mobilising and claiming against the state. It means getting access, a hearing and funding, which may depend on being able to demonstrate a constituency—often then called a community. There are many questions here about whose community. What are the conditions for individuals to enter it, or remain members? Who can speak on its behalf?

Representation is a complex issue, but there are several relevant meanings in this context. First, are people represented, or are they absent, invisible or unheard? Secondly, how are they represented, or misrepresented, for example, stereotypically or in sexist, racist constructions? Thirdly, who represents them? Are those who speak for them representative of them?

Many of those categories mobilised in the new social movements were largely spoken for until recently, especially in the making and authorising of public knowledge. In academia and policy making they may still be spoken for—or ignored. Those few who have been allowed 'in' are under heavy pressure to be representative, to speak for everyone from their presumed community (Mercer, 1988:12). 'The more power any group has to create and wield representations, the less it is required to be representative' (Williamson quoted in Mercer, 1988:12. See also Gunew, 1988:111, on the expectation that migrant women writers be representative; and Huggins and Tarrago on the pressures of being the only Aboriginal woman at women's conferences, 1990:147).

Here the politics of voice is crucial. Voices previously unheard politically are in contest both within and between groups, as they struggle to produce a speaking position (Morris, 1988:6). The struggle is both to overcome silence or marginality, and against stereotypic misrepresentation. There is a further struggle over who is recognised or enabled to speak on their behalf. Some individuals resist being heard only as representatives of a particular community. Some women do not have or want a 'community' in terms of their presumed race or ethnic identity.

Beyond the distinction between speaking for and speaking from, is the issue of speaking as:

> The moment I have to think of ways in which I will speak as an Indian, or as a feminist, the ways in which I will speak as a woman, what I am trying to do is generalize myself, make myself a representative ... There are many subject positions which one must inhabit, one is not just one thing. (Spivak in Gunew and Spivac, 1986:137; see also Bannerji, 1987)

How do people organise themselves into social space and discourse? (Bannerji, 1987). And who is authorised to speak? There is a complex politics of representation already noted in terms of category workers in the state. Those who claim to speak for a category or community frequently claim representativeness by virtue of being a member of that category or community.

This claim can be met by de-authorising people, declaring them inauthentic. Thus Aboriginal people who aren't 'traditional' or 'don't look Aboriginal' may find their right to speak on Aboriginal issues contested. Radicals from whatever background may be labelled as stirrers, or women radicals as lesbians and/or feminists, used as terms of abuse or to imply a deviance which supposedly debars them as legitimate spokespersons on the grounds that they are not representative of anyone. Thus too some minority women are invited to speak (including at some feminist gatherings) so long as they remain safely in exotica, or the past; so long as their difference is not politicised in such a way as to threaten or even involve the audience. If they do not behave predictably or are too successful, they may have their authenticity and right to speak questioned (Trinh, 1987:14; Marcus, 1990).

The struggle to come into representation is part of an expansion of the political arena. Thus feminists reject attempts to confine 'women' to issues to do with family, women and community, and in turn to keep these issues 'private' (Hamilton, 1989). This involves contesting the mystifying denial of the politics by those who seek to place their own position beyond political scrutiny. Here dominant groups normalise and naturalise their own identities and social interests, and accuse those who mobilised against them as being 'political' or 'ideological' in a way that they pretend not to be.

On the other hand, community representatives can claim their membership of groups as giving them insider knowledge (Said,

1985:15). Here culture is reclaimed as oppositional force (cf Williams, 1987:25), to de-authorise 'experts' and others from outside who have for so long spoken for or about them (Huggins, 1990; Atkinson et al., 1985; Morris in Beckett, 1988a:76). But does this mean that only Aboriginal people speak for Aborigines? Can only Aboriginal women speak for Aboriginal women, and only older urban Aboriginal women speak for themselves, and so on?

There are issues here to do with the politics of voice and listening to the oppressed. Is there necessarily virtue in oppression? (cf Sivanandan, 1983; Hall, 1988b). Certainly there is pain, damage and anger, which has to be dealt with. There is also learning and experience that can now be politicised and collectively theorised. There are possibilities of reclaiming language, and of building a culture of opposition. Yet mobilising a constituency or community along boundaries drawn in and for dominance may reinforce those boundaries and so continue to trap people within them. It may also make the category an easy target for state management.

IDENTITY POLITICS

There are many questions to do with insider and outsider status here (Said, 1985:15). Identity politics can often be moralistic politics as previously silent and silenced groups mobilise around their own oppression or exclusion, and make moral claim. Here the community can be hijacked by its more powerful members, including patriarchs or paid state agents for whom culture is a disguise or legitimises inequality or exploitation within the category. 'Culture' may be used to deny the rights of women or other relatively powerless members to speak, to close against younger people and exclude from the community radicals and others whose behaviour the powerful ones see as not appropriate. Politics, including sexual politics, are part of every community; and power is an intrinsic feature of every community, too.

Who can speak? Who can speak for whom? What can be said? What cannot be spoken or asked? (Spivac in Gunew and Spivac, 1986). How are people heard? For there are different listening positions as well as different speaking positions available to different people. Questions of audience can also relate to the fear that when difference has been used for so long against people, to speak of differences within the community may subvert a shared political project, or facilitate state or racists' divide-and-rule strategies.

Dominant-group racism and culturalism reify, homogenise and essentialise the categories. So too can some oppositional forms, including an identity politics which posits ancestry or gender as explanation of difference or giver of virtue. People may have shared interests and social identities, but, as we have seen, the big categories of race, ethnicity and gender disguise both differences within and common interests across the boundaries. Recognising difference without recognising affinity or connections across category boundaries can undermine opportunities for alliances and for inclusive claim which may be necessary to effect significant change (Meekosha and Pettman, 1991).

Culture isn't just a disguise or a mobilising or containing strategy. Cultural expectations do inform our ways of being, knowing and understanding. Access to dominant cultural capital, including knowledge of the English language, is crucial to get on in Australia. Culture is a basis for association, affiliation, familiarity and confidence, safety and belongingness. In its name too, people are constrained from choices and made to pay for their presumed origins; but they can also organise and claim on these grounds. Meanwhile cultures are constantly in the process of construction and contest, both within communities and in their dealings with and representations to outsiders.

Cultures are not set, separated, or bounded by impenetrable borders. The impact of industrialisation and urbanisation, the commodification of relations, the differential incorporation of different groups within the labour market and the penetration of the institutions of the state at all levels of civic culture, have placed people into complex relations with each other. The places for practising culture apart from the dominant one are severely limited. Dominant cultural representations are structured and imposed through institutions like the law and education. Individuals negotiate their own meanings and ways, within the more or less confining spaces they occupy in relation to both community and the wider system. They may or may not recognise representations of 'their' culture, whether those who speak are from outside or inside the community (Grossberg, 1989:29).

The politics of culture are played out within communities as well as between them. Culture as a political project can be reactionary, oppositional, radical or accommodationist. So it is necessary to ask who is constructing the categories, and who is resisting or reinforcing particular differences and identities. It is also necessary to ask *what is identity for?* (Bourne, 1987:22; Jordan in Parmar, 1989:63).

FEMINIST CRITIQUES OF IDENTITY POLITICS

It may help to distinguish between the political and the analytical purposes of categories (Barrett, 1987). Analytically it is necessary to deconstruct the categories and ask how women experience them, and where different women are positioned within them. Yet identity politics is strong politics, with powerful emotional appeal as well as instrumental use (Howard, 1988). There may be discrepancies and contradictions between theorising about identity, and the lived experiences of those whose associations and politics are being theorised about. It is also necessary to contest the 'naturalisation' of categories and boundaries, especially those imposed on subordinate groups, without denying the validity of identities based on shared experiences and common social location (cf Mason, 1990; Hollinsworth, 1991).

Feminism in its various forms often privileges women's experience, both as affirming that women do know a lot about being women, and as a strategy to de-authorise those who have excluded or spoken for women. Early feminist emphasis on consciousness raising gave individual women a voice and a hearing in a (supposedly but not always) safe environment. It also provided the opportunity to reflect on those experiences and trace patterns and connections between women. 'The personal is political' was an empowering slogan, as well as a revealing reading of gender relations and sexual politics.

Some constructions of identity politics were political (Cohambee River Collective, 1982), but others had the effect of reducing the political to the personal, and so became therapy rather than politics (Bourne, 1987). In this context relations of domination and subordination were disguised and power was personalised, so that the enemy often became individual men, or white women or heterosexual women. This could lead to demobilisation and to the personal paralysis of guilt (as opposed to reflecting on and owning one's speaking positions). It could also lead to women not being prepared to leave 'home'—the safe places shared with those who were seen as being the same or having had the same experiences (Reagon in Smith, 1983; Parmar, 1989).

Thus identity politics can militate against alliances and against solidarity and support for particular women or issues. 'Organising around one's own oppression' is good and necessary politics, but if it means only doing that the more marginal or politically weak women are again left alone (Meekosha and Pettman, 1991). It provides no basis for dealing with difference, other than by avoiding it.

Identity politics can also give an appearance of fixed and essential difference, and so again disguise the shifting, relational, positional nature of identity. It needs to be countered by asking 'no longer who am I, but when, where and how am I (so and so)?' (Trinh in Parmar,

1990:57). Identity politics also segment oppressions which actually exist in mutually constitutive relationships. It segments individual women, asking them to choose which they are—woman, black, socialist or lesbian, for example, when the woman concerned may be all these and more (Bannerji, 1987:12).

7 Academia

There are many sites where public knowledge about Others—and about us—is being produced. Cultural production includes both popular and 'quality' media, and literature; and cultural and critical studies are currently areas of intense interrogation of difference and identity.

Much knowledge of Others is also being produced within or under the sponsorship of bureaucratic institutions (Meekosha, 1989), and a range of policy documents now exist which can be analysed as sites of meaning and political definitions of what the problems are, as well as who it is who has them (Yeatman, 1988). Increasingly academic research is dependent on bureaucratic consultancies, in which the contract brief may lay out not only what is to be researched, but how it is to be done. Often only 'safe' or ideologically congruent researchers are funded. Researchers have little or no control over the uses to which their research is put—nor even if it will be published (Meekosha, 1989). This increasingly bounded relationship highlights a host of issues concerning the role of the academic in knowledge-making about Others, and the rights of those who are being researched, in a situation increasingly subject to economist definitions of social problems and solutions. It relates back to the state's role in reformulating political claims and managing difference.

Higher education institutions are a site for producing authorised or sometimes revisionist or oppositional knowledge. They are also an employer of people, and a deliverer of (education) services. They are a key site in the reproduction of racism and sexism, and possibly for anti-racist and anti-sexist struggles. These roles stand in complex relationship with each other, although we segment them here.

The connections between academics and policy makers are many, various and uneven. The close association historically between some anthropologists and Australian government policies towards Aboriginal people has been subjected to some scrutiny (e.g., Cowlishaw, 1986, 1990b). More recently a number of individuals like H. C. Coombs have been extremely influential through both their academic writings and their appointment to advisory committees. Anthropologists have become expert witnesses in a range of inquiries which have themselves generated much publicly available knowledge, notably through land rights hearings (Bell, 1986), but also through, for example, the Royal Commission into Aboriginal Deaths in Custody. Here anthropologists are joined by sociologists, psychologists and criminologists, again almost all non-Aboriginal. Partly for this reason the Commission has set up Aboriginal Issues Units with Aboriginal heads in each state, and appointed an Aboriginal Royal Commissioner, Pat Dodson, to investigate the underlying causes of the deaths (*Land Rights News*, July 1990:23; Hazelhurst, 1989). The extensive evidence now being collected in a systematic way from Aboriginal people about their experiences of policing and racism is of a rather different kind. The very repetition of experiences and understandings through the Commission and through the National Inquiry into Racist Violence, as well as through complaints to the Human Rights Commission and to different state anti-discrimination boards, represents a dramatic hearing for those whose views have long gone unheeded.

Sociologists have had some input into the ideological construction of multiculturalism, where Jerzy Zubrzycki was chief architect in the Fraser government's time, and into subsequent elaboration of ethnicity or culture as a basis for identifying and managing special needs (see de Lepervanche, 1984). Other sociologists have been equally active in their critique of multiculturalism and of the work of those who are seen to have significant inputs to bureaucratic understandings of social problems to do with migration and ethnicity (Jakubowicz, 1984; see also the exchanges in the *Journal of Intercultural Studies*, 1989). Some sociologists have also asserted and examined the role of gender in constituting ethnic relations and indeed culture itself (e.g., Bottomley and de Lepervanche, 1984; Martin, 1986).

The intellectual politics of feminism are rather different from the mainstream disciplines, for feminism began as an engaged and oppositional discourse (Stanley, 1990:15). While the links between feminist academics and the women's movement are problematic, feminist academics recognise that they have a personal interest in revealing gender issues in power and knowledge structures (Grosz in Caine et al., 1988:97). Their identity and right to speak as 'women' has come under attack from outside academia, including from other feminists, but a claim to an impartial position vis á vis teaching or researching about women is impossible within feminist discourse. They work and politic in different ways and with varying energy, but within an understanding that they do have social interests as women in feminism. Thus while most anthropologists and socialists of race and ethnicity study groups other than those they come from, feminism is women dominated (see Marcus, 1988; Stone, 1989; Moi, 1989; Evans, 1990, on whether men have a role in feminist scholarship).

Universities and other places of research and teaching are crucial sites in elaborating and validating certain kinds of knowledge, which enter administrative, popular or practice domains in ways that may reinforce or unsettle our understandings of social problems, provide language for explaining or obscuring connections, and widen or fore-close conceivable political options. Increasingly, credentials from a tertiary institution are a necessary prerequisite not only for middle management and policy formulation jobs, but for a range of service deliverers, community workers and local knowledge makers. Indeed, Aboriginal Studies and Multicultural Studies electives have often been developed in connection with a range of human service courses, although the more overtly political and threatening Women's Studies were often more difficult to establish (*Woman's Studies*, 1990). Thus Aboriginal, multicultural or women's issues are often raised in terms of clients, consumers or students.

ABORIGINAL STUDIES, MULTICULTURAL STUDIES AND WOMEN'S STUDIES

Many academic courses and materials in the humanities and the social sciences long ignored women, Aboriginal people and people from non-English-speaking backgrounds, in their reproduction of the Master Discourse, where the imperial white male was the Subject and norm of society and politics. Absences and silences were revealed and protested through the rise of the social movements and of radical scholarship in many often disconnected fields. Especially from the mid-1970s, small centres in Women's Studies, Aboriginal Studies or Multicultural Studies appeared in some tertiary institutions. They also appeared as electives, either in the established disciplines or as part of service or 'troubled person's industry' courses which had now discovered more social problems.

These centres and electives were added in, and rarely challenge the central bodies of knowledge. They often had newly appointed specialised staff, and their programs remain under-funded and largely elective. They are kept structurally apart from the main business, and simultaneously take pressure off the mainstream disciplines to address differences.

The new centres are constrained by their 'studies' designation, and by the construction of their contents and concerns as soft and feminised in their association with women or with jobs largely done by women (like education, social work or nursing). They were also seen as 'political' because they (hopefully) spoke to people's own needs and claims, and their funding was in part connected, no matter how vaguely, with a politically mobilised constituency (Evans, 1990:457).

Already suspect in terms of the university discourse of neutral and objective knowledge, and uneasily related to usually highly individualised tertiary teaching and research, the staff within these units or the elective fragments soon faced overload. They attracted students, often re-entry or older students who chose their offerings in search of a personal quest or with a politics of engagement. They also attracted students who found many mainstream lecturers or courses alienating, and much time was taken up in advice and counselling work for which staff received no time allowance. In addition mainstream lecturers often refer students and others to the specialist studies or elective lecturers for readings, a hearing or unofficial supervision, rather than re-educate themselves to be able to provide for non-traditional students or develop their own competence in the newer studies area.

Thus the existence of special studies centres or electives, essential as they are to recognise difference and respond to student and community or constituency demands, may have the effect of taking pressure off the institution, while also containing the offerings and their workers in marginal areas. In addition the add-on and category nature of the response means that yet again Women's Studies, Aboriginal Studies and Multicultural Studies, or whatever are their elective designations within other disciplines and courses, are usually quite separate organisationally and in content and personnel.

Women's Studies are overwhelmingly white, although there is increasing concern about this position, partly as feminist discourses both here and in the overseas journals and conference exchanges are increasingly interrogating difference among women. Much Aboriginal Studies and Multicultural Studies is still (with honourable exceptions) unconcerned with gender, or makes women visible in a single lecture or section of readings that contain them in the margins. This segregation works against a recognition of the constitutive and interactive relations involved; and Aboriginal women and ethnic-minority women may fall between the institutional territory boundaries (cf Christian, 1989).

The segmented/parallel teaching has been aggravated by the failure of the early hoped-for expansion, in centres or from them, replaced by budget cuts and intense competition for dwindling resources in which marginal, contract, low-status and often female staff are badly placed to compete. The situation is somewhat different for some Aboriginal Studies programs, where Department of Aboriginal Affairs and now the Aboriginal and Torres Strait Islander Commission (ATSIC) funding has been 'extra' to the institution. However, this often means courses or centres are dependent on short-term funding, which comes with apparently endless evaluations and scrutiny. Much staff time is then spent in preparing reports and submissions, and coping with the disruption of yet another outside gaze. Hard-pressed to develop methods of evaluating non-traditional students, objectives and outcome, they often find their scholarship and practices criticised for not being academic enough.

The centres and electives, and the inclusion of material on women, Aborigines and migrants in some mainstream and foundation courses, has gone some way to overcoming the normalised absence of those constituted as Other in academic knowledge. But the objects of the new attention can still be represented in ways that reproduce common sense categories and understandings about difference. This is particularly true where the focus was on 'them', wrenched out of the historical and political context and relationships that constitute them as different in the first place (Pettman, 1988d). The 'social problem' approach of much of the literature on Aborigines and migrants or representations of them as helpless and hapless victims may unintentionally reproduce racism, rather than equip students with a critical understanding of the politics of the construction of social differences in ways that penalise some differences and privilege others. This becomes even more damaging as students then take up jobs or go into social situations where they act on their understandings. It also compounds the difficulties for those students who find themselves represented in ways that are racist or sexist.

Here then are issues to do with coming into representation (Hall, 1988b). Becoming visible is not enough; indeed it may make for more vulnerability, intervention or offence. Those who make even a token attempt to include Others when they have done no serious work on their own perhaps unintended racism and sexism, nor worked through the social significance of their own racial, ethnic or gender location, nor grappled with feminist, anti-racist and critical scholarship on their own areas of research and teaching, may do more harm than good. Yet leaving the mainstream offerings as they often are—racist, sexist, imperialist, middle class and heterosexist—leaves education and academics as intrinsically part of the problem. Any serious attempt to add in women or race or cultural difference will unsettle mainstream ways of knowing, and subvert central concepts and categories. If the search is pursued, the consequent unravelling and reconnecting will reveal the constitutive and interactive nature of the social relations of difference—relations that are simultaneously gendered, racialised, ethnically-located and classed.

Simply knowing more about 'them' doesn't lead to tolerance (Pettman, 1984). We must also scrutinise why 'we' want to know more about 'them', especially when knowledge has for so long been used against them (Trinh, 1990). Do we want to know more about them in order to manage them better? This can be part of a control or containment strategy of the kind noted in chapter 5. Yet the contradictions are as always everywhere, for those who want to learn more about others so as to do their own job better, for example, may have control or liberatory motivations for the use of their knowledge and for their jobs.

Those who come to learn bring different motivation, social interests and experiences to any hearing, reading or conversation in these areas. Thus many of those non-Aboriginal people who enrol in a graduate Aboriginal Studies program may already be working in areas that bring them in contact with Aboriginal people. These contacts may have revealed their previous training as woefully inadequate or damaging, or have generated new questioning and awareness of difference that stimulates an intellectual engagement with their own situation. And of course some students change and redefine in the process of learning, as some teachers do. In this sense the centres and electives are spaces that are negotiated by many players, each bringing different resources and interests to the negotiations, but pressed upon by the wider politics of the institution and the society beyond it.

In any exchange it is important to know who the audience is, or in the case of teaching who the students are. Tertiary institutions are providers of services to which there is unequal access. This is especially pertinent because the institutions act as gatekeepers to both the traditional professions like law and medicine, and to a range of 'helping' industries and services with whom various minority groups have profoundly problematic relationships. Women, Aboriginal people and people of non-English-speaking backgrounds seek access to and success in the credentialing institutions to strengthen their individual position within the labour market, and/or to enable 'localisation' or fairer representation of their category claims within other institutions.

Thus it is necessary to know who the students are—who gets admitted, who completes their courses, who does well and at what cost? There are questions about who can get in, in terms of entry requirements. Recent provision for mature age entry, special bridging courses or admission for Aboriginal students, and quotas for disadvantaged students have widened access in a number of tertiary institutions; although counter-changes in terms of fees may discourage unsponsored or individual applicants. While some students or those groups who are drastically under-represented as students may require special programs, it may be politically and institutionally preferable to have more generally open and inclusive procedures in place.

There is also the question of what students are offered and how they are treated within the institution. Are there courses which are useful and relevant to them? Are they taught in congenial and appropriate ways? Does the institution offer support, or is it up to the individual student or lecturer to establish and maintain this support?

Women's Studies are mainly but not entirely and not without contest for women (Marcus, 1988; Evans, 1990). It is much less clear who Aboriginal Studies and Multicultural Studies are for, and most students in these courses are still majority students (and in my observation mainly women). Indeed there are a number of Aboriginal people who argue that it is precisely 'whites' who do need to be taught Aboriginal Studies—and preferably taught by Aboriginal people. There are increasing numbers of students from non-English-speaking backgrounds, but they may not identify or be identified as such. There are some Aboriginal students, especially in Aboriginal Studies or in Aboriginal support programs giving access to courses like social work or education. This makes teaching doubly complex. For example, asking students to explore their own racism when members of the target groups are present may cause offence, yet proceeding with little notion of what preconceived ideas, fears and expectations are may be counter-productive. Building an interactive and mutually respectful classroom situation while deconstructing racism and sexism is a highly political and ethically charged engagement.

The different motivations of the students is a key. Thus some Aboriginal students may enrol in Aboriginal Studies, or ethnic-minority students in Multicultural Studies, precisely to retrieve or recover something about themselves; or alternatively be reluctant attenders fulfilling requirements of their recruitment into a DAA or ATSIC job. Yet a tutor or other students may look to them as experts, expecting them to 'know' things about 'their' culture that they could not analyse or articulate about their own. Alternatively, the minority students may find all credence given to 'authorities' and texts produced about but from outside their communities, and that their own experiences and understandings are seen as somehow naive or emotional. This in turn raises issues to do with how we authorise what we say; and about the politics of experience, of which more later. It also raises questions about the ethics of teaching other adults, and responsibility towards them in terms of the intervention which teaching undoubtedly can be—a topic that appears to have received rather less attention than the somewhat different situation of ethics in research and interview engagements (Pettman, forthcoming, b).

What is taught and how it is taught is not restricted to what goes on in the classroom. Library resources and other materials are needed to support both teachers and students in their pursuit of an understanding of difference or of the society in which differences are played out.

In teaching and in reading recognising plurality isn't enough. Plurality needs to be placed within the structure of power relations. A critique of de-politicised difference is visible if marginal in multiculturalism (Jakubowicz, 1984), and is increasingly available through feminist theorising around difference (Caine et al., 1988; Eisenstein and Jardine, 1987; Bacchi, 1990). The discourse around Aboriginality may utilise bounded and essentialised notions of culture, but recognition of Aboriginal difference in terms of indigenous status and the experience of racism, including state racism, reveals political power relations and a sense of what is at stake. Much of feminism also presents difference in oppositional terms in the binary men/women, not without its own problems. Thus there are questions here to do with what is taught and how it is taught; whether dominant versions are reinforced, avoided or confronted; what or who is unsettled; how to engage with difference; how to create and use spaces, but not get trapped inside them.

It is extremely difficult to generalise in situations of change and with the politics of different institutions, states and government policies. Notions of academic freedom also often save departments and individuals from the close attention of others. So it is necessary to ask where and how race and gender are taught, how difference is represented or explained, and whether there are anti-racist and/or anti-sexist projects within higher education institutions.

Here the normalised absence/pathologised presence treatment of women, Aboriginal people and ethnic minorities in teaching and research is related to the invisibility or marginality of members of those groups in the institution, although the connections between the substantive dimension of knowledge-making and the industrial politics of who is employed and where within the institution is problematic. It is, however, necessary to ask who is teaching and researching about Others, and about the nature of our society. And does it matter?

ACADEMIA AND EQUAL EMPLOYMENT OPPORTUNITY

There are few women academics, and especially few women at senior levels as decision makers and players with access to committees and conversations of power, either to protect their own interests or to sponsor their preferred candidates, areas and projects (Gale, 1990).

Women's Studies centres are strategic spaces, but they are small, marginal and do not exist in all places (*Women's Studies*, 1990). There are also isolated or individual feminists who may be the only ones in a particular department (and the point about any token is that one is enough). There may be other women who are academics, although still usually few in number, but they may deliberately or disinterestedly reject any involvement in teaching or research on women, and may be ignorant of or hostile to feminist scholarship in their area. Women academics may also be clustered in particular areas, again usually in association with feminised occupations, and with topics to do with women or gender relations, and unseen and unheard within a range of strategic academic arenas. Women academics may also find themselves left to 'mind the shop' in disciplines like law and economics, where academic salaries are relatively unattractive compared to private or government employment.

Women's Studies are usually taught by women (with some of the resistance to renaming it Gender Studies an attempt to keep it so, Evans, 1990). The women are middle class by attainment if not by upbringing or inclination; they are overwhelmingly white and largely of English-speaking background; and they are likely to be aged from late thirties to late forties. There are a few younger feminists elsewhere in academia; but the shutdown in jobs over the last decade leaves a log-jam of tenured and senior male academics who settled in during the boom years.

Although it is overwhelmingly women who teach, research and write for Women's Studies, Aboriginal Studies and Multicultural Studies are still dominated by 'outsiders', especially in research and academic publications. Dominant-group men and women are involved, although again according to the familiar gendered pattern which relegates women largely to untenured and junior positions, except in some service-related and feminised teaching areas. Some women not from English-speaking backgrounds may be recruited, although they may not identify with a 'community', or in the case of women academics from overseas may not have a local community.

Aboriginal people are now found in small numbers in academia, usually in association with Aboriginal Studies or support programs, often with DAA/ATSIC or Department of Education, Employment and Training (DEET) funding. They include lecturers, tutors, coun-sellors and student advisers, typists and receptionists. Aboriginal people are still drastically under-represented as tertiary students, reflecting the damaged history of Aborigines and schooling. Aborigi-nal graduates often move on, for they are better paid and rewarded in the Aboriginal Affairs industry than in academia, or they choose to work in Aboriginal organisations.

Those Aborigines working in academia were often recruited with Aboriginality as a qualification—a welcome widening of established definitions of relevant skills and experience in this and other areas. However, this can be used against them to imply that it is the only reason they got the job, undermining their professional status and denying them a significant voice. It may also increase resentment against them as jobs generally are harder to get. They are often presumed to have competence only in Aboriginal issues, even where their first love is maths or literary theory. This expectation forecloses opportunities outside the Aboriginal area, and locks them into jobs that do not have a career track. This is especially so for those engaged in support roles, in programs that are politically vulnerable and institutionally marginal, where jobs are often subject to short-term funding and uncertain futures.

Aboriginal staff are often expected to know everything about both Aboriginal culture and the local communities, although even here their legitimacy may be challenged by those who question their authenticity or the right to speak for Aboriginal people. They are both recognised as exceptional and expected to be representative (Huggins and Tarrago, 1990). They are required to provide endless professional advice to colleagues on matters curricular or student, which are rightly the responsibility of the enquirers. If there are only one or two Aboriginal staff, they may find themselves on numerous equal opportunity and other committees, with no time credit for their often exhausting and demoralising committee and consultation work. Those who constantly point out silences, misrepresentations or simplistic responses soon get a reputation for being angry or difficult, and may be avoided or excluded from access to information they need to negotiate their way through the institution (cf Gurnah,

1989/90; also Morris on women in isolated and alienating academic contexts who are seen as nagging, i.e., engaging in 'unsuccessful repetition of the same statements', powerless to transform the situation, 1988:15). On the other hand Aboriginal staff who try to pick their fights and let a lot go by, or simply do not care, or happen to share a dominant view anyway, may find they are being used against their more critical colleagues as the authority and authoriser regarding things Aboriginal. They may then face accusations from other Aborigines of being 'coconuts' or of seeking their own interests at others' expense.

A further concern of Aboriginal staff is that their experiences of racism are not taken seriously by their colleagues or by the institution, and that they can never be sure that any action will be taken when they go to the trouble, in an unsupportive environment, to register a complaint. While the need to provide support and counselling for non-traditional students is increasingly recognised, Aboriginal academic and support staff need support too.

Common complaints of Aboriginal staff in tertiary education include others' use of inappropriate language, teachings or views that render Aboriginal people and their political claims invisible or trivialise or misrepresent them, racist jokes or offensive language involving other staff or students, and recurring comments like 'you don't look Aboriginal'. There is rarely a clear anti-racist policy with procedures and designated people who have enough authority to get compliance or action while also being open enough to be approachable. Lacking too are guidelines for negotiating and consulting with Aboriginal people. Thus a complaint or incident is often taken out of Aboriginal hands or becomes part of an elaborate and exhausting bureaucratic process.

Aboriginal staff can find themselves accused of being too involved, too emotional or too political—accusations that feminists are all too familiar with. At the same time they are expected to give endless support and counselling to Aboriginal students, to liaise with the local communities and to buffer and mediate between the institution and Aboriginal people. Some sympathetic whites in these programs also engage in much nurturing and mediating, and so come close enough to witness and sometimes be a target for the frustration and anger generated by racism and sexism.

ANTI-RACISM AND ANTI-SEXISM

Here there is the problem of institutional change, and of the possibility of using institutions that are thoroughly implicated in the reproduction of racism and sexism to combat those very processes and practices. So beyond issues of what is taught and who is employed to teach or research is the question of persuading the institution to address racism and sexism seriously (Pettman, 1990; Pettman, forthcoming, b).

How then can the powers that be, the academics, the staff association or union be convinced to recognise that racism and sexism are everyone's business, and not only those who teach about and/or are from 'the minorities'? How do racism and sexism, separately or together, become agenda items in both substantive and industrial terms? It is necessary to ask who is or isn't employed, and to ask where work on race and gender is being done—taught, researched and written about—and whether they are ever being put together. It is also necessary to ask where feminist and anti-racist and critical scholarship is being taken seriously, for academics are working in an institution and in disciplines and intellectual traditions that are both gendered and deeply implicated in protecting and projecting the master subject.

It can be argued that it is the ethical and professional responsibility of each academic to examine their own attitudes and behaviour for racism and sexism, and to develop strategies and skills to teach competently and inclusively. Such competence is unlikely in the face of ignorance about the social significance of one's own race, ethnicity and gender.

Working for a more inclusive institution is made more difficult by the continued academic, political and administrative segmentation of issues to do with Aborigines, people from non-English-speaking backgrounds and women, again conceived as alternative and exclusive identities. Equal opportunity is still often coded to mean 'women', and special admissions programs for Aborigines, for example, may be resented by others who feel marginalised or devalued in higher education institutions. It may be politically desirable to develop policies and practices that do not target particular minority groups, but rather provide forms of access and support that are more inclusive and accommodate the range of different experiences and interests; but again the particular situation of Aboriginal people needs addressing as well. There are also difficulties with monitoring and evaluating programs for staff or students which require categorising people in terms of race or ethnic background. Here it is easier to monitor changes in terms of gender. Asking people their ethnic identity will give shifting and multiple answers, and some may oppose such questions, as their own biography or politics may have led them to different strategies for negotiating identity, especially in the workplace.

So again it is necessary to recognise and affirm different experiences and to overcome the exclusion and silencing of so many, but without locking people into externally imposed categories or pursuing a politics that reproduces and validates common sense racism. It is also necessary to avoid the essentialism of locating identity, knowledge or political position in any fixed relation with origin.

TEACHING AND RESEARCHING ABOUT OTHERS

It is not tenable to argue that only Aborigines can teach about or research racism in Australia; nor that all Aborigines or all women or Aboriginal women will agree or present a single view or value; nor that morality, right politics or truth lie necessarily with the oppressed (Gunew, 1988). However, subordinated groups have profoundly different but not transparent experiences and interests, and the continued domination of public power by elite white Anglo males is unacceptable. Spivak asks

> can men theorize feminism, can whites theorize racism, can the bourgeois theorize revolution, and so on. It is when *only* the former groups theorize that the situation is politically intolerable. Therefore it is crucial that members of these groups are kept vigilant about their assigned subject-positions. (Spivac, 1987:253)

Those who become aware of their own speaking position/s, and of the absence or silence of the objects of study, may seek to allow 'them' to speak for themselves. Strategies here include inviting visiting speakers, using oral history sources and non-academic writings, for example, autobiographies and political or popular tracts as texts. Films, interviews and video productions may also provide opportunities to speak to those formerly excluded from social discourse. Democratic pedagogy which aims to empower all adult learners and recognises what they bring to their own learning can also open up teaching and learning positions. These strategies aim to create a space in which those usually silent/silenced can speak. They recognise Others' experiences and the validity of their ways of talking or writing, thus challenging the master discourse in both its content and its authorising forms. They also raise questions about the nature of evidence, and about appropriate ways of critiquing 'non-academic' writings, especially the literature of resistance (Harlow, 1987).

There are also issues to do with audience, and who members of minorities are writing for or speaking to (Huggins and Tarrago, 1990:143). Much autobiographical writing by Aboriginal women, for example, is of the family history and truth-telling narrative, as are 'migrant women's writings'. They and the 'I-story' are decidedly out of fashion in literary or cultural studies currently (Gunew, 1988). Yet their impulse—to tell other stories, to provide positive images, to explain (to themselves as well as to others) how it might have come to this—are personally and socially significant. And it is an irony that while many oppressed people are now asserting their status as subject, the very notion of the subject is under attack, especially in literary and cultural theory (Morris, 1988:15; Christian, 1988). Here Stanley regrets 'the resurgence of theory from those who were once the certified namers of other women's experiences and who are now likely to become the certified deconstructors of the same' (1990:154).

Feminism early taught us that the personal is political; and both feminism and other forms of critical theory and practice have now taught us that the personal is not political enough (Fox-Genovese, 1979/80). Women exchanging experiences and reflecting on their feelings may be delighted and immensely relieved to discover that other women have similar experiences. This knowledge can form the basis for understanding the problem as systemic or social, rather than as evidence of personal failure or misadventure. Women can then find new ways to name their concerns, to politicise their experiences and enable them to make connections with other women. But there is no inevitable or easy relationship between experience, theorising and acting.

'The category of experience is in many ways a problematic one' (Barrett, 1987:32). Meaning is constructed by position and relationship, rather than by what 'really' happened. This is not to say that memory is not true or accurate; rather that it is a reconstruction which speaks to where the person is now, and to the social setting within which that person now stands. Celebrating identities which up to now have been stigmatised is a political act, but celebrating them without situating them within the politics of difference and the power relations within which they are constructed simply encourages a cultural relativist position. It also infuses identity politics with a kind of moralism, so that 'just to name yourself as part of a given group is to claim a moral backing' (Barrett, 1987:32).

According special privilege to accounts of personal experience as 'true' does allow some people to be heard, and does affirm the liberatory call to 'break the silence', which forced rape, child abuse and other deadly secrets onto the political agenda (McIntosh, 1988). It has encouraged women to organise around their own oppression, to recognise that they do have valid knowledge about their own condition, and to resist and contest namings of themselves and their problems by more powerful others. This is politically crucial if they are to determine and mobilise in support of their own interests.

Sites of difference are also sites of power (Barrett and McIntosh, 1985:35), and dominant groups have long used divide and rule strategies that represent differences as natural, thereby separating oppressed groups from each other and imprisoning people within the boundaries.

> The very theme of difference, whatever the differences are represented to be, is useful to the oppressing group—any allegedly natural feature attributed to an oppressed group is used to imprison this group within the boundaries of a Nature which, since the group is oppressed, ideological confusion labels 'nature of oppressed person ... ' to demand the right to Difference without analysing its social character is to give back to the enemy an effective weapon. (Questions Féministes, quoted in Trinh, 1987:18)

Identity and experience become ways of authorising what we say. They may be useful strategies for undermining and unsettling the master discourse, if used to reflect on our own as well as others' positionality. They may be part of feminist challenges to the disciplines. These challenges are advancing in contested theory, but still highly uneven and marginal in practice.

Subjecting different knowledge bases and methodologies to feminist and anti-racist scrutiny means listening to and learning from those usually excluded from academia. It also means pursuing the implications of theorising about difference in one's politics and work practices, as well as organising to develop anti-racist and anti-sexist strategies towards a more open and inclusive workplace.

FEMINIST RESEARCH

Issues of who speaks for whom, and who produces knowledge about whom, arise in terms of feminist research on women. It might be assumed that women are better placed to research women by virtue of what they share as women, and because women are reputedly better at listening and empathising (Stacey, 1988:22). Alternatively women researchers may be more dangerous to other women precisely because they *seem* to be less so.

The politics and ethics of feminist research were raised by Oakley in 1981 (1984) in her critique of interviewing, taught as a male role, involving a neutral interviewer attempting to control the interview process. Oakley noted the capacity of interviewees to sabotage the process, including by asking questions and by encouraging or assuming friendships, and suggested that feminist interviewers could attend to these dilemmas by observing the responsibility to reciprocity.

McRobbie asks who we do feminist research for, and points to conflicts between feminist academic researchers and practitioners—social workers, teachers, youth workers, also often women and quite often feminist—over whose accounts become the official version of the problem (1982). The division of labour in terms of kinds of skills and different kinds of writing is key here; together with the recognition that many of the groups interviewed—youth, single mothers, and so on—have very different age, class, and race or ethnic locations from those who construct knowledge about them. McRobbie's analysis of the unequal power relations of the interview situation reveals dangers of exploitation and patronising exchanges, and poses ethical dilemmas about intrusive or upsetting questioning.

What do feminist researchers do when women ask them to leave something out (Stacey, 1988), or if they tell them something the researchers think they should not have divulged? Finch concludes that 'my interviewees need to know how to protect themselves from people like me' (Finch, 1984:80). Researchers may come across information that could be very damaging to the informants. What, for example, if she is abusing her own or another woman's child? (cf Wise in Stanley, 1990a). What if she is participating in activities that are illegal, or could be made to pay by a violent spouse or vindictive local policeperson? Research that is reported through radio or television programs or given subsequent publicity through the media may have more immediate consequences than through the obscure or removed academic journals, but confidence is an ambiguous thing to guarantee.

How researchers respond to interviewees is also a moot point. The interview is a form of intervention, and the role researchers play to elicit information may itself direct the response, in an elaborate play in which shrewdness is no monopoly of the interviewer. How then do researchers 'present' at the interview? Identifying as a woman for example or as a mother or a co-educator may establish a connection or open a conversation that puts others off guard. Alternatively a researcher's self-disclosure may be seen by some women as an imposition; or her construction of a particular version of herself may be ultimately manipulative (Ribbens, 1989:584). Attempts at a more sharing or collaborative process may also run into difficulties, as the interviewees might not tell the researcher what she thinks happened (Ferrier, 1990), or may not agree with or be hurt by how researchers write them. Many women lack access to the kinds of power that enable them to exercise control over the process.

But not all non-academic women are innocent victims. What if researchers decide to research 'up' for a change, and find powerful right-wing women's projections of themselves unpalatable? Are all women's views and experiences of equal value? (Bourne, 1987; Stanley, 1990b:58). What about those who organise to deny other women rights, for example to abortion, or to land rights?

There is no necessary sympathy of positions between women. If women teachers or schoolgirls express strongly racist or homophobic views should researchers contest these responses, or hear them out and perhaps appear to affirm them? Reproducing people's language and categories in the write-up may give them a voice, and that voice may reproduce racism or homophobia.

Not that feminist research is necessarily true or liberatory either. Against heavy and sometimes bitter debate about who and what is feminist, some insist on the pluralism of academic feminism, and on acknowledging that while feminist research as a whole may be marginal, there are still feminist silences within it (Stanley and Wise in Stanley, 1990a:46).

Feminist researchers often find many women are willing and helpful informants (McRobbie, 1982:56). Their generosity and patience may speak to their vulnerabilities or loneliness. Research into a community, locality, industry or union may also reveal many women who believe that they do have a story that is worth telling and that others—younger women, other minority women—may learn from. Or they may simply enjoy a hearing or performance when time and space are rarely given to tell 'their' story. Here Ferrier sees interviewing as an act of collaboration between two people, which requires negotiation of the terms about what will be said and how (1990). But the tellings say more about them now than the past they are re-creating. They reveal more through an analysis of the politics of representation and notions of positionality, as what we 'know' is shaped in complex interaction with where we are placed, historically and socially (Morris, 1988; de Lauretis, 1989).

Ribbens notes the difference between private and public accounts (1989:580). Feminist research into those areas of women's lives so often invisible or ignored may bring unwanted attention or interpretations to bear, and are actually involved in shifting the boundaries between personal, private, and public (Ribbens, 1989:589). This may be especially so for women from minority backgrounds who have so often seen knowledge of them constructed for the purposes of controlling them; and for whom withholding knowledge about themselves may be an act of resistance against an intrusive state or its helpers (Edwards, 1990:487).

THE POLITICS AND ETHICS OF RESEARCH

Aboriginal women in particular are used to intrusions and make informed judgements about who to talk with and what to say (Huggins, 1990:114). Aboriginal people often complain of being over-researched, and little good it has done them (Bellear, 1988:68). Now there are a range of procedures and vetting processes in place. Thus Land Rights Councils and community councils are more likely to give access to those who have demonstrated an interest and commitment to Aboriginal interests over time. A rather different process is involved as some communities or organisations seek researchers to gather information or inform their own cases. Here again women may be marginalised in those organisations where contacts with the mainstream are run mainly as men's business. This may exclude both feminist researchers and community women from the research process and from the construction of publicly available knowledge.

Aboriginal people are increasingly aware that government departments, archives and museums hold a huge amount of information about them (Fourmile, 1989), and some seek white academic assistance in working their way through the records held about their families or communities (Huggins, 1987/88; Edwards and Read, 1989; Ferrier, 1990:134–35). Many Aboriginal people are involved in doing oral history, often as family or community development or cultural retrieval projects. Research here can generate a lot of anger and pain as past injustices and failures come to light. Research is an intervention. Is an outsider and/or professional researcher involved at this stage in any way responsible for the effects? The project may also involve the construction of a history for certain public purposes—what is the researcher to do if the construction offends her notions of authenticity and accuracy?

The political and ethical issues of researching women and/or besieged minorities become clear when the stories may be used as part of the evidence. This is so in land rights claims where, for example, women may wish to assert a claim which they see Aboriginal men and white men as ignoring (Bell, 1986), or where different groups of Aboriginal people may be in dispute over ownership (Lilley, 1989). It also raises questions about providing evidence which may undermine the dispossessed claim, a debate which recently occurred in a New Zealand case where an anthropologist demonstrated settler attachment to land and place during a Maori land claim (*Anthropology Today*, 1990).

These issues recur where telling stories or publishing research may reveal damage and conflict within stigmatised communities or groups, which may then be used against them. This fear and contests over who owns the problem and who has the right to speak led to a number of Aboriginal women objecting to a white feminist anthropologist writing about the rape of Aboriginal women by Aboriginal men in a feminist journal (Bell and Nelson, 1989; Larbalestier, 1990). It can also inhibit lesbians from publicly naming violence in some lesbian relationships as a problem.

Here researchers are obliged as everywhere to recognise their own speaking position, and the social identities and interests which colour their own readings; but also to ask what speaking and listening positions are available to others? There are questions of audience here and the uses to which public knowledge about Others may be put (Huggins and Tarrago, 1990). It doesn't necessarily mean being silent or silenced, although those are possible responses (Gunew and Spivac, 1986; Bannerji, 1987). It does mean preparing for readings which must locate 'the problem' within its context, and engaging with possible racist or sexist readings and hearings.

There is no longer an innocent subject, both in the sense that 'no politics remains innocent of that which it contests' (Fox-Genovese, 1979:80–81) and in terms of moving beyond representations of the essentialised and heroic woman/native/other innocent victim (Hall, 1988b; Trinh, 1989). Likewise there is no innocent reading or first encounter, for we are positioned within complex and dynamic social relations and social history which structure and inform our every encounter. It is within this recognition of structure and history that feminist theory and practice now seeks to locate both the specific interests of different women and the possibilities for connection and alliance across the differences.

8 Feminism in conversation with itself

Feminism has powerful import in asserting that sex power places women differentially compared with men. There is a structure of power that positions women systematically and generates particular relations and experiences that are women's. Women have different relationships to citizenship, militarisation, the labour market and to reproduction in its wider senses. Women are also vulnerable to particular kinds of violence, including regularly to violence of men who are supposed to care about them, and with whom they are in intimate relations.

It is simply not possible to make sense of the lives, choices, opportunities and constraints of people, women or men, without recognising the personal and social consequences of their sex.

Most feminists argue further that those consequences of sex are not fixed, determined or inevitable in shape or texture, but rather shift over time and place (de Lauretis, 1989:5). This assertion generated the sex and gender distinction, and recognition of femininity and of women as social constructions (Howard, 1988). This was a radical position against a biologicalism which naturalised and essentialised obvious sex differences as an explanation for women's subordination and oppression, which thus seemed to be inevitable.

Identifying women and men as social constructions revealed sexism as an ideology, and pointed to the ideological reproduction of the category 'women' and elaboration of its meaning in ways that both reflected and reinforced women's placement socially and materially. It also directed attention to sets of social practices which confirmed or subverted women's placement.

This project was necessary to identify sex and gender relations as generative rather than as simply an added factor of social life, and also to establish a social construction of gender that would allow for a politics of women's equality or women's liberation. It was a brave, daring, highly political reading of 'women' that generated much energy and learning in pursuing the nature of the ideology and practice of sexism and the material relations of gender.

Feminist analysis and politics are not monolithic, and feminists pursue different and changing paths in this project. Some feminists focus on sex roles, stereotypes and socialisation, others on the nature of women's work, or of men's violence, or in recovery projects revealing earlier feminisms, women's writings and so on. Different feminisms have emerged, often dividing along crucial dimensions. Radical feminists looked to women in themselves, to sex, gender and patriarchy as key. Others variously labelled marxist or socialist feminists focused on class and capitalism, and asked where the women were in these processes. They were often already politically engaged in left politics and had come to recognise, personally and intellectually, that this dimension was not enough. While continuing to assert the crucial constitutive relationship of class and productive relations, they asked questions about the nature of women's work both in and beyond the workplace, developing concepts of social reproduction and joining radical feminists in their (rather different) challenging of the confinement of women within the 'private' sphere.

Other feminists opted for more or less materialist explanations, and some asserted different kinds of representations of women, which sometimes mirrored pre-feminist or even patriarchal views. Thus maternal feminists stress female and feminine virtues and values that were those traditionally or popularly associated with women— the nurturing, caring, loving, sharing, emotional, intuitive woman. Here the category women is reclaimed, inverted and fused with positive values, honouring it as black or cultural nationalism did with demeaned race categories (Alcoff, 1988:411–14).

Some pacifist feminists advocated a social cultural shift in the public domain from masculine to feminine values. These moves recognised and mobilised around powerful dimensions of women's experiences and notions of self. There were then a range of positions, from highly political and radical reconstructions of maternalism as a political and ethical resource, through to a confirmation of the boundaries and 'authentic' feminine characteristics which could have the effect of continuing to entrap women within a virtuous, private and domesticated domain.

There are fierce debates around who owns feminism, reflected in feminist journals like *Australian Feminist Studies* and *Hecate* in Australia, and including *Feminist Review* and *Women's Studies International Forum* internationally. There are also fierce debates about the place of men in feminism and/or in struggles for gender equality (Marcus, 1988; Stone, 1989). Some participants in these debates deploy binary and essentialist representations, including some whose theoretical politics supposedly rejected this construction. There is also impatience from those feminists who think that men have already received too much attention, and that interest in gender studies or in men's studies means men are again occupying most of the public space, even in those few precious areas that women have secured for women (Marcus, 1988; Maynard, 1990).

There now is considerable debate over the originally useful sex/gender distinction (e.g., Lorber and Farrell, 1991; Nicholson, 1990). This is in part a re-run of the older equality/difference debates sometimes represented as marxist/socialist feminist on the one hand and radical feminist on the other, although these distinctions often refer more to a tendency than to single-mindedness or fixed boundaries. Individuals and groups shift over time. Feminism is often highly eclectic, and never fixed. Again it may be more useful to speak of feminisms than of feminism in the singular (de Lauretis, 1989:8), although it is still useful to speak of feminism to identify both a field of discourse and a political project towards understanding and eliminating women's subordination.

There is a growing suspicion among feminists, even those who earlier argued another position, that women are after all quite different from men (de Lauretis, 1989). A number of those who assert that women are made not born observe the tenacity and totality of gender power in all its different variations, and wonder if that power is constructed on another deeper difference. Feminism is currently engaged in a complex reformulation of difference, in terms of difference between men and women. This is reflected in writings and discussions about the sexed body and embodiment, feminist psychoanalysis, feminist ethics and notions of women as speaking, reasoning and moralising in a different voice (Goodnow and Pateman, 1985; Eisenstein and Jardine, 1987; Caine et al., 1988, Nicholson, 1990). These more recent interests have led to an increasingly complex series of feminist positions in the light of the multi-faceted nature of women's oppression and gendered power relations.

Feminism is not only an academic pursuit, but also a political project. Different explanations clearly have different implications for feminist practice. Feminist theorising is informed by strategic concerns, as women find themselves in situations which demand action now. Theoretically they may be committed to overthrowing patri-archy, but today they have to work in a particular workplace, live in a particular family, negotiate a particular street, or aim to keep the refuge open. The difficulty (among others) then becomes to devise strategies for now, while simultaneously working to change the situ-ation. Thus feminists find themselves fighting for child-care as a women's issue because it is overwhelmingly women who are primar-ily or solely responsible for children, while also pursuing social changes that will not leave women, or at least individual women, so responsible.

It is now twenty years since the second-wave western feminism became politically visible. Since then there has been much work, theorising and arguing, taking many forms. Feminists have identified and analysed many normalised absences and misrepresentations that collude in women's oppression (Grosz in Caine et al., 1988:55). Gendered power relations and social practices have been analysed in a range of societies and sites, and through different disciplines and theoretical perspectives (Eisenstein and Jardine, 1987; Caine et al., 1988). There has been effort to give voice and hearing to women, to represent women's experiences and complex politics of ideological contestation and material power and place within overall structures of subordination and exclusion.

The last twenty years have also seen much feminist theorising and action, political mobilisation and state and other response. So sex-role socialisation is no longer enough, for it leaves structures untouched and assumes an equality model that many feminists now question. Equal employment opportunity is no longer enough, as it has been minimally effective in some areas, and it has mainly helped already relatively privileged women. Some feminist-supported mea-sures like no-blame divorce or the recognition of women's sexuality may have been counter-productive, encouraging many men to be even more irresponsible towards women and children. Other changes did not make the difference they were supposed to. There have been many developments in theory and politics with feminism in conver-sation with and against itself.

The last twenty years have also been years of critical theory, some of it feminist, feminist-informed or useful to feminism. The language has changed, for example from ideology to discourse, with complex elaborations about knowledge-making and experience in different disciplines. There are now better understandings of the nexus between the family, the household, the labour market and the state, and more recognition of the specificity and variety of women's expe-riences. And against this post-modernism casts doubt on, informs and sometimes speaks from the feminist project (Nicolson, 1990).

So 'feminism' and 'women' twenty years on reveal rich and often troublesome variety and specificity. This variety has been revealed in part through interrogating sexism and sex power. But it has also emerged through engagements with and in response to the struggles of many different women against 'dominant' feminism, demonstrating again that power is a relational concept both within and between categories.

Women organised in anger and defiance, persistently and bravely, or even reluctantly and sometimes apologetically against men or male power, and forced (some) men to notice. Other women, or some of the same women, organised against those women they saw as using class and/or race power to co-opt the women's movement. These struggles within feminism signalled the end of the innocent female subject.

Women associated with the early second-wave of feminism are now often represented as white, middle class, of the dominant culture, abled, perhaps as heterosexual, although the energy of many lesbian women involved is not always discounted. Dominant-group women were best placed to make waves but, as with first feminism, the women were much more various, including many working-class women.

The different uses of categories, for analytical and categorical purposes, need noting here. It is necessary to deconstruct the categories to understand the politics of their making, while also utilising or mobilising the categories for political purposes. Some representations of feminism as exclusive, privileged and selfish seek to deauthorise feminists as somehow inauthentic or at least unrepresentative of women, to deny their right to speak for women, the moral constituency they claim as both cause and backing.

Indeed many but by no means all of those women who organised, mobilised and especially who had access to public forums, publications and so on, were of dominant groups in terms of racial and cultural difference and of class. Other women were fighting for their survival and often naming themselves as women in the fight, though not necessarily tactically or politically as feminists.

Again there are the complex issues of the relationship between academic feminism, political feminism and women, challenges from within the women's category, and an apparent lack of fit between feminist theorising and some women's understanding of their own lives. Thus black feminists mounted critiques of 'white' feminism which entailed further negating moves and inversion and interrogation of the categories (*Feminist Review* no. 17, 1984; Collins, 1990;

Huggins, 1987). Black feminists and some black women who refused to call themselves feminist pointed out to white women the kinds of things that white women had been pointing out to men. They pointed to the absences, the silences, the exclusion of other women through language, practices, definition of interests and exercise of power. They pointed to white women universalising their own experiences as 'women's'. Carby (1982) summed this up in her demand 'White women Listen!', asking 'Who exactly do you mean when you say WE?'

Black feminists went on to identify stereotypic misrepresentations of black women revealing the familiar 'normalised absence/ pathologised presence' representation of black women even within many feminist discourses and texts. Some went so far as to conclude that white feminism was by its nature and in terms of the social interests of its influential players incapable of becoming inclusive of 'women'. Others countered by contesting white women's ownership of feminism, and argued that in true feminism racism was not a possibility, accusing of female aggrandisement those who called themselves feminist but failed or refused to address the experiences of most women (Smith in Hull, 1982:49; Walker in Hull, 1982:41).

Black feminists went further to argue that black women could not simply be added in. Rather core concepts and categories of white feminism analysed and mobilised around patriarchy, the family, reproduction, work and the state would be unsettled and changed through analysis of the very different experiences and social locations of black women (Carby, 1982; Huggins, 1987). This critique spoke powerfully to race power—to the vast and traumatic historical experiences of colonisation and slavery which still determine global national power and the very different experiences of people who are socially defined as black.

Black feminists then looked to race both as explanation and as a political project. They along with other minority women put difference on the feminist agenda in another dimension, as differences between women. They raised the issue of possible conflicts of interests and differential power among women. Thus black feminists did not only say they and their political priorities and experiences had been left out. They also said that white women had left out crucial dimensions of their own social identities and of the structuring of power in their own societies, pointing especially to race and cultural difference and in many cases to class. They pointed out that some women were simultaneously oppressed and oppressors, with power over other women and over some other men (Joseph, 1981; Hooks, 1984).

There are contradictions and ironies here. Just as speaking of 'women' could appear to confirm biological divisions formerly mobilised against women, using the categories of black and white as in 'black feminism' versus 'white feminism' could appear to confirm biological divisions of race and colour, with ambiguity about other kinds of difference, including where cultural difference, minority status, language, migration, religion and so on fitted (Anthias and Yuval-Davis, 1983).

Thus black feminists revealed another binary opposition in terms of a crucial dimension of social power. For a number of black feminists the determinative power structuring relations, including relations between white and black women, was race (Huggins, 1987). Here again the relationship between the biological category and the social construction, and between the categories and the individual, was problematic.

Going beyond this to try to put sex power and race power together revealed white men on top, black women at the bottom, but white women and black men in highly ambiguous positions, although in some black feminist representations black men were less in power and opportunity and more oppressed than white women (Joseph, 1981).

Or might it depend on the audience? Where black feminists or womanists are addressing their comments to white women or white feminists, the political project is different from when they address men within their own communities (presuming of course that they have a community). A black American feminist collective noted 'We struggle with black men against racism, while we also struggle with black men about sexism' (Combahee River Collective in Hull, 1982:13). Race, then, is a political resource mobilised by women marginalised by, among others, white women and within white feminism.

It might also depend on the time and stage of the struggle. Particular feminist interventions are made within particular political contexts, although they may later be read in the light of subsequent events. Thus Carby's agenda-setting challenge was to white feminists for whom race and racism appeared invisible. Once racism was on at least some feminist agendas, black feminists and other feminists were able to pursue the task of recognising differences of various kinds among women, and to analyse multiple oppression—although some feminists had already made a beginning here (Anthias and Yuval-Davis, 1983; Parmar, 1989).

Thus black feminist critiques drew attention to the personal and political significance of white as a political colour, in ways parallel to early feminists drawing men's attention to the significance of their own gender. The critiques also highlighted the concept of a dominant culture and moved beyond patriarchy, where the bonding was not simply one of men against women. This critique then had a crucial role in unsettling feminism, and prompted further elaboration of the specificity and variety of women's experiences and interests.

So how should dominant-group women address their whiteness and their privileged access to cultural capital? How are they placed in terms of race and culture? What are minority women's social interests? And what does a political project around race and gender look like? What does acknowledging race differences and cultural differences do to feminism? How have colonisation and racism structured race power and placed the different women, black and white, within the structure? How is it reproduced and what is the continuing material, ideological and personal significance of race and cultural difference today?

Deconstructing women to reveal the dimension of race power is not, however, the end of the story. There have been criticisms of black feminism as a new subordination, a new binary which is not enough. There have been challenges from other groups of women who saw themselves as marginalised within or through feminism. The category 'woman' was deconstructed through their various critiques. Thus working-class women spoke to different experiences of work and the family, of welfare and the state. The politicisation of sexuality and sexual choice as more than lifestyle, debates about heterosexuality, increasing understanding of the social significance of age and disability, and contests around different ideologies and politics all led to fracturing along various dimensions (Meekosha and Pettman, 1991).

There is now increasing recognition of the constitutive relations of difference, analytically and conceptually, materially and politically, ideologically and personally (Barrett, 1987; Caine et al., 1988; Howard, 1988; de Lauretis, 1989). This has led to elaboration of the specificities of women's experiences, recognising them as multiple and contingent. Interrogating race and gender thus also means deconstructing 'black', which in turn signals the end of the innocent black subject (Hall, 1988b). This doesn't mean that race isn't important, any more than gender isn't important. But it does mean that race or gender alone or even together do not add up to the ways different women experience being women or being black.

There is the issue here too of the colour dimension, of the very different constructions of white versus black, of categories of women of colour, or Asian, for example. There are also differences among women revealed through analyses of the social interests of ethnic-minority women, to do with culture, language, religion and the experience of migration and migrantness. Thus the recognition of difference becomes a series of differences often represented as binary, but each naming of opposition leads to another exclusion or set of exclusions that further segments women politically and often personally (Bannerji, 1987:12).

Binary representations also produce a hierarchy of oppressions, and prioritise a particular determining force in social relations, when each dimension is constituted interactively and relationally (Ramazanoglu, 1989; Harriss, 1989; Briskin, 1990). They can also encourage a clear domination–oppression divide that represents women or black women, for example, as passive victims. Thus Newton and Rosenfelt argue for moves beyond the 'tragic essentialism' of these representations to 'the Both-ands of experience: that women at different moments in history have been both oppressed and oppressive, submissive and subversive, victim and agent, allies and enemies of men and of one another' (1985:xxiv).

Once woman as a unitary category goes, the question shifts from 'where are the women?' to also asking 'which women?' Sensitivity to difference may recognise the variety and specificity of women's experiences, and the resulting groups may become smaller and more particular (Curthoys, 1989:147–8; Harriss, 1989:37). The consequent elaboration of differences might get closer to women's actual experiences, although experience itself is not innocent either (Barrett, 1987:32). We are becoming more aware and more critical of the different ways of writing and politicising experiences and interests and feminism. But still some of the women written and theorised about refuse to recognise themselves in the theorising.

The recognition of differences among women and the stress on specificity does allow for a segmentation of the task. There can be organisation around issues and sites, identifying racism and sexism in terms of practice and effects, which in turn facilitate strategies and make sense to the women involved (Knowles and Mercer, 1990). But alternatively groups can get so specific that most people have left already, caricatured, for example, as a group of older black disabled lesbian eco-feminists. Some women are all of these; but such a fragmentation may leave stranded and unsupported the least politically organised groups of women, as we each respectfully go off and organise around our own oppression, or give theirs back to them (Meekosha and Pettman, 1991).

This move may converge in effect if not intent with the divide and rule strategy of dominant interests, helping to demobilise women and to set different groups of women against each other. There are very complex politics here about how not to appropriate others' struggles, but still to recognise connections among women, to deal with conflicts among women and take responsibility for our actions or position. This last point can make for moralistic or guilt politics, which are not useful, although some minority women may feel that a bit of guilt and/or silence on the part of relatively purposeful or privileged women is long overdue. And the power differentials, unequal opportunities and choices, and some women's apparent collusion in oppressive or exploitative social relations do have to be dealt with.

It is necessary to move beyond the biologism that says that simply being born male, or white, makes one inevitably guilty (Bourne, 1987; Stone, 1989; Moi, 1989; Parmar, 1989). Reducing power to individuals' culpability, complicity or victimisation is often personally paralysing and politically demobilising. Yet each person is differentially positioned in this society now, for example as a woman, as white, as English-speaking or not. Segmenting and creating binary oppositions disguise the complex and interrelated structuring of power (Trinh, 1987:7; Ramazanoglu, 1989:141). So it is always necessary to ask who has power in any given situation or relationship. Differences are played out as relations of domination, subordination and resistance, though again across shifting boundaries and through contested and often contradictory sets of relationships on the ground.

It is also necessary to ask about the politics of difference and identity, for knowing another's category and power positions does not predict that person's politics:

> [M]uch organizational grief could be avoided if people understood that partnership in misery does not necessarily provide for partnership for change: when we get the monsters off our backs all of us may want to run in very different directions. (Jordan in Parmar, 1987:13)

A politics of affinity is a far more useful basis for alliance than essentialised identities are (Adams, 1989:32).

A complex politics offers different and changing possibilities for alliances, affiliations and identities, as we play in/up to/against/ along with the structure (Reagon, 1983; Parmar, 1989). There are genuine conflicts and differences of interests, although difference doesn't necessarily make for conflict, and there are almost always possibilities for congenial or at least tolerable personal, social and political engagements. Difference and identity are never fixed or final. Differences are significant but they are also positional and relational. They are frequently organised and articulated around issues, and in specific situations (Knowles and Mercer, 1990). They require location within wider sets of social relations and political projects so that the connections, conflicts and commonalities between them can be seen. This search is indicated in Haraway's urging 'an argument for *pleasure* in the confusion of boundaries and for *responsibility* in their construction' (1987:13).

It is necessary to situate or contextualise women's differences and political projects and social interests (Haraway, 1988). It is also necessary to situate feminist writing in terms of their particular projects. Writings are significant because they are accessible to (some) others who are not party to the encounters or disputes that generate them. Yet they often appear in journals, especially academic journals, after a lot of skirmishes, organisations and kitchen conversations, and after conflicts, reconciliations or collaborations on the ground (Christian, 1988).

What then are the possibilities of moving beyond category politics, with an inclusive political project, a project that is feminist, anti-racist and anti-colonialist? Central to this project is how to treat difference in theory and practice, and how to talk and work across the category boundaries. It means owning one's own speaking position/s, social interests and politics, and locating multiple and contingent identities and politics within structures and social relations. It means finding a language to interrogate difference, secure home bases and build alliances in a critical engagement—not of conformity or of agreement, but recognising where it is appropriate to work together and where separately. It means recognising the specificity of women's interests and their various alliances with other women and with some men. It means recognising unequal power and conflicting interests while not giving up on community or solidarity or sisterhood.

To be continued . . .

Bibliography

ABC (1990) 'Are All the Women White?' *The Coming Out Show*, 21–22 September

Adams M. (1989) 'There's no Place Like Home: on the Place of Identity in Feminist Politics', *Feminist Review* 31, pp. 22–33

Alcoff, L. (1988) 'Cultural Feminism versus Post-Structuralism: the Identity Crisis in Feminist Theory', *Signs* 13, pp. 405–36

Alcorso, C. (1987) 'Outwork and Migrant Women: Some Responses', *Migration Action* 11, 3, pp. 1–13

Alexander, C. (1984) 'Aboriginals in Capitalist Australia: What it Means to Become Civilised', *Australian and New Zealand Journal of Sociology* 20, 2, pp. 233–42

Alomes, S. (1988) *A Nation at Last?*, North Ryde: Angus and Robertson

Amos, V. and Parmar, P. (1984) 'Challenging Imperial Feminism', *Feminist Review* 17, pp. 3–20

Anderson, B. (1983) *Imagined Communities: Reflections on the Origin and Spread of Nationalism*, London: Verso

Antcliff, S. (1988) 'Behind the Rhetoric: a closer look at the New Right', *Australian Quarterly* 60, 1, pp. 63–9

Anthias, F. and Yuval-Davis, N. (1983) 'Contextualizing Feminism: gender, ethnic and class divisions', *Feminist Review* 15, pp. 62–75

Anthropology Today (1990) 'Cultural Politics in New Zealand' Discussion, 6, 3, pp. 3–9

Atkinson, J. (1990) 'Violence in Aboriginal Australia: Colonialism and its Impact on Gender', *Refractory Girl* 36, pp. 21–6

Atkinson, M., Langton, M., Wanganeen, D. and Williams, M. (1985) 'A Celebration of Resistance to Colonialism', in M. Hill and A. Barlow, *Black Australia* 2, Canberra: Australian Institute of Aboriginal Affairs

Attwood, B. (1988) 'Understandings of the Aboriginal Past: History or Myth', *Australian Journal of Politics and History* 34, 2, pp. 265–71

—— (1989) *The Making of the Aborigines*, Sydney: Allen & Unwin

Australian Bureau of Statistics (1986) Information Paper Census 86, Aborigines and Torres Strait Islander Count, Canberra: Australian Government Publishing Service

Australian Institute of Criminology (1990) Report of the National Inquiry into Violence, Canberra: Australian Institute of Criminology

Bacchi, C. (1980) 'Evolution, Eugenics and Women', in E. Windschuttle ed., Women, Class and History, Melbourne: Fontana/Collins, pp. 132–50

—— (1990) Same Difference: Feminism and Sexual Difference, Sydney: Allen & Unwin

Baldock, C. and Cass, B. eds (1983) Women, Social Welfare and the State, Sydney: Allen & Unwin

Ballard, J. (1987) 'Ethnicity as a Mask of Confrontation' in C. Jennett and R. Stewart eds, Three Worlds of Inequality, South Melbourne, Macmillan

Bandler, F. (1983) The Time Was Ripe: the Story of the Aboriginal-Australian Fellowship 1956–69, Sydney: APCOL

Bannerji, H. (1987) 'Introducing Racism: Notes Towards an Anti-Racist Feminism', Resources for Feminist Research 16, 1, pp. 10–12

Banton, M. (1987a) Racial Theories, Cambridge: Cambridge University Press

—— (1987b) 'What We Now Know About Race', New Community 13, 3, pp. 349–62

—— (1987c) 'The Battle of the Name', New Community 14, 1/2, pp. 170–5

Barbalet, J. (1988) Citizenship, Milton Keynes: Open University Press

Barker, M. (1981) The New Racism, London: Junction

Barnsley, J. (1988) 'Feminist Action, Institutional Reaction', RFD/DRF 17, 3, pp. 18–21

Barrett, M. and McIntosh, M. (1985) 'Ethnocentrism and Socialist Feminist Theory', Feminist Review 20, pp. 24–47

Barrett, M. (1980) Women's Oppression Today, London: Verso

—— (1987) 'The Concept of Difference', Feminist Review 26, pp. 29–41

Beckett, J. (1987) Torres Strait Islanders: Custom and Colonialism, Cambridge: Cambridge University Press

—— (1988a) Past and Present: the Construction of Aboriginality, Canberra: Aboriginal Studies Press

—— (1988b) Aboriginality, Citizenship and the Nation-State, Social Analysis 24, pp. 3–18

—— (1989) in M. Howard ed. Ethnicity and the State in the Pacific, Tokyo: United Nations University

Bell, D. (1983) Daughters of the Dreaming, Melbourne: McPhee Gribble/Allen & Unwin

—— (1986) 'In the Case of the Lawyers and Anthropologists', Journal of Intercultural Studies 7, 1, pp. 20–9

—— (1990) 'A Reply to "the Politics of Representation"', Anthropological Forum 6, 2, pp. 158–66

Bell, D. and Napurrula Nelson, T. (1989) 'Speaking About Rape is Everyone's Business', Women's Studies International Forum 12, 4, pp. 406–16

Bell, J. (1986) an interview in Hecate XXII, 1–2, pp. 64–75 •

Bellear, L. (1988) 'Koori History and the Bicentenary', Lilith 5, pp. 68–70

Bennett, S. (1989) Aborigines and Political Power, Sydney: Allen & Unwin

Berndt, C. (1978) 'Digging Sticks and Spears, or, the two-sex model', in F. Gale ed., Woman's Role in Aboriginal Australia, Canberra: Australian Institute of Aboriginal Studies

Berndt, R.M. and Tonkinson, R. eds (1988) *Social Anthropology and Australian Aboriginal Studies*, Canberra: Aboriginal Studies Press

Bhabha, H. and Parekh, B. (1989) 'Identities on Parade', *Marxism Today*, June, pp. 24–9

Bhatt, C. (1986) 'Funding the Flames: The Creation of Black Crisis Managers', *Emergency* 4, pp. 43–7

Bhavnani, K. and Coulson, M. (1986) 'Transforming Socialist-Feminism: the Challenge of Racism', *Feminist Review* 23, pp. 81–92

Bottomley, G. and de Lepervanche, M. eds (1984) *Ethnicity, Class and Gender in Australia*, Sydney: Allen & Unwin

Bottomley, G. (1984a) 'Racism: Sociological Perspectives', *New Left Review* 89, pp. 24–31

——— (1984b) 'Mediterranean Women in Australia: An Overview' paper to a Symposium of Mediterranean Women's Organisations', Delphi, Greece

——— (1988) 'Ethnicity, Race and Nationalism in Australia: Some Critical Perspectives', *Australian Journal of Social Issues* 23, 3, pp. 169–83

Bourne, J. (1987) 'Homelands of the Mind: Jewish Feminism and Identity Politics', *Race and Class* 29, 1, pp. 1–24

Boyle, H. (1987) 'We Don't Want to be Massacred any More', *Land Rights News* 2, p. 4

Bradley, S. (1987) 'Aboriginal Women in the Australian Workforce', *Aboriginal History* 11, 2, pp. 143–55

Briskin, L. (1990) 'Identity Politics and the Hierarchy of Oppression' *Feminist Review* 35, pp. 102–8

Briscoe, G. (1988) 'Capitalism, Culture and Land Rights', in B. Wright et al., *Contemporary Issues in Aboriginal Studies* 2, Sydney: Firebird Press

Brittan, A. and Maynard, M. (1984) *Racism, Sexism and Oppression*, London: Basil Blackwell

Brock, P. (1989) *Women, Rites and Sites: Aboriginal Women's Cultural Knowledge*, Sydney: Allen & Unwin

Broom, D. ed. (1984) *Unfinished Business: Social Justice for Australian Women*, Sydney: Allen & Unwin

Broom, D. (1987) 'Another Tribe: Gender and Inequality', in C. Jennett and R. Stewart eds, *Three Worlds of Inequality*, Melbourne: Macmillan

Broome, R. (1982) *Aboriginal Australians*, Sydney: Allen & Unwin

Brown, C. (1981) 'Mothers, Fathers and Children: From Private to Public Patriarchy', in H. Hartmann (1981) *Women and Revolution: The Unhappy Marriage of Marxism and Feminism*, London: Pluto Press

Brown, K. (1986a) 'Establishing Difference: Culture, "Race" and the Production of Ideology', *Australian and New Zealand Journal of Sociology* 22, 2, pp. 175–86

——— (1986b) 'Keeping Their Distance: the Cultural Production of Racism', *Australian and New Zealand Journal of Sociology* 22, 3, pp. 387–98

Brown, R. (1989) 'Maori Spirituality as Pakeha Construct', *Meanjin* 48, pp. 252–8

Bryan, B. et al. (1985) *The Heart of the Race: Black Women's Lives in Britain*, London: Virago

Bryson, L. (1988) 'Welfare Issues in the Eighties' in J. Najman and J. Western eds, *A Sociology of Australian Society*, Melbourne: Macmillan

Bureau of Immigration Research (BIR) (1991) *Australia's Population Trends and Prospects*, Canberra: Australian Government Publishing Service

Burgmann, M. (1984) 'Black Sisterhood: Urban Aboriginal Women and their relationship to the white Women's Movement', in M. Simms, *Australian Women and the Political System*, Melbourne: Longman Cheshire

Bulkin, E., Pratt, M. and Smith, B. (1984) *Yours in Struggle: Three Feminist Perspectives on Anti-Semitism and Racism*, New York: Long Haul Press

Burns, A. (1990) 'Mother-headed Households', *The Australian Quarterly* 59, 3-4, pp. 387-400

Butlin, N. (1983) *Our Original Aggression*, Sydney: Allen & Unwin

Cahill, D. (1988) 'Asians and the Great Immigration Debate of 1988', *Asian Migrant* 1, 6, pp. 201-5

——— (1989) 'Refugees in Australia: Policy and Practice', *Asian Migrant* 2, 3, p. 81

Caine, B., Grosz, E. and de Lepervanche, M. eds (1988) *Crossing Boundaries: Feminisms and the Critique of Knowledges*, Sydney: Allen & Unwin

Caine, H. and Yuval-Davis, N. (1990) 'The Equal Opportunity Community and the Antiracist Struggle', *Critical Social Policy* 29, pp. 5-26

Carby, H. (1982) 'White Woman Listen! Black Feminism and the Boundaries of Sisterhood', in CCCS *The Empire Strikes Back*, London: Hutchinson

——— (1986) 'Lynching, Empire and Sexuality in Black Feminist Theory', in H. Gates ed. *'Race', Writing and Difference*, Chicago: University of Chicago Press

Carmody, K. (1988) 'Aboriginal Oral History: Some Problems in Methodology', Canberra: Australian Institute of Aboriginal Studies Conference

Carmody, M. (1990) 'Keeping Rape on the Political Agenda', National Women's Conference 90 *Proceedings*, Canberra

Carrington, K. (1990) 'Aboriginal Girls and Juvenile Justice', *Journal for Social Justice Studies* 3, pp. 1-18

Carroll, B. (1972) 'Peace Research: The Cult of Power', *Conflict Resolution* xvi, 4, pp. 591-616

Cass, B. (1988) 'The Feminisation of Poverty' in B. Caine et. al. eds *Crossing Boundaries*, Sydney: Allen & Unwin

Castles, F. (1985) *The Working Class and Welfare*, Sydney: Allen & Unwin

Castles, S. and Kosack, G. (1975) *Immigrant Workers and Class Structure in Western Europe*, London: Oxford University Press

Castles, S. (1984) *Here for Good: Europe's New Ethnic Minorities*, London: Pluto Press

Castles, S. et al. (1988) *Mistaken Identity: Multiculturalism and the Demise of Nationalism in Australia*, Sydney: Pluto Press

Castles, S. (1990) 'Immigration and Multiculturalism: Perspectives for the 1990s', *Migration Action* March, pp. 15-18

Centre for Contemporary Cultural Studies (CCCS) (1982) *The Empire Strikes Back: Race and Racism in 70s Britain*, London: Hutchinson

Chase, A. (1981) 'Empty Vessels and Loud Noises: About Aboriginality Today', *Social Alternatives* 2, 2, pp. 23-7

Choo, C. (1990) *Aboriginal Child Poverty*, Melbourne: Brotherhood of St. Lawrence

Christian, B. (1988) 'The Race for Theory', *Feminist Studies* 14, 1, pp. 67-80

——(1989) 'But Who Do You Really Belong To—Black Studies or Women's Studies?', *Women's Studies* 17, 1, pp. 17–23

Clapham, D. and Smith, S. (1990) 'Housing Policy and "Special Needs" ', *Policy and Politics* 18, 3, pp. 193–205

Clifford, J. and Marcus, J. eds (1986) *Writing Culture: the poetics and politics of ethnography*, Berkeley: University of California Press

Cohen, P. and Bains, H. eds (1988) *Multi-Racist Britain*, London: MacMillan

Collins, J. (1988) *Migrant Hands in a Distant Land*, Sydney: Pluto Press

Collins, P. (1990) *Black Feminist Thought*, Boston: Unwin Hyman

Collmann, G. (1988) *Fringe Dwellers and Welfare: Aboriginal Response to Bureaucracy*, St Lucia: University of Queensland Press

——(1988) 'I'm Proper No.1 Fighter, Me: Aborigines, Gender and Bureaucracy in Central Australia', *Gender and Society* 2, 1, pp. 9–23

Combahee River Collective (1982) 'A Black Feminist Statement' in G. Hull et al. eds, *All The Women Are White, All the Blacks are Men, But Some of Us Are Brave*, New York: Feminist Press

Connell, R. (1990) 'The State, Gender and Sexual Politics', *Theory and Society* 19, pp. 507–44

Connolly, C. (1990) 'Review of Fay Weldon's Sacred Cows', *Feminist Review* 35 pp. 113–18

——(1991) 'Washing our Linen: One Year of Women Against Fundamentalism', *Feminist Review* 37 pp. 68–77

Coombs, H.C., Brandl, M. and Snowden, W. (1983) *A Certain Heritage*, Canberra: Australian National University

Cornell, S. (1988) 'The Transformation of Tribe: Organisation and Self-concept in Native American Ethnicities', *Ethnic and Racial Studies* 11, 1, pp. 27–45

Cowlishaw, G. (1986) 'Race for Exclusion', *Australian and New Zealand Journal of Sociology* 22, 1, pp. 3–24

——(1987) 'Colour, Culture and the Aboriginalists', *Mankind* 22, 2, pp. 221–37

——(1988) *Black, White or Brindle: Race in Rural Australia*, New York and Melbourne: Cambridge University Press

——(1990a) 'Where is Racism?', *Journal for Social Justice Studies* 3, pp. 51–62

——(1990b) 'Helping Anthropologists: Cultural Continuity in the construction of Aboriginalists', *Canberra Anthropologist* 13, 2, pp. 1–29

Cowlishaw, G. and Morris, B. eds (1990) 'Contemporary Race Relations in Australia', *Journal of Social Justice Studies* 3

Croft, S. (1986) 'Women, Caring and the Recasting of Need — a Feminist Appraisal', *Critical Social Policy* 16, pp. 23–39

Cunneen, C. (1990a) 'Aborigines and Law and Order Regimes', *Journal for Social Justice Studies* 3, pp. 37–50

——(1990b) *Aboriginal–Police Relations in Redfern*, Sydney: HEROC

Curthoys, A. (1970) 'Historiography and Women's Liberation', *Arena* 22, pp. 35–40

——(1983) 'Rewriting Australian History: Including Aboriginal Resistance', *Arena* 62, pp. 96–110

——(1989) *For and Against Feminism*, Sydney: Allen & Unwin

Curthoys, A. and Markus, A. eds (1978) *Who are our Enemies? Racism and the Working Class in Australia*, Neutral Bay: Hale and Iremonger

Dale, J. and Foster, P. (1986) *Feminists and State Welfare*, London: Routledge and Kegan Paul

Daly, A. (1990) 'Women in the Workforce and Family Structure in Australia', *Journal of the Australian Population Association* 7, 1, pp. 27–39

Daniels, K. (1985) 'Feminism and Social History', *Australian Feminist Studies* 1, pp. 27–40

Daniels, K. and Murname, M. eds (1989) *Australia's Women: A Documentary History*, St Lucia: University of Queensland Press

Davis, A. (1983) *Women, Race and Class*, New York: Vintage Books

—— (1990) *Women, Culture and Politics*, New York: Vintage Books

de Beauvoir, S. (1970) *The Second Sex*, New York: Bantam

de Lauretis, T. ed. (1988) *Feminist Studies/Critical Studies*, Bloomingham: Indiana University Press

—— (1989) 'The Essence of the Triangle, or Taking the Risk of Essentialism Seriously', *Differences* 1, 2, pp. 3–38

de Lepervanche, M. (1980) 'From Race to Ethnicity', *ANZ Journal of Sociology* 16, 1, pp. 2–37

—— (1984) 'Immigrants and Ethnic Groups', in S. Encel and L. Bryson eds *Australian Society*, 4th edn, St Kilda: Longman Cheshire

—— (1989) 'Breeders for Australia: a National Identity for Women?', *Australian Journal of Social Issues* 24, 3, pp. 163–81

de Lepervanche, M. and Bottomley, G. eds (1988) *The Cultural Construction of Race*, Sydney: Studies in Society and Culture

DeShazer, M. (1990), 'Sisters in Arms', *NWSA Journal* 2, 3, pp. 349–73

DIEA Department of Immigration and Ethnic Affairs (1984) *About Migrant Women: Statistical Profile 81*, Canberra: Australian Government Publishing Service

—— (1986) *Immigrant Women's Issues*, Canberra: Australian Government Publishing Service

—— (1987) *And ... Giving Our Lives To This Country: Spanish-speaking Women in the Workforce*, Canberra: Australian Government Publishing Service

Dill, B. T. (1983) 'Race, Class and Gender: Prospects for An All-Inclusive Sisterhood', *Feminist Studies* 9, 1, pp. 131–50

Dixon, M. (1986) *The Real Matilda: Women and Identity in Australia 1788–1975*, Ringwood: Penguin

Dominelli, L. (1989) 'An Uncaring Profession: Racism in Social Work', *New Community* 15, 3, pp. 391–403

Drakakis-Smith, D. (1981) 'Aboriginal Underdevelopment in Australia', *Antipodes* 13, 1, pp. 2–37

Eade, J. (1990) 'Nationalism and the quest for authenticity', *New Community* 16, 1, pp. 493–503

Edwards, A. (1988) *Regulation and Repression: The Study of Social Control*, Sydney: Allen & Unwin

Edwards, C. and Read, P. (1989) *The Lost Children*, Doubleday

Edwards, R. (1990) 'Connecting Method and Epistemology: a White Woman Interviewing Black Women', *Women's Studies International Forum* 13, 5, pp. 477–90

Eisenstein, H. and Jardine, A. eds (1987) *The Future of Difference*, New Brunswick: Rutgers University Press

Eliadis, M. et al. (1989) *Issues for Non English Speaking Background Women*, Office of Multicultural Affairs: Australian Government Publishing Service

Elshtain, J.B. (1987) *Women and War*, New York: Basic Books

Enloe, C. (1981) 'The Growth of the State and Ethnic Mobilisation: The American Experience', *Ethnic and Racial Studies* 4, 2, pp. 123–36

—— (1988) *Does Khaki Become You? The Militarization of Women's Lives*, London: Pandora

—— (1990) *Bananas, Bases and Beaches: Feminism and International Politics*, London: Pandora

Evans, M. (1988) 'Choosing to be a citizen: the time path of citizenship in Australia', *International Migration Review* 22, 2, pp. 243–64

Evans, Mary (1990) 'The Problem of Gender for Women's Studies', *Women's Studies International Forum* 13, 5, pp. 457–62

Evans, R., Saunders, K. and Cronin, K. eds (1975) *Exclusion, Exploitation and Extermination: Race Relations in Colonial Queensland*, Sydney: ANZ Book Company

Evans, R. (1982) 'Don't You Remember Black Alice, Sam Holt? Aboriginal Women in Queensland History', *Hecate* VIII, 2, pp. 7–21

Fabian, J. (1983) *Time and the Other: How Anthropology Makes its Other*, New York: Columbia University Press

Fatin, W. (1990) 'Women in the State', *National Women's Conference Proceedings*, pp. 11–15

Fesl, E. and Markus, A. (1986) 'Land Rights: The Wrong Numbers', *Australian Society*, May 3–4

Fesl, E. (1990) 'The English Language and Kooris', *Social Alternatives* 9, 2, pp. 35–7

Ferrier, C. (1990) 'Resisting Authority', *Hecate* 16, 1/2, pp. 134–9

Finch, J. (1984) ' "It's Great Having Someone to Talk To": the Ethics and Politics of Interviewing Women' in C. Bell and H. Roberts eds, *Social Researching: Politics, Problems, Practice*, London: Routledge and Kegan Paul

Fox-Genovese, E. (1979–80) 'The Personal is Not Political Enough', *Marxist Perspectives* 8, Winter pp. 94–113

Foster, L. and Stockley, D. (1988) 'The Rise and Demise of Australian Multiculturalism 1973–88', *Politics* 23, 2, pp. 1–10

—— (1989) 'The Politics of Ethnicity: Multicultural Policy in Australia', *Journal of Intercultural Studies* 10, 2, pp. 13–32

Fourmile, H. (1989) 'Who Owns The Past? Aborigines as Captive of The Archives', *Aboriginal History* 13, 1, pp. 1–8

Framework 36 (1990) Third Scenario: Theory and the Politics of Location

Franzway, S., Court, D. and Connell, B. (1990) *Staking a Claim: Feminism, Bureaucracy and the State*, Sydney: Allen & Unwin

Fraser, N. (1987) 'Women, Welfare and the Politics of Need Interpretation', *Thesis Eleven* 17, pp. 88–106

Fulcher, C. (1989) 'Policy, Practice and Social Theory: Towards an Agenda', National Social Policy Conference paper, Sydney: University of New South Wales

Gaitskell, D. (1982) 'Are Servants ever Sisters?', *Hecate* VIII, 1, pp. 102–12

Gale, Fay ed. (1978) *Woman's Role in Aboriginal Society*, Canberra: Australian Institute of Aboriginal Studies

―――― (1983) *We Are Bosses Ourselves: the Status and Role of Aboriginal Women Today*, Canberra: Australian Institute of Aboriginal Studies

―――― (1990) 'Women Must Set Own Agenda', the *Australian*, 26 September

Gale, Fay and Wundersitz, J. (1986) 'Aboriginal Visibility in the "System" ', *Australian Social Work* 39, 1, pp. 21–6

Gale, Fran (1989) 'With One Accord? the Participation of Immigrant and Australian Women in Trade Unions', paper to the APSA conference, Sydney: University of New South Wales

Game, A. and Pringle, R. (1983) *Gender at Work*, Sydney: Allen & Unwin

Gardner, S. (1986) 'Is Racism "Sexism Extended?" Literature, History and Moral Panics', *Hecate*, pp. 75–97

Gender and History (1990) Special Issue on Autobiography and Biography 2, 1

Gilbert, K. (1973) *Because a White Man'll Never Do It*, Sydney: Angus and Robertson

―――― (1977) *Living Black*, Ringwood: Penguin

Gilroy, P. (1987) *There Ain't No Black in the Union Jack: The Cultural Politics of Race and Nation*, London: Hutchinson

Goldberg, D. (1987) 'Raking the Field of the Discourse of Racism', *Journal of Black Studies* 18, 1, pp. 58–77

Goodall, H. (1987) 'Aboriginal History and the Politics of Information Control', *Oral History Association of Australia Journal* 9, pp. 17–33

Goodnow, J. and Pateman, C. eds (1985) *Women, Social Science and Public Policy*, Sydney: Allen & Unwin

Gordon, P. and Klug, F. (1986) *New Right, New Racism*, London: Searchlight

Greek–Australian Women's Workshops (1988) *Women of the Mediterranean*, Melbourne: Centre for Migrant and Intercultural Studies, Monash University

Green, M. and Carter, B. (1988) 'Races and Race Makers: The Politics of Racialisation', *Sage Race Relations Abstracts*, 13, 2, pp. 4–30

Greenfield, C. and Williams, P. (1987–8) 'Aboriginal Women, Newspapers and the Politics of Culture', *Hecate* XIII, 2, pp. 76–106

Greer, P. (1989) 'Report to the Domestic Violence Service', *Aboriginal Health Worker* 13, 4, pp. 14–20

Grieve, N. and Burns, A. eds (1986) *Australian Women: New Feminist Perspectives*, Melbourne: Oxford University Press

Grimshaw, P. (1982) 'Australian Women in History, Black and White: A Comparative Study', Second Women and Labour Conference, Melbourne: University of Melbourne

―――― (1985) 'Women in History: Reconstructing the Past' in Goodnow, J. and Pateman, C. eds *Women, Social Science and Public Policy*, Sydney: Allen & Unwin

Grossberg, L. (1989) 'The Context of Audiences and the Politics of Difference', *Australian Journal of Communication* 16, pp. 13–35

Guidieri, R. and Pellizzi, F. eds (1988) *Ethnicities and Nations*, Austin: University of Texas

Gundara, J. (1988) 'Western Europe: Multicultural or Xenophobic?', Education and Development Conference Paper, London: Institute of Education

Gunew, S. (1983) 'Migrant Women Writers: Who's on Whose Margins?', *Meanjin* 42, 1, pp. 16–26

Gunew, S. and Spivac, G. (1986) 'Questions of Multiculturalism', *Hecate* XII, 1–2, pp. 136–42

—— (1988) 'Authenticity and the Writing Cure' in Sheridan, S. ed. *Grafts: Feminist Cultural Criticism*, London: Verso

Gunew, S. and Mahyuddin, J. eds (1988) *Beyond the Echo: Multicultural Women's Writings*, St Lucia: University of Queensland Press

Gurnah, A. (1989–90) 'Translating Race Equality Policies into Practice', *Critical Social Policy* 27, pp. 110–25

Gusfield, J. (1989) 'Constructing the Ownership of Social Problems', *Social Problems* 36, 5, pp. 431–41

Haggis, J. (1990) 'Gendering colonialism or colonising gender?', *Women's Studies International Forum* 13, 1/2, pp. 105–16

Hall, J. D. (1984) 'Women, Rape, and Racial Violence', in Snitow, A. et al. eds, *Desire: The Politics of Sexuality*, London: Virago

Hall, P. (1989) 'Women and Award Restructuring', *Refractory Girl* no. 33, pp. 13–17

Hall, R. (1989) *The Black Diggers*, Sydney: Allen & Unwin

Hall, S. (1978) 'Racism and Reaction' in Commission for Racial Equality, *Five Views on Multicultural Britain*, London: Commission for Racial Equality

—— (1980) 'Race, Articulation and Societies Structured in Dominance', in *Sociological Theories: Race and Colonialism*, Paris: UNESCO

—— (1988a) 'The Toad in the Garden: Thatcherism Among the Theorists', in Nelson, G. and Grossberg, L. eds, *Marxism the Interpretation of Culture*, London: Macmillan

—— (1988b) 'New Ethnicities', in ICA Document 7, *Black Film: British Cinema*, pp. 27–31

Hall, S. and Held, D. (1989) 'Left and Rights', *Marxism Today* June, pp. 16–23

Hamilton, A. (1986) 'Daughters of the Imaginary', *Canberra Anthropologist* 9, 2, pp. 1–25

—— (1987) 'Equal to Whom? Visions of Destiny and Aboriginal Aristocracy', *Mankind* 17, 2, pp. 129–39

Hamilton, C. (1989) 'Women in Politics: Methods of Resistance and Change', *Women's Studies International Forum* 12, 1, pp. 129–35

Hamilton, P. (1990) 'Inventing the Self: Oral History as Autobiography', *Hecate* 16, 1/2, pp. 128–33

Hampel, B. (1989) 'Social Analysis or Ideology?, Government Statements on Multiculturalism', *Journal of Intercultural Studies* 10, 1, pp. 1–12

Hanen, M. and Williams, A. (1989) 'Life Crises and Ageing People of non–English speaking Backgrounds', *Australian Journal on Ageing* 8, 4, pp. 3–4

Hanmer, J. and Maynard, M. eds (1987) *Women, Violence and Social Control*, London: Macmillan

Hanson, A. (1990) 'The Making of the Maori', *American Anthropology* 91, 4, pp. 890–902

Haraway, D. (1987) 'A Manifest for Cyborgs: Science, Technology and Socialist Feminism in the 1980s', *Australian Feminist Studies*, 4, pp. 4–42

—— (1988) 'Situated Knowledges: the Science Question in Feminism', *Feminist Studies* 14, 3, pp. 573–99

Harding, S. ed. (1988) *Feminism and Methodology: Social Science Issues*, Bloomingham: Indiana University Press

Hargraves, K. (1982) *Women at Work*, Ringwood: Penguin

Harlow, B. (1987) *Resistance Literature*, New York: Methuen

Harris, C. (1982) 'The "Terror of the Law" As Applied to Black Rapists in Colonial Queensland', *Hecate* VIII, 2, pp. 22–48

Harris, D. (1987) *Justifying the Welfare State*, London: Blackwell

Harriss, K. (1989) 'New Alliances: Socialist Feminism in the 1980s', *Feminist Review* 31, pp. 34–54

Hartmann, H. (1981) *Women and Revolution: The Unhappy Marriage of Marxism and Feminism*, London: Pluto Press

Hartsock, N. (1983) *Money, Sex and Power: Towards a Feminist Historical Materialism*, New York: Longman

Hatzimanolis, E. (1990) 'The Politics of Nostalgia: Community and Difference in Migrant Writing', *Hecate* 16, 1/2, pp. 120–7

Hazlehurst, K. and C. (1989) 'Race and the Australian Conscience: Investigating Aboriginal Deaths in Custody', *New Community* 16, 1, pp. 35–48

Head, B. (1989) 'The State and Political Culture', paper to APSA, Sydney: University of New South Wales

Hearn, J. (1982) 'Radical Social Work—contradictions, limits and political possibilities', *Critical Social Policy* 2, 1, pp. 19–34

Higginbotham, E. (1990) 'Feminism and the Academy', *NWSA Journal* 2, 1, pp. 105–11

Hindess, B. (1990) 'Political Equality and Social Policy', *Thesis Eleven*, 25, pp. 114–21

Hollinsworth, D. (forthcoming) 'Discourses on Aboriginality and the Politics of Identity in Urban Australia', *Oceania*

Hooks, B. (1981) *Ain't I a Woman? Black Women and Feminism*, Boston: South End Press

—— (1984) *Feminist Theory: From Margin to Centre*, Boston: South End Press

—— (1989) *Talking Back: Thinking Feminist, Thinking Black*, London: Sheba

Howard, J. (1988) 'Feminist Differings: Recent Feminist Literary Theory and Criticism,' *Feminist Studies* 14, 1, pp. 167–90

Howard, M. ed. (1982) *Aboriginal Power in Australian Society*, St Lucia: University of Queensland Press

—— (1982a) 'Australian Aboriginal Politics and the perpetuation of Inequality', *Oceania* liii, 1, pp. 82–101

—— ed. (1989) *Ethnicity and the State in the Pacific*, Tokyo: United Nations University

Huggins, J. (1987) 'Black Women and Women's Liberation', *Hecate* X111, 1, pp. 77–82

—— (1987/8) 'Aboriginal Women Domestic Servants in the Interwar Years', *Hecate*, 13, 2, pp. 5–23

—— (1990) 'International Indigenous Women's Conference Report', *Australian Feminist Studies* 11, pp. 113–14

Huggins, J. and Tarrago, I. (1990) 'Questions of Collaboration', *Hecate* 16, 1/2 pp. 140–7

Hull, G. T., Scott, P. B. and Smith, B. eds (1982) *All The Women Are White, All The Blacks Are Men, But Some Of Us Are Brave*, New York: Feminist Press

Human Rights Australia (1988) *Toomelah Report*, Sydney: HEROC

Human Rights and Equal Opportunity Commission (HEROC) (1991) *Report of the National Inquiry into Racist Violence*

Immigrant Women's Speakout Association of New South Wales (1990) *Annual Report for 1989*, Sydney: Lidcombe

Inglis, A. (1974) *Not a White Woman Safe—Sexual Anxiety and Politics in Port Moresby, 1920–1934*, Canberra: ANU Press

Jacobs, P. (1986) 'Miscegination in Western Australia 1930–1937', *Australian Aboriginal Studies* 2, pp. 15–23

Jakubowicz, A. (1984) 'Ethnicity, Multiculturalism and Neo-Conservatism', in Bottomley and de Lepervanche eds, *Ethnicity, Class and Gender in Australia*, Sydney, Allen & Unwin

—— (1985) 'Racism, Multiculturalism and the Immigration Debate in Australia', *Sage Race Relations Abstracts* 10, 3, pp. 1–15

—— (1989) 'The State and the Welfare of Immigrants in Australia', *Ethnic and Racial Studies* 12, 1, pp. 1–35

Jakubowicz, A. and Meekosha, H. (1991) 'Creating Knowledge About Ethnic Minorities', unpublished paper

Jennett, C. (1987) 'Incorporation or Independence? The Struggle for Aboriginal Equality', in Jennett, C. and Stewart, R. eds *Three Worlds of Inequality*, South Melbourne: Macmillan, pp. 57–93

Jennett, C. and Stewart, R. eds (1990) *Hawke and Australian Public Policy*, South Melbourne: Macmillan

Jennings, K. and Hollinsworth, D. (1987–8) 'Ways of Seeing and Speaking About Aboriginal Women' *Hecate* xiii, ii, pp. 113–33

Jenson, J. (1990) 'Different but not Exceptional?', *New Left Review*, pp. 58–68

Jones, D. and Hill-Burnett, J. (1982) 'The Political Context of Ethnogenesis', in Howard, M. *Aboriginal Power in Australian Society*, St Lucia: University of Queensland Press

Jones, J. (1985) *Labour of Love: Labour of Sorrow*, New York: Basic Books

Jones, P. (1990) 'Rushdie, Race and Religion', *Political Studies* 38, pp. 687–94

Jordan, D. (1985) 'Census Categories—Enumeration of Aboriginal People, or Construction of Identity?', *Australian Aboriginal Studies* 1, pp. 28–36

Joseph, G. (1981) 'The Incompatible Menage a Trois: Marxism, Feminism and Racism', in H. Hartmann ed., *Women and Revolution: The Unhappy Marriage of Marxism and Feminism*, London: Pluto Press

Julien, I. and Mercer, K. (1988) 'De Margin and De Centre', *Screen* 29, 4, pp. 1–10

Jupp, J. (1988) 'Immigration and Ethnicity', in Najman, J. and Western, J. eds, *A Sociology of Australian Society*, South Melbourne: Macmillan

—— et al. (1989a) *The Political Participation of Ethnic Minorities in Australia*, Canberra: Australian Government Publishing Service

—— (1989b) 'Australian Institutions' Response to Multiculturalism', *Migration Action* xi, 2, pp. 13–19

—— (1989c) *The Challenge of Diversity: Policy Options for a Multicultural Society*, Sydney: ANU Press

Kahan-Guidi, A. and Weiss, E. (1989) *Forzo e Coraggio—Give Me Strength*: Italian–Australian Women Speak, Broadway: Women's Redress Press

Kalantzis, M. (1990) 'Ethnicity Meets Gender Meets Class', in S. Watson ed., *Playing the State*, Sydney: Allen & Unwin

Kalowski, J. (1986) 'Women in a Multicultural Society', *Migration Action* viii, 1, pp. 10–14

Keeffe, K. (1988) 'Aboriginality: Resistance and Persistence', *Australian Aboriginal Studies* 1, pp. 67–81

Keesing, R. (1989) 'Creating the Past: Custom and Identity in the Contemporary Pacific', *The Contemporary Pacific* 1, 1/2, pp. 19–42

Keen, I. ed. (1988) *Being Black: Aboriginal Cultures in 'Settled' Australia*, Canberra: Australian Institute of Aboriginal Studies

Kelly, R. (1990) 'Aboriginal Women's Role in Society', *National Women's Conference Proceedings*, pp. 158–65

King, D. (1988) 'Multiple Jeopardy, Multiple Consciousness', *Signs* 14, 1, pp. 42–71

Kirby, V. (1989) 'Capitalising Difference', *Australian Feminist Studies* 9, pp. 1–24

Knapman, C. (1986) *White Women in Fiji 1835–1930: The Ruin of Empire?*, Sydney: Allen & Unwin

Knowles, C. and Mercer, S. (1990) 'Feminism and Anti-racism' in A. Cambridge and S. Feuchtwang eds, *Antiracist Strategies*, Aldershot: Avebury

Kovel, J. (1988) *White Racism: a Psychohistory*, London: Free Association Books

Kunz, E. (1988) *Displaced Persons: Calwell's New Australians*, Sydney: ANU Press

Labumore/Roughsey, E. (1984) *An Aboriginal Mother Tells of the Old and the New*, Melbourne: McPhee Gribble

Lam Thi Cuc, Luong Thuy Lieu and Cahill, D. (1989) 'Vietnamese Female Outworkers in Melbourne's Western Suburbs', *Asian Migrant* 2, 3, pp. 95–8

Langer, B. (1990) 'From History to Ethnicity: El Salvadoran Refugees in Melbourne', *Journal of Intercultural Studies* 11, 2, pp. 1–13

Langford, R. (1988) *Don't Take Your Love to Town*, Ringwood: Penguin

Langton, M. (1981) 'Urbanizing Aborigines: The Social Scientists Great Deception', *Social Alternatives* 2, 2, pp. 16–22

—— (1988) 'Medicine Square', in I. Keen ed., *Being Black: Aboriginal Cultures in 'Settled' Australia*, Canberra: Australian Institute of Aboriginal Studies

—— (1988b) 'The Getting of Power', *Australian Feminist Studies* 6, pp. 1–5

—— (1989) 'Feminism—What do Aboriginal Women Gain?' *Broadside* (National Foundation for Australian Women Newsletter) 2, p. 3

Larbalestier, J. (1980) 'Feminism as Myth: Aboriginal Women and the Feminist Encounter', *Refractory Girl* 20–21, pp. 31–9

—— (1988) 'For the Betterment of these People: the Bleakley Report and Aboriginal Workers', *Social Analysis* 24, pp. 19–33

—— (1990) 'Ideology and Aboriginal–European Relations in the Northern Territory' *Social Analysis* 27, pp. 70–82

—— (1990) 'The Politics of Representation: Australian Aboriginal Women and Feminism', *Anthropological Forum* 6, 2, pp. 143–57

Lattas, A. (1990) 'Aborigines and Contemporary Australian Nationalism', *Social Analysis* 27, pp. 50–69

Lattas, J. (1989) 'Feminism as a Proper Name', *Australian Feminist Studies* 9, pp. 85–96

Lawrence, E. (1982) 'Just Plain Common Sense: The Roots of Racism' in Centre for Contemporary Cultural Studies, *The Empire Strikes Back: Race and Racism in 70's Britain*, London: Hutchinson, pp. 212–35

Lesbock, S. (1983) 'Free Black Women And The Question of Matriarchy', in J. Newton et al. eds, *Sex and Class in Women's History*, London: Routledge & Kegan Paul

Lever-Tracy, C. and Quinlin, M. (1988) *A Divided Working Class*, London: Routledge and Kegan Paul

Lewis, E. (1987) 'Afro-American Adaptive Strategies', *Journal of Family History*, 12, 4, pp. 407–20

Lilley, R. (1989) 'Gungarakayn Women Speak: Reproduction and the Transformation of Tradition', *Oceania* 60, 2, pp. 81–98

Long, J. (1989) 'Leaving the Desert: Actors and Sufferers in the Aboriginal Exodus from the Western Desert', *Aboriginal History* 13, 1, pp. 9–43

Lorber, J. and Farrell, S. eds (1991) *The Social Construction of Gender*, London: Sage

MacKinnon, C. (1983) 'Feminism, Marxism, Method and the State: Towards Feminist Jurisprudence', *Signs* 8 pp. 635–58

—— (1989) *Towards a Feminist Theory of the State*, Cambridge, Mass.: Harvard University Press

McConnochie, K., Hollinsworth, D. and Pettman, J. (1988) *Race and Racism in Australia*, Wentworth Falls: Social Science Press

McCorquodale, J. (1986) 'The Legal Classification of Race in Australia', *Aboriginal History* 10, 1, pp. 7–24

McGrath, A. (1978) 'Aboriginal Workers for Northern Territory Settlers 1911–1939', Women and Labour Conference, Sydney: Macquarie University

—— (1987) *Born in the Cattle*, Sydney: Allen & Unwin

—— (1988) 'Born or Reborn in the Cattle?', *Meanjin* 47, 1, pp. 171–7

McHoul, A. (1988) 'Sociology and Literature: The Voice of Fact and The Writing of Fiction', *ANZ Journal of Sociology* 24, 2, pp. 208–25

McIntosh, M. (1988) 'Family Secrets as Public Drama', *Feminist Review* 28, pp. 6–15

McQueen, H. (1970) *A New Britannia*, Ringwood: Penguin

McRobbie, A. (1982) 'The Politics of Feminist Research', *Feminist Review* 12, pp. 46–57

Maddock, K. (1983) *Your Land is Our Land*, Ringwood: Penguin

Mama, A. (1989) 'Violence Against Black Women: Gender, Race and State Responses', *Feminist Review* 32, pp. 30–42

Mankind (1985) Discussion on Aboriginality, 15, 1

Mansell, M. (1989) 'How the Bicentenary Helped the Aboriginal Nation Grow', *Social Alternatives* 8, 1, pp. 9–11

Marcus, J. (1988) 'Australian Women and Feminist Men', *Hecate* 14, 2, pp. 98–106

—— (1989) 'Racism, Terror and the Production of Australian Autobiographies', unpublished paper

—— ed. (1990) *Writing Australian Culture*, Social Analysis no 27

Maris, H. and Borg, S. (1985) *Women of the Sun*, Ringwood: Penguin.

Markus, A. (1987) 'Land Rights, Immigration and Multiculturalism', in Markus,

A. and Rasmussen, R. eds, *Prejudice in the Public Arena: Racism*, Melbourne: Monash University, pp. 21–34

—— (1990) *Governing Savages*, Sydney: Allen & Unwin

Markus, A. and Rickfels, M.C. eds (1985) *Surrender Australia? Essays in the Study and Uses of History*, Sydney: Allen & Unwin

Marshment, M. (1983) Review of Alice Walker, *Race and Class* XXV, 2, pp. 91–4

Martin, J. (1978) *The Migrant Presence*, Sydney: Allen & Unwin

Martin, J. (1986) 'Non-English-Speaking Migrant Women in Australia', in N. Grieve and A. Burns eds, *Australian Women: New Feminist Perspectives*, Melbourne: Oxford University Press

Masian, S. (1990) 'The Profile of Filipino Women', in National Women's Conference *Proceedings*, Canberra

Mason, D. (1982) 'After Scarman: A Note on the Concept of Institutional Racism', *New Community* 10, 1, pp. 38–45

—— (1990) 'Categorisation, Identity and Social Science', *New Community* 17, 1, pp. 123–33

Matthews, J. (1989) 'Which Way to the Barricades?' *Australian Feminist Studies* 9, pp. 133–42

Mayberry, P. (1987) 'Women and Social Security', *Social Security Journal*, Winter, pp. 20–7

Maynard, M. (1990) 'The Re-Shaping of Sociology? Trends in the Study of Gender', *Sociology* 24, 2, pp. 269–90

Meekosha, H. (1989) 'Research and the State: Dilemmas in Feminist Practice', *Australian Journal of Social Issues* 24, 4, pp. 249–68

Meekosha, H. and Jakubowicz, A. (1989) 'Increasing Opportunity or Deepening Disappointment?', *Migration Action* xi, 1, pp. 9–19

Meekosha, H. and Pettman, J. (1991) 'Beyond Category Politics', *Hecate* 17, 2

Meese, E. and Parker, A. eds, (1989) *The Difference Within: Feminism and Critical Theory*, Philadelphia: John Benjamin

Mercer, C. (1987) 'The Nation: Be in it?' *Australian Left Review*, 101, pp. 8–15

Mercer, K. (1986) 'Racism and Sexual Politics', *Emergency* 4, pp. 56–61

—— (1988) 'Recording Narratives of Race and Nation' ICA Documents 7, pp. 4–14

Merlan, F. (1988) 'Gender in Aboriginal Life: A Review', in R. M. Berndt and R. Tonkinson eds, *Social Anthropology and Australian Aboriginal Studies*, Canberra: Aboriginal Studies Press

Migration Action (1989) Special issue on Migrant and Refugee Women, 11, 3

Mikhailovich, K. (1990) 'The Social Construction of the Victim—Women as Victims of Male Violence', in National Women's Conference *Proceedings*, Canberra

Miles, R. (1987a) 'Recent Marxist Theories of Nationalism and the Issue of Racism', *British Journal of Sociology* XXXVIII, 1, pp. 24–43

—— (1987b) *Capitalism and Unfree Labour: Anomaly or Necessity?*, London: Tavistock

—— (1988) 'Beyond the "Race" Concept: The Reproduction of Racism in Britain', in M. de Lepervanche and G. Bottomley eds, *The Cultural Construction of Race*, Sydney: Studies in Society and Culture, pp. 7–31

——— (1990) 'The Racialisation of British Politics', *Political Studies* 38, pp. 277–85

Miller, J. (1985) *Koori: a will to win*, Sydney: Angus and Robertson

Mizstal, B. (1990) 'Migrant Women in a Class Society', unpublished paper

Mohideen, R. (1990/91) 'Racism and the Women's Movement', *Womanspeak* Dec/Jan pp. 10–11

Moi, T. (1989) 'Men Against Patriarchy', in L. Kauffman ed., *Gender and Theory*, Oxford: Basil Blackwell

Moody, R. (1988) *The Indigenous Voice: Visions and Realities* vols 1 and 2, London: Zed Books

Moraga, C. and Anzaldua, G. eds, (1983) *This Bridge Called my Back: Writings by Radical Women of Colour*, New York: Kitchen Table

Morgan, S. (1987) *My Place*, Fremantle: Fremantle Arts Centre Press

Morris, B. (1990a) 'Making Histories/Living History', Social Analysis, 27 pp. 83–92

——— (1990b) 'Racism, Egalitarianism and Aborigines', *Journal for Social Justice Studies* 3, pp. 61–76

Morris, M. (1988) *The Pirate's Fiancee: Feminism, Reading and Post-Modernism*, London: Verso

Muecke, S. (1982) 'Available Discourses on Aborigines', in P. Botsman ed. *Theoretical Strategies*, Sydney: Local Consumption Publications, pp. 98–111

Mueller, A. and Newton, J. (1986) 'Women Learning About the State', *RFD/ DRF* 15, 1, pp. 4–7

Mulvaney, D. J. (1986) 'A Sense of Making History', *Australian Aboriginal Studies* 2, pp. 48–56

Mumford, K. (1989) *Women Working: Economics and Reality*, Sydney: Allen & Unwin

Murphy, J. (1986) 'The Voice of Memory: History, Autobiography and Oral Memory', *Historical Studies* 22, 87, pp. 157–75

Mum Shirl with Bobbi Sykes (1989) *An Autobiography*, Richmond: Heinemann

Mundine, K. (1990) 'Women in this land for another 60 000 years', in National Women's Conference *Proceedings*, pp. 166–9

Najman, J. and Western, J. eds (1988) *A Sociology of Australian Society*, Melbourne: Macmillan

Nathan, P. and Leichietner Japanangka, D. (1985) *Settle Down Country*, Alice Springs: Kibble Books

National Women's Conference (1990) *Proceedings*, Canberra: Write People

Newton, J. and Rosenfelt, D. eds (1985) *Feminist Criticism and Social Change*, New York: Methuen

Ng, R. (1986) 'The Social Construction of Immigrant Women in Canada', in R. Hamilton and M. Barrett eds, *The Politics of Diversity*, London: Verso

Nicholson, L. ed. (1990) *Feminism/Postmodernism*, New York: Routledge

Oakley, A. (1984) 'Interviewing Women: a Contradiction in Terms?', in *Telling the Truth About Jerusalem*, London: Basil Blackwell

O'Donnell, C. and Hall, P. (1988) *Getting Equal: Labour Market and Regulation and Women's Work*, Sydney: Allen & Unwin

Offe, C. (1982) 'Some Contradictions of the Modern Welfare State', *Critical Social Policy* 2, 2, pp. 7–16

Office of Multicultural Affairs (OMA) (1989) *National Agenda for a Multicultural Australia*, Canberra: Australian Government Publishing Service

Omi, M. and Winant, H. (1987) 'Racial Theory in the Post War United States', *Sage Race Relations Abstracts*, 1/2(2), pp. 3–44

O'Shane, P. (1976) 'Is There Any Relevance in the Women's Movement for Aboriginal Women?' *Refractory Girl*, September 12, pp. 31–4

—— (1984) in S. Mitchell *Tall Poppies*, Ringwood: Penguin

Palmer, P. M. (1983) 'White Women/Black Women: The Dualism of Identity and Experience', *Feminist Studies* 9, 1, pp. 151–80

Pallotta-Chiarolli, M. (1989) 'From Coercion to Choice: second generation women seeking a personal identity in the Italo-Australian Setting', *Journal of Intercultural Studies* 10, 1, pp. 49–63

Parmar, P. (1989) 'Other Kinds of Dreaming', *Feminist Review* 31, pp. 55–65

—— and Minh-ha, T. (1990) 'Woman, Native Other Interview' *Feminist Review* 36, pp. 65–74

Pateman, C. (1988) *The Sexual Contract*, Oxford: Basil Blackwell

Pearson, D. (1988) 'From Communality to Ethnicity: the Maori ethnic revival', *Ethnic and Racial Studies* 11, 2, pp. 168–91

Perkins, C. (1975) *A Bastard Like Me*, Sydney: Ure Smith

—— (1986) *The Administration of Aboriginal Development*, Canberra: Royal Institute of Public Administration

Peterson, N. (1985) *Capitalism, Culture and Land Rights*, Social Analysis no 18, pp. 85–101

Pettman, J. (1984) 'Racism and Education: Lessons from Britain', *Multicultural Australia Papers*, 30

—— (1987) 'Combatting Racism in the Community', in Markus, A. and Rasmussen, R. eds, *Prejudice in the Public Area: Racism*, Melbourne: Monash University

—— (1988a) 'Learning about Power and Powerlessness: Aborigines and White Australia's Bicentenary', *Race and Class* xxix, 3, pp. 69–85

—— (1988b) 'Whose Country is it Anyway? Cultural Politics, Racism and the Construction of Being Australian', *Journal of Intercultural Studies* 9, 1, pp. 1–24

—— (1988c) 'The Politics of Race', Peace Research Centre *Working Paper No. 54*, Canberra: Australian National University

—— (1988d) 'Racism and Aborigines', in B. Wright ed., *Contemporary Issues in Aboriginal Studies* 2, Sydney: Firebird Press

—— (1990) 'Racism and Sexism in Tertiary Education' Working Paper SACAE: Aboriginal Studies and Teacher Education Centre

—— (1991) 'Racism, Sexism and Sociology', in G. Bottomley et al. eds, *Intersexions: Gender/Class/Culture/Ethnicity*, Sydney: Allen & Unwin

—— (forthcoming, a) 'White Women and Racism', in S. Gunew and A. Yeatman eds, *Feminism and The Politics of Difference*

—— (forthcoming, b) 'Antiracist Strategies for Tertiary Education' in E. Martens ed., *Recent Studies in Cultural Diversity and Education*, Adelaide: National Centre for Cross-Cultural Curriculum and Staff Development

Phoenix, A. (1985) 'Theories of Gender and Black Families', in G. Weiner ed. *Just a Bunch of Girls*, London: Open University Press

Powell, L. (1983) 'Black Macho and Black Feminism', in B. Smith ed., *Home Girls: A Black Feminist Anthology*, New York: Kitchen Table

Prager, J. (1987) 'American Political Culture and the Shifting Meaning of Race', *Ethnic and Racial Studies* 10, 1, pp. 62–81

Price, C. (1989) *Ethnic Groups in Australia*, Canberra: Australian Immigration Research Centre

Pringle, R. (1988) *Secretaries Talk: Sexuality, Power and Work*, Sydney: Allen & Unwin

Radford, G. (1990) 'EEO for Women in the 1990s', in National Women's Conference *Proceedings* pp. 58–75

Ramazanoglu, C. (1989) *Feminism and the Contradictions' of Oppression*, London: Routledge

Randall, M. (1988) 'Feminism and the State: Questions for Theory and Practice', *RFR/DRF* 17, 3, pp. 10–17

Rasmussen R. and Tang, K. (1990) 'Asians in Australia and the Don Quixotes', *Asian Migrant* 3, pp. 21–4

Rapp, R. (1979) 'Anthropology: Review Essay', *Signs* 4, 3, pp. 497–513

Read, P. (1984) *The Stolen Generations*, Sydney: Ministry of Aboriginal Affairs

—— (1988) *A Hundred Years War: The Waradjuri People and the State*, Canberra: ANU Press

—— (1990) *Charles Perkins: A Biography*, Ringwood: Viking

Reagon, B. (1983) 'Coalition Politics: Turning the Century', in B. Smith ed., *Home Girls: A Black Feminist Anthology*, New York: Kitchen Table

Reece, B. (1987) 'Inventing Aborigines', *Aboriginal History* 11, 1, pp. 14–23

Reiter, R. ed. (1973) *Towards an Anthropology of Women*, New York: Monthly Review Press

Rex, J. and Mason, D. eds (1986) *Theories of Race and Ethnic Relations*, Cambridge: Cambridge University Press

Reynolds, H. (1972) *Aborigines and Settlers*, Stanmore: Cassell

—— (1981) *The Other Side of the Frontier*, Townsville: James Cook University Press

—— (1987) *The Law of the Land*, Ringwood: Penguin

—— (1990) *With the White People*, Ringwood: Penguin

Ribbens, J. (1989) 'Interviewing—An Unnatural Situation?', *Woman's Studies International Forum* 12, 6, pp. 579–92

Rich, A. (1976) *Of Woman Born: Motherhood as Experience and Institution*, New York: Norton

—— (1981) 'Disloyal to Civilisation', in *On Lies, Secrets and Silence*, London: Virago

—— (1986) 'Notes Towards a Politics of Location' in *Blood, Bread and Poetry* New York: Norton

Riley, D. (1987) 'Does Sex Have a History? Women and Feminism', *New Formations* 1 pp. 35–45

Robinson, F. and York, B. (1977) *The Black Resistance*, Camberwell: Widescope

Rollins, J. (1985) *Between Women: Domestics and their Employers*, Philadelphia: Temple University Press

Rosser, B. (1985) *Dreamtime Nightmares*, Canberra: Australian Institute of Aboriginal Studies

Rowland, R. (1988) *Woman Herself*, Melbourne: Oxford University Press

Rowley, C. (1974a) *The Destruction of Aboriginal Society*, Ringwood: Penguin
—— (1974b) *Outcasts in White Society*, Ringwood: Penguin
Rowse, T and Moran, A. (1984) 'Peculiarly Australian — The Political Construction of Cultural Identity', in Encel, S. and Bryson, L. eds, *Australian Society*, 4th edn, Sydney: Longman Cheshire, pp. 229–77
Rowse, T. (1986) 'Aborigines as Historical Actors: Evidence and Inference', *Historical Studies* 22, 87, pp. 176–98
—— (1988) 'Tolerance, Fortitude and Patience: Frontier Pasts to Live With?' *Meanjin* 47, 1, pp. 21–9
Royal Commission into Aboriginal Deaths in Custody (1988) *Interim Report*, Canberra: Australian Government Publishing Service
Rubin, G. (1975) 'The Traffic in Women: Notes on the Political Economy of Women', in R. Reiter ed., *Women and Anthropology*, New York: Monthly Review Press
Rutherford, J. ed. (1990) *Identity: Community, Culture, Difference*, London: Lawrence and Wishart
Ryan, L. (1986a) 'Aboriginal Women and Agency in the Process of Conquest: A Review of Some Recent Work', *Australian Feminist Studies No 2* pp. 35–43
Ryan, L. (1986b) 'Reading Aboriginal Histories', *Meanjin* 45, 1, pp. 49–57
Said, E. (1978) *Orientalism*, London: Routledge and Kegan Paul
—— (1985) 'Orientalism Reconsidered', *Race and Class* XXVII, 2, pp. 1–16
Sansom, B. (1980) *The Camp at Wallaby Creek*, Canberra: Australian Institute of Aboriginal Studies
Sassoon, A. ed. (1987) *Women and the State*, London: Hutchinson
Saunders, K. (1982) 'Pacific Islander Women in Queensland', in M. Bevege et al., *Worth Her Salt*, Sydney: Hale and Iremonger
—— (1990) 'Recent Women's Studies Scholarship, 1: History', *Hecate* 16, 1/2, pp. 171–80
Saunders, M. (1989) 'Mothers are Our Sisters: Agency, Responsibility and Community', *RFR/DRF* 18, 3, pp. 47–50
Sawer, M. (1989) 'Feminism and the State Workshop', *WEL National Bulletin* Nov–Dec, pp. 13–14
—— (1990a) *Sisters in Suits*, Sydney: Allen & Unwin
—— (1990b) 'Feminism and the State—Australia Compared', National Women's Conference *Proceedings* pp. 34–51
Scott, P. B. (1982) 'Debunking Sappire: Towards a Non-Racist and Non-Sexist Social Science', in Hull, G.T. et al., *All The Women are White, All The Blacks Are Men, But Some Of Us Are Brave*, New York: Feminist Press
Scutt, J. ed. (1980) *Rape Law Reform*, Canberra: Australian Institute of Criminology
—— (1987) *Different Lives*, Ringwood: Penguin
Segal, L. (1987) *Is the Future Female? Troubled Thoughts on Contemporary Feminism*, London: Virago
Seitz, A. (1989) 'Non-English Speaking Background Women, Some Issues and Concerns', in *Migrant Action* 11, 3, pp. 3–5
Sharp, R. and Brownhill, R. (1989) *Short Changed: Women and Economic Policies*, Sydney: Allen & Unwin
Shaver, S. (1989) 'Gender, Class and the Welfare State in Australia', *Feminist Review* 32, pp. 90–109

Sheldrake, P. (1989) 'Access and Equity Plan: Immigration, Local Government and Ethnic Affairs Portfolio', *Migrant Action* xi, 1, pp. 6–8

Sherington, G. (1990) *Australia's Immigration 1788–1988*, Sydney: Allen & Unwin

Shortus, S. (1988) 'Now and Then: the Nation-state and Nationalism 1888–1988', *Meanjin* 47, 2, pp. 194–201

Sivanandan, A. (1982) *A Different Hunger: Writings on Black Resistance*, London: Pluto

—— (1983) 'Challenging Racism: Strategies for the Eighties', *Race and Class*, XXV, 2, pp. 1–12

—— (1989) 'New Circuits of Imperialism', *Race and Class* 30, 4, pp. 1–19

Smith, Barbara ed. (1983) *Home Girls: A Black Feminist Anthology*, New York: Kitchen Table

Smith, Bernard (1981) *The Spectre of Truganini*, Boyer Lecture, Sydney: Australian Broadcasting Corporation

Solomos, J. (1986a) 'Varieties of Marxist Concepts of Race, Class and State: A Critical Analysis', in J. Rex and D. Mason eds, *Theories of Race and Ethnic Relations*, Cambridge: Cambridge University Press pp. 84–109

—— (1986b) 'Trends in the Political Analysis of Racism', *Political Studies* XXXIV, pp. 313–24

—— (1988) *Black Youth, Racism and the State*, Cambridge: Cambridge University Press

—— (1989) *Race and Racism in Contemporary Britain*, London: Macmillan

Speakout (1989) Immigrant Women's Speakout Association of NSW, *Annual Report*, Lidcombe

Spivak, G.C. (1988) *In Other Worlds: Essays in Cultural Politics*, New York: Methuen, pp. 241–68

—— (1989) 'Reading the Satanic Verses', *Public Culture* 2, 1, pp. 79–99

Stacey, J. (1988) 'Can There Be a Feminist Ethnography?', *Women's Studies International Forum* 11, 1, pp. 21–7

Stanley, L. ed. (1990a) *Feminist Praxis Research, Theory and Epistemology in Feminist Sociology*, London: Routledge

—— (1990b) 'Moments of Writing: Is There a Feminist Auto/biography?', *Gender and History* 2, 1, pp. 58–67

—— (1990c) 'Recovering Women in History from Feminist Deconstruction', *Women's Studies International Forum* 13, 1/2 pp. 151–8

Stanner, W. E. H. (1969) *Beyond the Dreaming*, Boyer Lectures, Sydney: Australian Broadcasting Corporation

Stasiulis, D. K. (1987) 'Rainbow Feminism: Minority Women in Canada', *Resources for Feminist Research* 16, 1, pp. 5–9

—— (1990) 'Theorising Connections: Gender, Race, Ethnicity and Class' in P. Li, *Race and Ethnic Relations in Canada*, Toronto: Oxford University Press

Stone, J. (1989) 'Reply to Julie Marcus', *Hecate* 15, 1, pp. 64–8

Storer, D. (1975) *But I Wouldn't Want My Wife to Work Here*, Fitzroy: Centre for Urban Research and Action

—— ed. (1985) *Ethnic Family Values in Australia*, Sydney: Prentice-Hall

Stromback, T. (1988) *Migrants, Ethnic Groups and the Labour Market*, Canberra: OMA Options Paper

Stubbs, P. (1985) 'The Employment of Black Social Workers', *Critical Social Policy* 12, pp. 6–27

Summers, A. (1975) *Damned Whores and God's Police*, Ringwood: Penguin

Sykes, B. (1975) 'Black Women in Australia', in J. Mercer ed. *The Other Half*, Ringwood: Penguin

Sykes, B. (1989) *Black Majority: An Analysis of 21 Years of Black Australian Experiences as Emancipated Australian Citizens*, Melbourne: Hudson

Tatz, C. (1979) *Race Politics in Australia*, University of New England, Armidale
——— (1982) *Aborigines and Uranium*, Richmond: Heinemann
——— (1990) 'Aboriginal Violence: A Return to Pessimism', *Australian Journal of Social Issues* 25, 4, pp. 245–60

Taylor, D. (1989) 'Citizenship and Social Power', *Critical Social Policy* 26, pp. 19–31

Thomas, N. (1990) 'Partial Texts', *Journal of Pacific History* xxv, 2, pp. 139–58

Thomas, S. (1988) 'Aboriginal Subjection and Affirmation', *Meanjin* 47, 4, pp. 755–61d

Thompson, D. (1990) 'Feminism and the Problem of Power', National Women's Conference *Proceedings* pp. 16–24

Thompson, P. (1978) *The Voice of the Past: Oral History*, Oxford: Oxford University Press

Tomlinson, J. (1986) 'Aboriginalising Child Care', *Australian Social Worker* 39, 1, pp. 33–6

Tonkinson, R. (1989) 'Aboriginal Ethnicity and Nation-Building within Australia' in M. Howard ed., *Ethnicity and the State in the Pacific*, Tokyo: United Nations University

Trigger, D. (1989) 'Racial Ideologies in Australia's Gulf Country', *Ethnic and Racial Studies* 12, 2, pp. 209–31

Trinh, Minh-ha (1987) 'Difference: A Special Third World Woman Issue', *Feminist Review* 25, pp. 5–20
——— (1989) *Women, Native, Other*, Bloomingham: Indiana University Press

Tsolidis, G. (1986) *Educating Voula: A Report on non-English Speaking Background Girls and Education*, Melbourne: Victorian Ministerial Advisory Committee on Multiculturalism and Migrant Education

Tucker, M. (1987) *If Everyone Cared: An Autobiography*, Melbourne: Grosvenor

Turner, B. (1990) 'Outline of a Theory of Citizenship' *Sociology* 24, 2, pp. 189–217

Vinson, T. et al. (1989) 'Class, Surveillance and Child Abuse', *Impact* 19, 3, pp. 19–21

Viviani, N. (1984) *The Long Journey: Vietnamese Migration and Settlement in Australia*, Melbourne: Melbourne University Press

Walby, S. (1988) 'Gender Politics and Social Theory' *Sociology* 22, 2, pp. 215–32
——— (1989) 'Theorising Patriarchy', *Sociology* 23, 2, pp. 213–34
——— (1990) 'From Private to Public Patriarchy', *Woman's Studies International Forum* 13, 1/2, pp. 91–104

Walker, A. (1982) 'Advancing Luna—and the Ida D. Wells', in *You Can't Keep A Good Woman Down*, London: The Women's Press
——— (1984) *In Search of Our Mothers' Gardens*, San Diego: Harcourt Brace Jovanovich

Wallace, M. (1978) *Black Macho and the Myth of the Superwoman*, New York: Dial Press

Ward, G. (1988) *Wandering Girl*, Broome: Magabala Books

Ward, I. (1988) Introduction in J. Kovel, *White Racism: A Psycho History*, London: Free Association Press

Ware, V. (1983-4) 'Imperialism, Racism and Violence Against Women', *Emergency* 1. pp. 25-30

Waring, M. (1988) *Counting for Nothing: What Men Value and What Women are Worth*, Sydney: Allen & Unwin

Waters, M. (1989) 'Patriarchy and Viriarchy', *Sociology* 23, 2, pp. 193-211

Watson, L. (1989) 'The Affirmation of Indigenous Values in a Colonial Education System', *Journal of Indigenous Studies* 1, 1, pp. 10-21

Watson, S. ed. (1990) *Playing the State: Australian Feminist Interventions*, Sydney: Allen & Unwin

Weaver, S. (1983) 'Australian Aboriginal Policy: Aboriginal Pressure Groups or Government Advisory Bodies?', *Oceania* 54, 1 and 2, pp. 1-22, 85-108

Webber, M. et al. (1990) 'Ethnicity, Gender and Industrial Restructuring in Australia 1971-1986', *Journal of Intercultural Studies* 11, 1, pp. 1-48

West, I. (1984) *Pride Against Prejudice: Reminiscences of a Tasmanian Aboriginal*, Canberra: Australian Institute of Aboriginal Studies

White, I., Barwick, D. & Meehan, B. eds (1985) *Fighters and Singers: The Lives of Some Aboriginal Women*, Sydney: Allen & Unwin

White, R. (1981) *Inventing Australia: Images and Identity 1688-1980*, Sydney: Allen & Unwin

Williams, C. (1988) *Blue, White and Pink Collar Workers in Australia*, Sydney: Allen & Unwin

Williams, F. (1987) 'Racism and the Discipline of Social Policy: A Critique of Welfare Theory', *Critical Social Policy* 20, pp. 4-27

——— (1989) *Social Policy: A Critical Introduction*, Cambridge: Cambridge University Press

Williams, J. (1985) 'Redefining Institutional Racism', *Ethnic and Racial Studies* viii, 3, pp. 323-48

——— (1987) 'The Construction of Women and Black Students as Educational Problems', in M. Arnot and G. Weiner eds, *Gender and the Politics of Schooling*, London: Hutchinson

Willis, A. M. and Fry, T. (1988-9) 'Art as Ethnocide: The Case of Australia', *Third Text* 5, pp. 3-20

Willis, S. (1985) 'Black Women Writers', in G. Greene and C. Khan eds, *Making the Difference: Feminist Literary Criticism*, London: Routledge and Kegan Paul

Wilson, P. (1982) *Black Death, White Hands*, Sydney: Allen & Unwin

Wolf, E. (1982) *Europe and the People without History*, Berkeley: University of California Press

Women's Business (1986) Report of the Aboriginal Women's Task Force, Canberra: Australian Government Publishing Service

Woman's Studies at Australian Universities—a Dossier (1990), Canberra: ANU

Wundersitz, J. (1990) 'Aboriginal Youth and Juvenile Justice', *Olive Pink Society Bulletin* 2, 1, pp. 5-7

Yeatman, A. (1988) *A Review on Multicultural Policies and Programs in Children's Services*, Canberra: Office of Multicultural Affairs

—— (1990) *Bureaucrats, Technocrats, Femocrats: Essays on the Contemporary Australian State*, Sydney: Allen & Unwin

Yuval-Davis, N. (1986) 'Ethnic/Racial Divisions and the Nation in Britain and Australia', *Capital and Class*, 28, pp. 87–103

Yuval-Davis, N. and Anthias, F. eds (1989) *Women—Nation—State*, London: Macmillan

Zubaida, S. (1989) 'Nations Old and New', *Ethnic and Racial Studies* 12, 3, pp. 329–39

Index

Aboriginal: academics 138, 146-7, *see also* Aboriginal history; children 114-15, removal of 30, 57, 66, *see also* children, mixed race; culture 19, 23, *see also* Aboriginality, culture; deaths in custody 70, 91, 130; families 30-1, 65-7, 114-15, and welfare agencies 66; history 21-4; land rights, *see* land; languages 114; male sexuality, representations of 27-8, 69; 'matriarchs' 30, 65-6, *see also* Aboriginal women; organisations, funding for 90; social relations 114-15; staff in tertiary education 138-9; women, *see* Aboriginal women; writers 141-2. *See also* Aboriginality, Aborigines

Aboriginal Affairs, Department of 88

Aboriginal Child Care Association, Victorian 115

Aboriginal Child Poverty, Report into 70

Aboriginal Issues Units 130

Aboriginal Legal Aid services 71, 90, 93

Aboriginal Studies viii, 2, 21, 22, 131-7

Aboriginal and Torres Strait Islander Commission (ATSIC) 89-90, 133

Aboriginal women vii-viii, 2, 15, 17, 18, 19, 21-2, 24-34, 55, 114; and colonisation chapter 2; in domestic service 31-2; exploitation/sexual abuse of 19, 20, 27-8, 71; and family 65-9; representations of 25-6, 27-8, 30, 59, 65-6, 72; and research 146-7; and sexual politics 26-8, 29; and the state 91-3; status of 24-6; in traditional society 24-6; and welfare 87-8; and white men 20, 28-9; and white women 32-4, *see also* black-white relations; and work 31-2; writings of 141-2

Aboriginal women's conference, 1990 (NSW) 93

Aboriginality viii, 11, 12, 20, 22, 81, 91, 107-17, 121, 122, 136

Aborigines 11, 14, 107-17; and Aboriginal history 21-4; and assimilation policy 8; categorised 7, 89-90; and citizenship 81; classifications/definitions of 8; and difference 106-17; displacement/ dispossession of 17-21, 26-7; and domestic violence 70-1; exclusion of 5, 6-7, 88; and land rights 26, 89; legal status of 7, 88; in police custody 57, *see also* Aboriginal deaths; and racism 6, 59, *see also* racism; representations/stereotypes of 23, 27-8, 55, 65-6; 109-11, 113, 116, 133, *see also* Aboriginal women; as representatives 124,

Staples, 63
state, the: Aborigines and 88–93,
111; and anti-racism/sexism
103–5; in Australian history 4–6;
and discourses 103–4; and
ethnicity 117–19; and femocrats
99–100; and migrants 93–8; and
multiculturalism 117–19; women
and viii, 6, 78–88, 91–3; working
in/against 100–3
state intervention 79, 102
state organisations 100–3, *see also*
welfare
stereotyping, *see* cultural
representations/stereotyping
sterilisation of women, forced 36
Stubbs, P. 101
students of Aboriginal, Multicultural
and Women's Studies 132–3, 134–5

Tatz, C. 108
teaching about others 141–7
teaching in tertiary education 137–9
terminology and ethnicity 12
Torres Strait Islanders 93
tourist trade 73
trade unions 45, 49, 95
Truginini 29

unemployment 10, 46; for migrant
women 47
universities 131

values, Aboriginal 109–10, 113–14,
see also Aboriginality
values, cultural 51–2
victims: Aborigines as 17–21; blacks
as 11; women as vii, 2
violence: in colonisation 18, 26–7;
domestic 69–72, 74–5, 81, 86, 93,
support for victims of 74–5; male
69–72; racist 27–8, 59, 130; sexist
27–8; and sexuality 72–5; and the
state 80
Von Sturmer, J. 111

wages 79
Walker, Alice 101
Weldon, F. 119

welfare agencies 79; and Aboriginal
families 65, 66
welfare services 101–2, 105; women
and 84–8
welfare state, the 82, 84–8
Whitlam government 20, 118
Winant, H. 11
women: Aboriginal, *see* Aboriginal;
Asian, *see* Asian; Australian,
stereotyping 75; and Australian
nationalism 6; black 172–6; as
care-givers 86–7; and categories
127; and citizenship 80–1; and
community 75–7; and ethnicity
14–16; exclusion from social/
industrial rights 83; exploitation of
80, *see also* Aboriginal women,
sexual abuse/exploitation; and
feminism chapter 8; Filipino 73–4;
and identity politics 127; Muslim,
see Muslim; refugee 44;
representations of 14–15, 84, 86;
role of 14–16, 63–4, 67–9, 75–6,
86–7, 119, *see also* division of
labour, employment, family; as a
social category 75–6; and the state
viii, 6, 78–88, 91–3; status of 83–4;
Torres Strait Islanders 93; and
trade unions 49–50; and welfare
84–8; white, representations of
27–8
Women Against Fundamentalism 119
Women, Race, Ethnicity and the
State (workshop, 1989) ix
Women's Conference, International
Indigenous (1989) 93
Women's Studies ix, 2, 21, 131–7
work, *see* employment
work, women's *see* division of
labour; employment; family;
labour market
workers, state 100–3
writers: Aboriginal 142–3; of
Aboriginal history 21–4; on
Aboriginal women 24–6
Yeatman, A. 82
Yuval-Davis, N. ix, 14, 68
Zubrzycki, Jerzy 130